PRAISE FOR THE PURSUIT OF KINDNESS

"This is a book about hope, optimism and kindness, but it is realistic, too: Éamonn Toland has taken a very long view, back to the earliest humans. His approach is global and extraordinarily ambitious, which it has to be, given the size and profundity of the topic. He uses the lessons of history and prehistory to suggest paths towards a kinder, more caring future in a world that has become increasingly polarised and intolerant. If climate change is to be halted, human societies will also have to change. The book is . . . essential reading for anyone who cares about the past, but fears for the future."

--Francis Pryor MBE, *Time Team* archaeologist and author of *Britain BC*

"*The Pursuit of Kindness* is an extraordinary game-changer, a compelling and original book that corrects a universal misunderstanding about the core nature of the human species that is particularly relevant to the current American and European political conflicts, as well as a gripping good read that leaves us both relieved and inspired to follow our natural instincts and work with each other for the common good."

--Alan Rinzler, editor of *Bury My Heart At Wounded Knee* by Dee Brown and Toni Morrison's *The Bluest Eye*

"Éamonn Toland has written an intriguing book about why we care about one another. Rich with stories, and fresh in its perspective, this book will make you think more about what it means to be human. The book is for everyone because everyone needs kindness."

--Fergus Shanahan, Professor Emeritus at University College Cork and author of *The Language of Illness*

"Entertaining, accessible and important, *The Pursuit of Kindness* is a sweeping analysis of why kindness and cooperation isn't just morally important but key to our survival as a species. Éamonn Toland has joined the ranks of Malcolm Gladwell and Steven Pinker."

--David Young, aka Seán Black, best-selling author of the *Lockdown* series

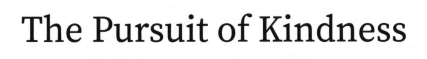

The Pursuit of Kindness

First published in 2021 by
Liberties Press
1 Terenure Place | Terenure | Dublin 6W | Ireland
libertiespress.com

Distributed in the United Kingdom by Casemate UK
The Old Music Hall | 106-108 Cowley Rd | Oxford | OX4 1JE | UK
casematepublishing.co.uk

Copyright © Éamonn Toland, 2021
The author asserts his moral rights.
ISBN (print): 978-1-912589-21-0
ISBN (e-book): 978-1-912589-22-7

2 4 6 8 10 9 7 5 3 1
A CIP record for this title is available from the British Library.

The Pursuit of Kindness

An Evolutionary History
of Human Nature

Éamonn Toland

Contents

SURVIVAL

I
Survival of the Kindest

Chapter One

Survival of the Kindest

"Love comes more naturally to the human heart than its opposite."[1]

NELSON MANDELA

Why are we kind? Are we born to love one another? Are we made in the image of our gods to be a moral animal, or do we have to learn how to be good and decent, to curb our self-centred instincts through culture, civilisation or religion?

How do we make moral choices? It's a question that has puzzled philosophers and theologians down through the ages – and then Charles Darwin published *On the Origin of Species* in 1859.

People all over the world have some familiarity with *On the Origin of Species* and have no doubt that the human race evolved over several million years to become the upright, intelligent, complex individuals inhabiting the earth today.[2] Many of these people also presume that evolution required people to battle against each other "red in tooth and claw", so that the weak fell by the wayside, while the strong passed their genes on to the next generation.

Darwin's theory suggests that a process called "natural selection" has had a profound influence on every living species, including human beings. Traits which were adaptive – which had increased our chances of survival – have been passed down from generation to generation.

Darwin liked a phrase that Herbert Spencer coined to describe the outcome: "survival of the fittest".

For decades, biologists believed that evolution and altruism were irreconcilable. Richard Dawkins once wrote: "Let us try to teach generosity and altruism, because we are born selfish." Francis Collins, a former Director of the Human Genome Project, believed that our selfless moral feelings conflict with the evolutionary urge to preserve our DNA, and could only have come to pass as a result of divine intervention.

They were both wrong.

*

The problem goes back to the original definition of altruism, as an act of generosity that comes at a personal cost. Scientists applied the idea to evolution, arguing that, if generosity blesses those who give, as much as those who take, then it isn't altruistic. Selfless behaviour that resulted in win-win, positive-sum outcomes didn't make the cut. Kindness didn't count unless it was at the cost of biological fitness. A literary conceit about "selfish" genes became a term of art. Natural selection was stuck in an intellectual cul-de-sac. Theoretically, the likelihood that true selflessness could persist in a species was reduced to the point of extinction.[3]

The old paradigm encouraged belief in two mutually incompatible propositions. On the one hand, genes were "blind replicators" which stumbled onto successful ways of producing copies and mutations of themselves through natural selection, including the extraordinary examples of collaboration found in the evolution of multi-cellular plants and animals. On the other hand, they were moralised as selfish actors, fine-tuning the species which carried them, so that their descendent genes could achieve a kind of immortality.

Kindness was a paradox – an aberration that had to be explained. An inner moral voice which made us feel good when we did good things, and feel bad when we did bad things, was either a figment of our imagination or an assimilated tradition which restrained our natural instincts through the rule of law and laborious cultural indoctrination in childhood.

Of course, not everyone feels bad when they do bad things. Roughly 1 percent of women and 3 percent of men suffer from anti-social personality disorder – more commonly referred to as sociopathy. They struggle to control impulses to manipulate others, with no regard to their feelings. Sufferers may deploy cognitive empathy to consciously and deliberately show consideration to others, but the emotional brakes on bad behaviour are faulty, if not entirely absent. In layman's terms, they lack a conscience.

So there are some people who can behave ruthlessly without remorse. But that still leaves us with a puzzle. Why do almost all of us (99 percent of women and 97 percent of men) have a conscience? And is it anything to write home about anyway?

Kin Altruism

They say it takes a village to raise a child. What they don't tell you is that the village will hand your child back the second she starts having a meltdown. Newborns are wired to respond to familiar voices. Three-day-old babies will adapt their suckling on a pacifier in order to hear their mother's voice, but not the voice of a stranger.[4]

Parenthood can be exhausting, particularly for humans, thanks to a unique shift in how early hominins evolved. By the beginning of the Pleistocene (more commonly known as the Ice Age), a period from about 2.6 million years ago to 11,700 years ago, our ancestors displayed one striking characteristic which differentiates us from our closest relatives, the common chimpanzees and bonobos: the ability to walk upright for extended periods of time. This gave hominins a larger foraging range, as well as the ability to spot predators above tall grasses.

Hominins' prefrontal cortex – the "executive function" of the brain, which mulls the consequences of conflicting actions – started to grow, helping them to anticipate, plan for and adapt to their environment. The legs of our bipedal ancestors lengthened, their fingers became more dextrous, and they developed arches on their feet to support their weight while running.

These hominins were smart, but there is a great deal we still don't know about them.[5] Sophisticated tools have been found from the early Pleistocene onwards, and at some point between 1.5 million and 0.5 million years ago, they learnt how to control fire – although, initially, they may have used it primarily for warmth and protection rather than cooking food. The archaeological record for pre-Neanderthal culture is much more limited. There is some evidence that hominins in the Fertile Crescent (from the Nile Valley to the Persian Gulf) were butchering large game animals methodically 250,000 years ago. This might indicate a degree of coordinated, collaborative behavior. Thus far, however, we have discovered no evidence of Homo erectus art or music, and, apart from the questionable claims for Homo naledi, a precursor of humans which became extinct 250,000 years ago, no evidence for ritual treatment of the dead.[6]

The legacy of our hominin ancestors – our ability to walk upright – has been key to our success, but it came at a cost. Our brains are five times larger relative to body size than those of other large mammals, and require four times as much energy. Consequently, the human body has to withstand far greater obstetric pressure and metabolic demands than that of a four-legged creature. This limits the size a baby can grow to at birth. In order to give birth safely, we have to emerge from the womb at a much earlier stage of development – when the neck muscles are not strong enough to support the weight of our heads.[7] Within a few days of birth, a baby held upright, with her head supported, will cheerfully swing her legs in a walking motion.

Flip her horizontal and cradle her under the chest, and she will revert to a crawl, months before she can do this on her own. In a very real sense, all human babies are born prematurely.

The slow pace at which our brains mature gives us the longest childhood of any creature on the planet, making us the "mama's boys" of nature. Parents and babies experience a surge of oxytocin, the so-called "hug hormone", by looking into each other's eyes.[8] The ongoing nurturing of our parents is crucial to our survival.[9] This massive investment in child-rearing encourages what evolutionary biologists call "kin altruism": we are wired to be kind to our kin, who will pass our genes on to the next generation.[10]

Human males spend far more time looking after their children than any other ape species, and often do so in monogamous relationships.[11] Sexual dimorphism – size differences between males and females – are much lower for humans than for many other apes, suggesting that in the distant past, human "alphas" did not routinely compete in order to acquire a harem of females. The average man is 9 percent taller and 20 percent heavier than the average woman, whereas a male silverback gorilla can be twice the size of the females with which he mates.[12] Women have had an incentive to find mates willing to dedicate themselves to raising their children. Genetic "fitness" has favoured attributes such as kindness, protectiveness, generosity and loyalty – at least within the nuclear family.[13]

There is evidence that single men fight over status where there is a dearth of single women, such as in the Wild West, but violence and criminality dropped sharply when these men settled down. This is consistent with child-rearing in monogamous relationships, although despite lower levels of sexual dimorphism, bonobos do not compete over sexual partners for very different reasons: they are wildly promiscuous.

Kin altruism continues to have powerful effects in hunter-gatherer societies, where close relatives spend more time living together, working together, protecting each other, and adopting each other's children. In the Developed World, relatives are more likely to aid each other in life-or-death situations, and parents invest heavily in their own children. Blood is still thicker than water.

In modern Western society, raising children correlates strongly with reduced crime and violence. In a study that tracked low-income young offenders in Boston over a forty-five-year period, the most significant predictor of recidivism was whether someone settled down and got a steady job upon his release. Only one in three men who got married was convicted of a further crime, compared to three out of four men who remained single.[14]

Kin altruism has been observed in other species. Monogamous behaviour has been observed in species where males spend a significant amount of time rearing their young, including the beautiful white-handed lar gibbons, prairie voles, California mice, the East African antelope, Kirk's dik-dik, convict cichlid fish, shingleback skink lizards, mute swans, penguins, and many other bird species.[15]

Reciprocal Altruism

Thanks to our mitochondrial DNA, we have been able to trace all modern humans back to a last common female ancestor, nicknamed "Eve".[16] By looking at how long it takes mitochondrial DNA to mutate, scientists have been able to calculate that Eve lived about two hundred thousand years ago.[17] Homo sapiens has been around as a distinct species for about three hundred thousand years: in evolutionary terms, no more than the blink of an eye.[18]

For most of that time, there were very few of us. Compared to other species, the human genome lacks diversity. Seventy thousand years ago, our entire ancestral population may have comprised a few thousand people.[19] We have lived in low population densities for at least 95 percent of our history. Based on the evidence of ancient camps and settlements, our global population may have been less than half a million people as recently as twenty thousand years ago. The implications of this are profound.

A hunter-gatherer band of a hundred people typically requires a home-range of 32 square miles in order to feed themselves.[20] This is small enough to allow them to walk to or from any point in their range within a day. Modern Tanzania, Kenya and Ethiopia, where many early hominin remains have been found, cover an area of just under 1 million square miles. This would have allowed a population of roughly 3 million people, living in around thirty thousand bands, to co-exist without significant pressure on food resources.

Our ancestral population of seventy thousand years ago occupied less than 1 percent of the immediately available foraging area. Before they had to cross the Sahara, sail the seas, or brave the mosquito-borne malarial lands of West Africa, they could expand into another million square miles across the rest of East Africa[21]. In the absence of permanent settlements, the potential for large-scale warfare and the spread of pandemic disease was limited. There was substantial scope for expansion without conflict among Homo sapiens.

When food and land are abundant, the fittest have a huge incentive to collaborate in hunting and gathering, warding off predators, sharing tools and match-making across bands, rather than competing over resources.[22] Bands of a hundred people need 40 percent less foraging area per person to survive than people living in bands of ten or fewer, although some bands fragment into nuclear families in seasons where vegetation is scarce and then re-form for large hunts at other times.[23]

We lived in this ample and abundant environment for at least 95 percent of our history as Homo sapiens. We helped fellow band-members to acquire food and safety even if they were not close relatives, while at the same time increasing the chances that they would do the same for us. We formed non-reproductive unions –

friendships – with others.[24] The psychologist Jonathan Haidt calls human beings "the world champions of cooperation beyond kinship".

Evolution selected for in-group bias, encouraging kindness towards those who have been kind to us, and creating the expectation that we had a right to see our kindness reciprocated. This mutually beneficial collaboration is also called "reciprocal altruism". One requirement of reciprocal altruism, the ability to distinguish familiar faces, is a hard-wired trait, as is the ability to learn a language.[25] Sophisticated reciprocal altruism may only exist in humans, although symbiotic and collaborative relationships can be seen in many other species[26]: sharks and cleaner fish, for example, or the domestication of dogs from wolves around fifteen thousand years ago, just before the rise of agriculture. As anyone who has had a dead mouse dropped on their doorstep can tell you, even cats know how to say thank you.

Reciprocal altruism doesn't stop fights from breaking out. Sometimes you don't need a biological incentive to find someone annoying. But in an era of very low population density, rather than challenge someone to mortal combat, with all the attendant risks that this involved, you could just move to the next valley, or a neighbouring band.[27] In this environment, any behavioural trait that helped us collaborate with each other would have an evolutionary edge.[28]

How We Got Out of Africa

Intrepid hunter-gatherer bands moved out of Africa long before the Mesolithic era began. Here's how:

1. We probably reached Australia 65,000 years ago; Siberia, Korea and Japan about 35,000 years ago; and the Americas between 35,000 and 25,000 years ago.[29]
2. We reached the southern part of Europe around 45,000 years ago, and followed the retreating glaciers northwards as the volatile

Pleistocene climate was replaced by the warmer Holocene about 12,000 years ago.[30] Over the last 10,000 years, European skin lightened to absorb vitamin D from sunlight in the colder northern latitudes.

3. There is evidence for the presence of Homo sapiens in the Near East as early as 125,000 years ago, and human teeth found in China have been dated to 80,000 years ago.[31]

Despite the fact that Sapiens and Neanderthals overlapped in Europe for thousands of years, it had been thought that when we reached out of Africa, we wiped out earlier species of hominins, either directly, through massacre, or indirectly, by occupying their habitat, forcing them into marginal areas where they could no longer cope.[32]

Recent research suggests that fight or flight were not the only options. There was at least a third "F". Up to 5 percent of European DNA is Neanderthal, and other early hominin Denisovan DNA from Siberia has been found in modern humans in places such as Papua New Guinea. Rather than being wiped out, at least some earlier hominins married up (or down: Neanderthal brains are bigger than ours).[33]

As it happens, humans have the largest penises of any ape species, more than twice the size of that of an average silverback gorilla. Other ape species, especially bonobos, also use sex to ease tensions, but there are some ways in which the human pursuit of love, not war, is unique.

The Morality Instinct

Charles Darwin observed that Homo sapiens is the only species which has an involuntary blush response when we do anything we feel ashamed of. Blushing seems designed to prevent us from doing wrong by revealing our inner emotional state to others. Scientists have asked whether our long-term incentives to collaborate led to a hard-wired moral framework which rewards good behaviour and punishes bad.

Toddlers try to soothe others spontaneously, or to open doors for people who are carrying heavy loads. To ascertain whether kindness was learned or instinctive, we needed to find a way to test children's responses before they learned a language, or the moral values of their parents.

Experiments by Paul Bloom on three-month-olds and six-month-olds have proven that nature, rather than nurture, is responsible for giving us a "rudimentary moral sense" – although this moral sense is very influenced by environmental factors thereafter. When looking at shows featuring a puppet which is trying to push a ball uphill, or roll a ball to other puppets, three-month-olds will watch a good guy who helps, or a neutral guy who does nothing, rather than a bad guy who tries to hinder or steal the ball.

When offered the puppet characters after the show, six-month-olds "overwhelmingly" choose the good puppet over the neutral puppet, and the neutral puppet over the bad puppet. This moral sense can be punitive as well as kind. A twelve-month-old child used the good guy to hit the bad guy over the head. Our built-in righteousness may come with a hard-wired sense of wrath.[34]

We used to think that it was a dog-eat-dog world. In order to survive, we had to be cognisant of that fact. But this brutal and nihilistic concept does not fit our modern view of evolution. The latest research from biology, archaeology and psychology has shown us that, at the earliest stages of human existence, our hunter-gatherer ancestors prevailed not by being stronger, but by working together.

Evolution does not insist that we are naughty or nice. A behavioural trait will prosper if it increases the chances that our genes will make copies of themselves. Since modern Homo sapiens evolved, about three hundred thousand years ago, we have had powerful motives to collaborate, rather than compete.

Traits that improved collaboration increased our chances of survival.[35] We are wired to be kind, and to expect kindness in return. The development of a conscience helped us to thrive. Our genes are not "selfish".[36] Those of us schooled in the old idea of evolution have had to rethink what we mean by natural selection.

If modern ethnographies of hunter-gatherer bands are anything to go by, we were never perfect. We bitched and moaned and gossiped. We shamed cheats, and punished those who bullied or hexed others – sometimes putting them to death. But we also loved, and laughed, and shared. We fought off predators together. We looked after each other. For tens of thousands of years, survival of the fittest for our species meant survival of the kindest.

Chapter Two

The Psychology of Morality

"Nothing in the Golden Rule says that others will treat us as we have treated them. It only says that we must treat others in a way that we would want to be treated."[37]

ROSA PARKS

Our basic moral sense evolved to help us survive in a world where a stranger was just a friend we hadn't met, where we knew no more than 100 to 150 people well, and ran into perhaps ten times that number from neighbouring bands. Philosophers have been arguing for centuries about how that moral sense works, with Kant favoring the head and Hume favoring the heart. Recent psychological research by Joshua Greene and others shows that there is also room for the gut, in a set of instinctive moral taboos.

Here are brief summaries of the core elements of this basic moral sense.

Understanding Our Aversion to Killing Innocent Strangers

We can test intuitive taboos with a classic moral dilemma. Are you willing to kill one innocent stranger if it means that five other innocent people will survive? Only one in fifty would kill a person to harvest her organs, so that five others can live, but we show a lot more flexibility in a scenario known as "the trolley problem".[38]

Imagine that you're standing beside a large stranger overlooking trolley tracks, when five other strangers become trapped in the path of a trolley that cannot stop before it kills them all. If you push the stranger onto the track, he will die, but the other five people will be saved. You cannot sacrifice yourself because you are too light to stop the trolley.

Should you push the large stranger under the trolley? What if you had to flick a switch to divert the trolley to a different track, but this still meant that one stranger would die instead of five?

Only one in three people would push a person off a bridge to stop a trolley from killing five others. On the other hand, nearly nine out of ten of us would press a lever to divert the trolley, knowing that someone will be killed by it on another track.[39]

In the first scenario, you can't save the five people stranded on the track without physically pushing the stranger under the trolley yourself. In the variation, you spend far less effort to flick a switch and save the trapped people. The death of the stranger on the other track is an unfortunate side-effect, called "the doctrine of double effect" by Thomas Aquinas, but this philosophical distinction is not the reason why people are more willing to flick a switch than to push someone off a bridge.[40]

Scientists used brain-imaging MRI scanners to see which parts of the brain lit up when they were considering the trolley problem. They wanted to see whether more blood flowed to parts of the brain associated with vigilance and emotional rapport, or to areas which are involved in abstract reasoning.

The results were definitive. When people were asked to push an innocent person off a bridge, they instinctively recoiled. Both the amygdala, which makes reflexive flight-or-fight decisions, and the ventromedial prefrontal cortex of the brain, which is involved in emotional and moral judgements, experienced a surge of blood-flow.

When respondents had to flick a switch, pull a lever, or use some other indirect method, it became a strictly utilitarian decision about saving five lives versus one. One of the most recently evolved parts of the human brain, the dorsolateral prefrontal cortex, which is associated with working memory, risk analysis, and abstract reasoning, perked up.[41]

Our instinctive respect for the rights of innocent strangers is based on our aversion to "prototypical violence".[42] Whether we push the stranger onto the tracks, or use a pole to nudge him over the edge, our brains tell us that this is the wrong thing to do. But this hard-wired moral mode is blind-sided when no personal force or touching is required to kill the stranger – something Joshua Greene calls "modular myopia".

When we don't use personal force to kill the stranger, our intuitive moral mode in the amygdala and ventromedial prefrontal cortex doesn't become as active in making the ethical decision. Our dorsolateral prefrontal cortex does the math that saving five people is better than saving one, even though we had to kill the one in order to save the five. If ethical decisions were made purely on this basis, we would always be on the lookout for trapdoors in footbridges.

These hard-wired moral faculties have not, however, made nurture irrelevant. In fact, as a collaborative species, we are heavily influenced by peer pressure and cultural norms, as psychologists and anthropologists have shown.

Using Equivalent Retaliation

Studies of hunter-gatherers show that they apply punishments to those who try to cheat, sharing less food with them, and shaming those who try to hide food. Their use of moral suasion has been shown to be highly effective in resolving conflicts without recourse to violence.[43]

In an effort to understand the way this behaviour works, in the 1970s political scientist Robert Axelrod invited game theorists to submit different strategies for collaboration and cheating. These were placed in a computer simulation to see which would be most effective. The most successful one, created by Anatole Rapoport, started by sharing initially, then responding to whatever the other bots were doing. Soon bots that shared with each other and shunned cheats dominated the population. Rapoport called his strategy "tit for tat".

A tit-for-tat strategy may be the optimal way to maximise collaboration and minimise cheating when people share resources on an ongoing basis. As we shall see below, tit-for-tat behavior may have become instinctive when it comes to striking bargains.

Testing Your Instinctive Fairness

The tit-for-tat instinct to strike fair bargains is exemplified in "the ultimatum game". In this experiment, two strangers are isolated in different rooms. They are told that they can split a sum of money, say a hundred dollars, if they can agree on how they should divide it between them. One person is authorised to make an offer, and if the responder in the other room accepts it, then the money is divvied up. If the offer is refused, neither participant receives anything.[44]

There is a clear incentive to be as greedy as possible. However, in the United States, the most common offer made was a fifty-fifty split, and the average offer was 44 percent. The lower the offer, the angrier the second person was likely to become. Anyone offering 20 percent to the other person was likely to be refused half the time.[45]

In societies where generosity is used to display status, people were willing to offer far more than in the United States. On the other hand, among the Machiguenga of Peru, the average offer was under half the average in the United States. Researchers argued that the extent of daily cooperation and market exchange explained two-thirds of the difference. Machiguenga families did not participate in large-scale hunts, and made very little of their living through trade. They offered less, and were less likely to reject low-ball offers.

What is remarkable is that any participant in any culture was willing to reject any offer at all. Logically, people should be willing to be $1 better off at no cost to themselves, even if they know that a stranger has pocketed $99 as result.[46] The ultimatum game suggests that our instinct to punish stinginess on a tit-for-tat basis persists even when there is no prospect of benefiting from the retaliation in a later exchange.[47] This does not mean that people are foolish to reject stingy offers instinctively. If there was even the slightest chance we would meet again, as there would have been in the Stone Age, a tactically irrational impulse from our "lizard brain" may well have conferred a long-term strategic benefit.

Signalling Social Status

Social status is intimately linked to reproductive success. Hunter-gatherer bands have little tolerance for boastfulness, and a respected hunter expects his peers to belittle his skills. This is what anthropologists call "insulting the meat".[48] Despite temptations to lie and cheat, you need to signal your kindness to others in order to boost your social status in an environment where modesty and generosity are rewarded.[49]

Ideally, prospective partners will find out by themselves how wonderful you are. If they are seeking a mate who is kind, protective, generous and loyal, one of the most powerful ways to show them you're a mensch is in how you behave towards others. Every opportunity you give people to praise you for your kindness is another deposit in the bank of reproductive fitness.[50]

Psychologists have tested this further, in a variation of the ultimatum game known as "the dictator game". The first player is asked to share a sum of money with a second player, who cannot veto any offer.

There is no financial penalty for stinginess in sharing out the hundred dollars, even if the first player decides to keep the lot.

Remarkably, the first player continues to share money with an anonymous stranger – albeit the average offer made in the United States is closer to 20 percent than fifty-fifty. If the refusal of a stingy offer in the ultimatum game made little sense, giving money in the dictator game makes no sense at all, unless the "dictator" is avoiding the stigma and reduced social status associated with stinginess.

To test whether "dictators" were naturally generous, or just worried about what others thought of them, psychologists came up with "the double-blind dictator game". "Dictators" were told that their offers would be put in sealed envelopes, and randomly assigned to other players. Being seen to be greedy was no longer a factor. The generosity of the offers made by the "dictators" fell when the risk of social censure or embarrassment was removed.

Responding to Peer Pressure

Collaboration and moral behaviour are also heavily influenced by subconscious cues we pick up from our surroundings. Researchers in Groningen, in the Netherlands, ran a series of experiments to test "the broken-window theory" – which holds that people are more likely to break the law in an environment where rules are already being flouted.

The broken-window theory, first introduced in a 1982 article by social scientists James Q. Wilson and George L. Kelling, proposes that policing and otherwise eliminating visible signs of minor crimes like vandalism, public drinking, parking violations and graffiti helps create an atmosphere of order and lawfulness which prevents more serious crimes.

The Dutch researchers found that more than one in four of us would steal money sticking out of an envelope in a mailbox covered in graffiti, but only one in eight of us would take the money if the mailbox was clean. Nearly nine out of ten motorists ignore signs saying "No trespassing" to take a shortcut to their cars if bicycles are illegally chained to railings nearby, but less than one in three will trespass if the bicycles are removed.[51]

The experiments support the idea that the laborious efforts of community workers and law-enforcement officials to clean up neighborhoods have reduced the incidence of anti-social behavior, but they also indicate that adherence to moral standards is contingent – influenced by what others have got away with before. Moral obligation increases where it is clear that others are following the rules.

Social programmes are now being influenced by environmental cues. In one study, placing a pair of angry eyes above a bike-rack reduced theft by 60 percent.[52] Whether aggressive stop-and-frisk programs, which disproportionately target Hispanic and African-American youth, have helped or hindered society is much more controversial.

Studies also show that, in addition to being influenced by the behaviour of our closest neighbours, we generally do not lend strong emotional or financial support to distant strangers by means of abstract reasoning alone.[53] We will give more to a less worthy cause closer to home which has touched our hearts.[54] To engage our intuitive moral mode, we need the sensory cues and peer pressure that surround us. We need to build rapport in order to be kind. It is not just sports teams that benefit from home advantage.

We are capable of extraordinary kindness, selflessness and empathy towards people we have just met. But we do need to meet them in some way in order to humanise their plight. As Paul Bloom said about the "spotlight" effect of empathy, we cannot process the deaths of millions in a faraway country in the same way that we sit glued to the television if a child is trapped down a well.

And as Stalin, of all people, said: "If only one man dies of hunger, that is a tragedy. If millions die, that's only statistics."[55]

Chapter Three

How Collaboration Evolved into Conflict

"A people free to choose will always choose peace."

RONALD REAGAN

For a kind and caring species, we have a remarkably poor record when it comes to empathising with strangers unless we can make a sensory connection. Collaboration may have been the key to our survival, but it is not hard to imagine that we spent a lot of time grousing about the jerks next door who tried to hoard food, or didn't fetch wood for the camp-fire. One thing we didn't do, however, was wage war. The archaeological evidence suggests that, as recently as fifteen thousand years ago, warfare was rare to non-existent.[56]

Unfortunately, as populations started to explode, warfare rapidly became widespread. The hunter-gatherer societies which were so effective when it came to sharing resources among band-members were now threatened with starvation as food supplies were lost to rivals. Bands coalesced into larger groups which could deter incessant raiding. We developed cultural solutions to reduce the risk of devastating conflict. We can trace the journey from kindness to conflict through archaeological digs and ancient cave-art, as well as the ways we sought to mitigate violence through the creation of kingdoms, sharing myths of common ancestry, and arranging patriarchal marriages.

The Influence of Population Growth
and Expansion

Humans are not the fastest creatures on earth, but we do possess great reserves of stamina. Seventy thousand years ago, the easiest way to hunt antelope was probably to track them until they were exhausted, and then corner and spear them. As populations expanded, we became more creative. The use of throwing-spears, javelins, blowpipes, and bows and arrows became widespread over the last twenty thousand years. There were mass-extinctions of mega-fauna whenever Homo sapiens entered a new territory.

The last phase of the Old Stone Age, the Upper Paleolithic, has been dated to between fifty thousand and fifteen thousand years ago. This was an exciting period when modern humans developed sophisticated art and jewellery alongside new hunting techniques.[57] Prey animals have been painted in caves for more than forty thousand years, perhaps for their spiritual significance. Some academics believe that we adopted better weapons because of a genetic breakthrough in intelligence, but it may also have been because animals were becoming harder to catch by a growing population. Necessity may have been the mother of invention.

If warfare was a routine cultural phenomenon, we would expect Homo sapiens to draw attention to it in the images we left behind. But despite the proliferation of highly effective hunting weapons, and thousands of images of hunting scenes, Cro-magnon cave paintings in dozens of caves across southern Europe do not depict any battle scenes from forty thousand to fifteen thousand years ago.[58]

The closest we get to artistic evidence of warfare earlier than fifteen thousand years ago is four unarmed, ambiguous figures impaled by spears, painted in three caves in France. They may be human or demi-gods, since two of them have tails. They may have been sacrificed, or found guilty of a capital crime. Even if we assume that they were victims of battle, their rarity reinforces the idea that warfare was not a routine feature of human life before populations started to explode.[59]

Our ancestors had no hesitation in depicting a massive uptick in battle scenes in later art. With soaring populations following the adoption of agriculture fifteen thousand years ago, images of rival groups of archers started to appear on cave walls.

The Paleontological Evidence of Increasing Warfare

Archaeologists have a spotty record in interpreting early human remains. It can be hard to tell how someone died. Seventy-five percent of violent deaths leave only soft-tissue injuries, so the absence of marks on skeletal remains is not conclusive. Cuts made by predatory animals must be distinguished from homicide or post-mortem burial rituals.

Highly influential books written by respected archaeologists like Lawrence Keeley (*War Before Civilisation*) and Keith Otterbein (*How War Began*) have argued that warfare is endemic in recorded human history. Some suggest that non-state band-cultures are intrinsically warlike, despite examples like the Gobero in Niger, which seems to have had no deaths from warfare in the eight thousand years of its existence, from sixteen thousand to eight thousand years ago.

Claims that we humans are inherently and universally warlike rely on ethnographies of modern hunter-gatherer societies.[60] Even among peaceful bands, punitive homicide rates are high – mainly for bullying or cursing others, or, to a much lesser extent, adultery.[61] One murder every century in a band of one hundred people is the equivalent, for example, of a homicide level over 2.5 times that of New York City in 2014.[62]

Punishing cheats and bullies may have been an intrinsic component of a collaborative moral sense, but extrapolating from contemporary hunter-gatherers into prehistory has to be done with caution. We can infer a great deal about how our ancestors foraged, or their cultural beliefs, by looking at modern hunter-gatherers, but we cannot simulate the freedom to roam that our ancestors enjoyed in an era of very low population density and abundant resources – and the corresponding impact on levels of warfare.[63]

Apart from modern ethnographies, the closest we can get to systematic violence in the very early archaeological record is an 800,000-year-old site in Spain which shows evidence of cannibalism among early hominins. Cannibalism, however, is a mortuary ritual in many cultures – to honour beloved relatives rather than celebrate the defeat of fallen enemies.

So proponents of the endemic-warfare theory have struggled to come up with reasons for warfare in an era where population densities were very low and resources plentiful. Climatic conditions were more volatile during the Ice Age, but with diverse sources of food being widely available, especially for adaptable Homo sapiens, it is hard to see how occasional climate-shifts over decades would lead to frequent conflict between scattered bands of hunter-gatherers. It is likely that our male hominin ancestors occasionally fought each other over females – there is some sexual dimorphism, after all – but in recorded history, men typically fight over status where there is a dearth of young women. As gender-ratios normalise, men tend to settle down and raise families, and conflict declines rapidly and substantially.

The archaeologists and anthropologists Jonathan Haas and Matthew Piscitelli of the Field Museum in Chicago have shown that the archaeological record for warfare in the Upper Paleolithic, from fifty thousand to fifteen thousand years ago, is "not silent". It simply isn't there. Just under three thousand skeletons have been excavated from this era, in more than four hundred sites. Apart from a handful of skeletons, in a handful of places, which may show signs of deliberate human violence, there is no evidence for warfare in the Upper Paleolithic.[64]

If our ancestors had been evenly distributed around the world, there would have been little environmental pressure to change the hunter-gatherer way of life, but the growth of sedentary bands created local population bottlenecks, where access to resources was more circumscribed.[65] We do not have a precise global head-count at the end of the last Ice Age, about twelve thousand years ago, but HYDE, the History Database of the Global Environment, calculates a population of 2 million people. Other sources place it in a range of between 1 million and 10 million, with an upper estimate of 20 million people.[66] As sedentary groups were surrounded by nomadic hunter-gatherer bands, migration to other regions was no longer a readily available option. When the climate became less volatile at the start of the Holocene era, twelve thousand years ago, we used agriculture to boost food yields as we were gradually encircled by other bands

Since they could not maintain an adequate supply of food by moving elsewhere, sedentary groups focused their attention on increasing the yield from wild seedlings they planted, and harvesting milk, meat and horsepower from domesticated animals. As the first farmers cultivated the land, they developed Neolithic tools of polished stone to help them.

Agriculture may have been invented separately in several parts of Eurasia and Africa, and was certainly invented independently in North and South America. As Jared Diamond has pointed out, the native plant species in the Fertile Crescent, including wheat, barley, peas and lentils, as well as the native animal species, such as cows, goats, sheep and pigs, gave the sedentary bands in that region an enormous head-start.[67]

The effect was explosive. In five thousand years, the HYDE database estimates that the global population grew from 2 million to 18 million people. By the time of Christ, ten thousand years after the invention of agriculture, the global human population may have risen more than a hundred-fold, to between 150 million and 330 million people.[68]

Fifteen thousand years ago, people cooped up in sedentary population bottlenecks had to find ways to increase local food-supplies in order to survive. Over the next ten thousand years, as population densities rose, warfare gradually appeared in the prehistoric archaeological record across the Fertile Crescent, and we were forced to develop cultural innovations designed to reduce the risk of devastating conflict.

From Kindness to Competition

Agriculture did not spread across Eurasia instantly. The received wisdom for much of the twentieth century was that agriculture arrived in Britain with waves of invading farmers, who wiped out the aboriginal population.[69]

While it seems that agriculture spread through migration rather than word of mouth, the genocide theory has undergone some revision. If 90 percent of the hunter-gatherers were eliminated, one of the weapons may have been biological. Europeans who travelled to the New World carried diseases which had crossed over from farm animals, wiping out millions of Native Americans in pandemics. Like Covid-19, Bronze Age farmers may have taken into Britain diseases against which the local hunter-gatherers had no immunity.

With the benefit of genetic testing, we can confirm that Neolithic farmers from the Middle East had a substantial impact on paternal DNA in Britain, and later migrants like the Beaker People were violent, but many Britons descend from the original hunter-gatherers in their maternal line.[70] The only complete destruction was of the native auroch, a large wild cow, which was supplanted in the Bronze Age by domesticated cattle from the Middle East.

In areas such as Britain, where wild-food sources were plentiful and the population relatively low, it took approximately six thousand years before plant and animal species from the Fertile Crescent were adopted in the local region. The spread of migrants, crops and animal species towards north-west Europe proceeded at the leisurely pace of roughly one kilometre per year.[71]

Why it took so long for agriculture to reach Britain's shores remains a source of speculation. The simplest answer may be that, in the absence of population bottlenecks, hunter-gatherers did not need to change their ways.

The domestication of plant and animal species brought with it a massive increase in food-yields, but it also created problems which were unknown among nomadic hunter-gatherer societies. A static supply of food required vigilance to protect crops and flocks from theft, whether by animals or neighbouring bands. It required skills in animal husbandry, irrigation and fertilisation. It also sparked the evolution of private property.

Hunter-gatherers could share because this was a highly efficient way of ensuring a steady supply of food at a time when killing large prey animals relied heavily on dumb luck. Farming required back-breaking work, but it resulted in a more predictable outcome. The more effort you put in – gods willing – the more you received: as you sow, so shall you reap. It was only fair that you claim the fruits of your labour. The people you could count on to work without skiving or malingering were your immediate kin. Around ten thousand years ago, Pre-Pottery Neolithic wheat-farmers in the Fertile Crescent started to organise farm labour around families rather than communal villages.[72] For the first time, our neighbours had something worth stealing.

While hard work increased the odds of a good harvest, it did not eliminate the risk of blight or bad weather. With rising populations, a bad harvest brought the spectre of famine, and squabbles over how to store and share the surplus in years of plenty. High population densities and poor sanitation among tribes and domesticated animals increased the risk of epidemic disease. A lack of food security, and the potential for dominance over larger regions, motivated chieftains to go to war. Malnourishment increased, average height decreased, and life-expectancy fell. We were in the era of Hobbes' *Leviathan*, as life became "nasty, brutish, and short".

In 1964, Fred Wendorf was working on a UNESCO archaeology project to document Jebel Sahaba in the Nile Valley, near the Sudan-Egypt border, before it was flooded by the Aswan Dam. At Site 117, his team stumbled across the ancient corpses of sixty-one men, women and children. The skeletons were dated to between thirteen thousand and fourteen thousand years old, making it the oldest mass burial site known to archaeology, and quite unlike the small nomadic burial sites of earlier periods. But it also has another claim to fame.

Unlike other burial sites in the region which have been dated to the same era, nearly half the bodies had suffered violent deaths from arrows or other objects, and many of the victims had suffered previous violent blows which had healed. Whether most were killed in a single ambush, or as a result of multiple skirmishes, is not certain, but the prevalence of healed wounds suggests that conflict had taken place over a period of time. We do not know whether all the victims were members of the same band, or if warriors from different sides were buried together. But in any case, these are the oldest known war-graves in the world.

We cannot know for sure what motivated the hunter-gatherer warriors of Jebel Sahaba – although rapid climate-change along the Nile is a likely culprit, with semi-sedentary bands forced to compete for dwindling food resources.[73] We have no idea how they justified the killings to themselves, since they did not leave written records.

It would be another five thousand to seven thousand years before the first cities were founded, in places like Jericho in the Jordan Valley, and Uruk and Eridu in modern-day Iraq. Some were initially built without defences, but by the time the first fully fledged system of writing was invented in Sumeria, around five thousand years ago, walls and defensive fortifications were in use across Mesopotamia.

As populations expanded in Sumeria, they became increasingly dependent on outside trade for crucial resources such as wood. Poor drainage and climate change increased salinity, and once-eliable sources of food became vulnerable. Swamps were drained and irrigated, bringing rival city-states into closer proximity.[74] As food-supplies became insecure, tensions over scarce resources became more common, and people sought ways to solve these conflicts without recourse to war.

Making Peace in a Time of War

A key way in which we sought to make peace was by merging bands. Bands of roughly a hundred people may have been ideal for hunting and gathering, but in the early days of agriculture, lethal raiding by small bands encouraged societies to scale up. To avoid being conquered and possibly enslaved, or worse still, suffering famine after raiding parties stole or destroyed their food, bands and tribes had powerful reasons for coming together through alliance or conquest.[75]

Based on archaeological evidence from pre-Columbian Mexico, when hungry, fearful bands coalesced into relatively stable kingdoms more than five hundred years ago, the average death-toll from battle as a percentage of the population may have dropped three-fold.[76] There were fewer independent warlords and inter-group rivalries, and arbitration by kings reduced favouritism in intra-group disputes.

Internecine conflict required a concentration of authority to direct military force, but once they took power there was no guarantee that autocrats would prioritise the people over their own interests. Nearly 4,500 years ago, for example, the Sumerian city of Lagash revolted against the corrupt Lugalanda and replaced him with the pious Urukagina, who cut taxes and punished criminals in an extensive campaign of reform.[77]

Kingdoms required kings and administrators to rule them, as opposed to egalitarian bands where decisions were generally made collectively. The importance and status of authority-figures increased. Some families became much richer than others, as material capital in land and livestock was passed down through generations.[78] As agricultural societies grew, they became more hierarchical. The potential for polygamous alpha-behaviour gave some warrior-kings a spectacular genetic payoff, as they fathered children with hundreds of women. Some geneticists estimate that one in two hundred men alive today share a common Mongolian male ancestor who lived a thousand years ago, a little before the time of Genghis Khan.

At the other end of the hierarchy, slavery has been present in agricultural societies in one form or another from the beginning of recorded history — as payment of a debt, as punishment for a crime, in tribute to a king, or in military conflict, when the lives of the vanquished were forfeit.

Sumerian texts recount the capture of foreigners as slaves, and in *The Iliad*, Homer's epic, Hector laments that his wife and son will be enslaved if the Trojans are defeated. At the milder end of the spectrum, slavery resembled indentured servitude, and was not always hereditary.

Enslavement has been easier where we deny our kinship to the enslaved, categorising out-groups as "them" rather than "us", as foreigners – even if they look like us, or speak the same language. The term for "slave" in ancient Sumerian was a synonym for a person from the mountains. A female slave was called "mountain girl" and a male slave was called "mountain man".[79]

Plato's ideal society was one where everyone, from kings to slaves, knew their place – unlike the anarchy of democracy. Especially when we were no longer closely related biologically, we fostered kin altruism culturally, by telling stories. Social cohesion was enhanced through myths of common ancestry which built tribal solidarity on the basis of a shared noble heritage. The twelve tribes of Israel were descended from the twelve sons of Jacob, the Yoruba were descended from the Emperor Oduduwa, and the Han Chinese were descended from the Yellow Emperor. By four thousand years ago, kings were building solidarity by instituting laws to protect the vulnerable, and assuming titles such as "Defender of the Orphan", "Husband to the Widow", "Rescuer of the Fearful" and "Saviour of the Distressed".[80]

In some cultures, kin altruism was also bolstered by the practice of fostering noble children with other warlords, where they became adoptive siblings as well as hostages – an insurance policy against raiding by rivals. Social cohesion was also strengthened by merging kingdoms into empires, quelling fractious tribal disputes, and holding diverse groups together with the promise of peace, stability and justice – for instance in the Pax Romana, the 206 years from the accession of Caesar Augustus to the death of the last great Emperor, Marcus Aurelius.

From Partners to Property

As societies became hierarchical, men began to dominate politically and economically, with limitations on female participation in public life varying across cultures. Writers have speculated about why this happened, citing everything from the development of warrior-castes to the accumulation of private property. But the value of women as creators of biological kin altruism – showing kindness towards your blood relatives – also encouraged the rapid growth of patriarchy as a means of reducing conflict.[81]

Ensuring that the right match-ups happened between rivals required a great deal of cultural engineering. Personal and intimate choices about who we want as our partners became strategic decisions about war and peace.

Women became assets. By bartering their bodies in marriage, clans cemented alliances between groups. By having children with rival warlords, patriarchies avoided succession crises which could plunge kingdoms into civil war. And by creating and enforcing strict rules and honour-codes relating to chastity and fidelity, they minimised doubt about the biological legitimacy of heirs. For a species which had lived in egalitarian bands for tens of thousands of years, this no doubt created tensions. People needed to believe that profound inequality on the basis of sex was not just a necessary evil to avoid war.

Patriarchies cultivated myths of female inferiority or weakness in order to persuade citizens that this was the natural order of things. Evidence that women were the intellectual equals of men was not part of the official narrative. Challenging social rules on marriage and fidelity became taboo. Rebelling, by marrying someone from the wrong group, could lead star-crossed lovers to the same fate as Romeo and Juliet.

The Rise of Patriarchy

This shift from partnership to patriarchy did not happen all at once, nor did it happen everywhere in the same way, and it didn't affect the lower classes to the same extent as the elites. The Greek historian Herodotus was scandalised 2500 years ago when he discovered that high-born Egyptian women could witness contracts and go to the public market.[82] In the Renaissance, the Spanish Inquisition despaired of the unlettered peasantry, who believed that "simple fornication" between unmarried partners was not a sin.[83]

Sexual attraction which led women to stray from arranged marriages became dangerous, particularly in aristocratic circles. Julia, the popular, witty, intelligent and famously promiscuous daughter of Augustus Caesar, allegedly said that she only had affairs when she was legitimately pregnant. She was forced into exile nevertheless, and may have died from malnutrition.[84] Female sexual allure and independence were suspect. According to most Christian mythology, Eve, notoriously, caused Adam to be banished from Eden when she handed him the forbidden fruit of self-awareness.

The transition to patriarchy can be seen in the evolution of the Old Testament, or Hebrew Bible. The story of Deborah, a female judge and prophet, is told in chapters four and five of the Book of Judges. Although Deborah is married to a man called Lapidoth, she is formidably powerful in her own right. Roughly 3200 years ago, before Israel became a kingdom, Deborah is the leader who rallies the army, under Barak, to rout the Canaanite army leader Sisera – who is killed by a woman called Jael after fleeing the battle.

A few centuries later, the new relationship between property and matrimony is described in the Book of Ruth. Ruth and her mother-in-law Naomi are childless widows who flee to Israel, where they suffer in poverty. Their story ends happily ever after when Ruth marries a rich kinsman of her dead husband Mahlon, called Boaz. However, the marriage can only take place after a closer relative relinquishes his claim to Mahlon's property, including his widow, by formally handing Boaz a sandal. This symbolic gesture leads to Ruth becoming the great-grandmother of the celebrated King David.

Fast-forward to 2500 years ago, to the Jews of the diaspora in Persia. We meet a beautiful Jewish orphan who lives with her older cousin Mordecai. The Book of Esther describes how King Xerxes I exiled his consort Vashti for refusing to parade in front of the court wearing only a crown. Xerxes hosts a beauty contest – which Esther wins, without revealing that she is Jewish.

Esther asks the king to appoint her cousin Mordecai as an official in his government. At the same time, the king's viceroy, Haman, seeking revenge over Mordecai for not having bowed down to him, buys a royal decree for ten thousand talents which allows the massacre of every Jew in Persia. Hearing this, Esther invites the king to a banquet, reveals that she's Jewish, and begs Xerxes to repeal Haman's genocidal decree. He does so – then orders that Haman be hanged from the gallows he had built for Mordecai, and appoints Esther's cousin as his new viceroy.

Esther succeeds, despite the fact that her appearance in the king's presence without a royal summons was punishable by death. Seven hundred years after the leadership of Deborah, Esther negotiates her way through an aristocratic patriarchy which objectifies women, and in which failure is fraught with potentially lethal risks.

Thereafter, apart from the erotic love-poetry of the Song of Songs, female voices fade from the narrative in the Hebrew Bible. As elsewhere, accounts of female heroism became half-remembered legends.[85]

Chapter Four

The Struggle for a More Open Society

"Those who do not remember the past are condemned to repeat it."

GEORGE SANTAYANA

People have been grappling with the task of creating a more open and plural society for thousands of years. The recent polarisation seen in the rise of Brexit and Donald Trump has shocked liberals, and led to fears that the gains made since the Enlightenment are under threat. However, we have been here many times before. Norms of tolerance which have persisted for centuries can be rapidly overturned when calamity strikes, and blame-storming leads to the persecution of the vulnerable.

The rise of patriarchal arranged marriage allowed societies to broker peace through kin altruism, but as a disempowered group, women were at risk of persecution as well as exploitation in moments of crisis. In one area, however, women have had a strong, if not always successful, influence: freedom of conscience.

Progressive female voices encouraged tolerance, including the Edict of Milan in 313, the first legal edict on freedom of worship in Western history. Thirteen hundred years before the Enlightenment, the laws of Church and State protected religious minorities. Elite figures in the Dark Ages taught that it was delusional to believe that sorcerers spoilt crops, poisoned wells or spread plague. Lynch-mobs seeking scapegoats for plague, famine, the pollution of water, or bad weather risked the death-penalty if they executed people for sorcery. State-sanctioned witch-trials fell into abeyance for more than a thousand years.

But progress was neither inevitable nor irreversible. Having been scapegoated for blasphemy when the Roman Empire suffered military defeats, Christians in their turn mollified the wrath of God by suppressing heresy, paganism and sexual desire within their ranks, especially in times of crisis. Female sexuality was traduced by theologians after the Sack of Rome in 410.

Eventually, the invention of the printing press allowed misogynistic fake news about sorcery to "go viral" in 1487, culminating in the "gynecide" of the Renaissance witch-hunts in the sixteenth and seventeenth centuries, in which at least three-quarters of the accused were female.

Women became perpetrators as well as victims. On the rare occasions when they rose to power in the Renaissance, in the absence of a suitable male heir, they were pivotal in the foundation of the Spanish Inquisition (1477), the Saint Bartholomew's Day Massacre (1572), and scorched-earth tactics (1602) which facilitated a sectarian colony on European soil, in a contested territory that would eventually become one of the biggest challenges for Brexit.

Female Influence on Religious Freedom 1700 Years Ago

Religious persecution upset centuries of tolerance – over which women had exerted a profound influence, most importantly in 313 in the form of Helena, the mother of the Roman Emperor Constantine the Great, who was devoted to her.[86]

Constantine knew less of his father Constantius. He had divorced Helena for a more strategic alliance when Constantine was still a child. Little is known of Helena's early life, other than that she sprang from humble origins before becoming the consort of an ambitious Roman aristocrat, and that she had a profound Christian faith.

By the third century, Christianity was still a minority religion, practiced by no more than one in ten of the population – mostly fools, women, children and slaves, according to the pagan intellectual Celsus.[87] But Christians were usually left to their own devices, despite having been blamed by Nero for the Great Fire of Rome in the year 64.[88]

The problem, from a Roman point of view, was not the Christian devotion to a new cult, but their unwillingness to honour the deities who protected the Empire in times of crisis. Refusing to engage in public homage of the gods led to tensions with the State, especially during major crises such as plagues and famines, or after military defeat, when people sought a scapegoat to blame for the loss of the favour of the gods.[89]

We know from looking at ancient tree-rings that the Roman Empire experienced erratic harvests from 200 to 650. The mix of rising populations and unpredictable crop-yields led to a series of invasions and military defeats. The Emperor Diocletian had another idea: the gods had allowed the Empire to be defeated due to the profanity of the Christians.

Roman emperors, faced with existential threats from barbarian hordes which could bring war, pestilence, enslavement or famine to their heartland, had little use for loving their enemies, turning the other cheek, or praying for those who persecuted them. Warring factions continued to target Christians in the civil war that followed Diocletian's abdication in 305.

From 303 to 313, thousands of Christians were executed in the arena, or burnt to death after being gruesomely tortured. Thousands more were forced into apostasy by public sacrifice to the gods. In North

Africa, Christians were allowed to repudiate their faith by handing over their sacred texts. Priests who handed them over (*tradere* in Latin) were called *traditores*, or traitors.[90]

Then, in 311, Constantine saw a Christian symbol in the sky, with the words: "By this sign, conquer."[91] The next day, he won the decisive battle of Milvian Bridge. It was not the first sign that he had seen. The previous year, he had had a vision of Apollo, and in 307 he had invoked Hercules during his second wedding ceremony. He was fond of the religion of Sol Invictus, the official sun-god of the later Roman Empire, and patron of soldiers, whose primary feast day was on 25 December; Constantine had Sol Invictus coins minted as late as 320.[92]

It was not unusual for an emperor to follow more than one cult. Attributing victory in battle to the favour of the gods was not a new phenomenon either, but putting the Prince of Peace, Jesus of Nazareth, into the frame was unprecedented.[93]

We almost certainly have Helena to thank for both Constantine's sympathy towards Christianity and his tolerance of all religions. Having witnessed the failure of the Diocletian persecutions, he was careful not to alienate pagans by adopting a muscular form of Christianity. The solution was to formalise the traditional Roman pluralist attitude towards all faiths.

The Edict of Milan, issued by Constantine and the Eastern Emperor Licinius in 313, stated that "no one whatsoever should be denied freedom to devote himself either to the cult of the Christians or to such religion as he deems best suited for himself, so that the highest divinity, to whose worship we pay allegiance with free minds, may grant us in all things his wonted favour and benevolence".[94]

Helena was formally baptised as a Christian soon after her son became emperor. In the move to Christianity, goddesses of fertility and wisdom such as Athena, Isis, Rhea and Tyche were replaced by the Virgin Mary and an array of saints, who interceded to grant good weather, fertility, safe childbirth and protection from enemies.[95]

Constantine tried to prevent sectarian spats among Christians, including Adoptionists, who claimed that Jesus was fully human and created; Sabellians, who believed there was no distinction between Jesus and God; Homoiosians, who said that Jesus was "like" God the Father; Homoiousians, who said that Jesus was "of similar substance" to God the Father, and Homoousians, who argued that Jesus and God the Father were of identical substance and, together with the Holy Spirit, formed the Holy Trinity in one God.These conflicts had to be resolved, even if Constantine struggled to see how such "idle and trivial" distinctions could cause so much tension.[96] Unlike earlier disputes, fissures between the pillars of the Church could now undermine the foundations of the State. The most intractable dispute was between Alexander, the Bishop of Alexandria, who believed in the Holy Trinity, and his excommunicated presbyter Arius, who believed that Jesus was created by, and subordinate to, God the Father.[97]

Constantine wrote a letter rebuking Alexander and Arius, stating that their quarrel was not over "precepts of the Divine Law . . . the Divine commandment in all its parts enjoins on us all the duty of maintaining a spirit of concord".[98] To maintain that spirit, he summoned Church patriarchs to his palace at Nicaea in 325, where they adopted the Nicene Creed – which is still used by mainstream Christian denominations today.

Constantine continued to oppose Christian intolerance throughout his life, writing that it was "contrary to the divine law that we should overlook such quarrels and contentions . . . whereby the Highest Divinity may perhaps be roused not only against the human race but against myself",[99] and telling a group of bishops that they did "nothing but that which encourages discord and hatred and, to speak frankly, which leads to the destruction of the human race".[100]

This from a man who had executed Licinius, his main political rival, in the same year as the Council of Nicaea, and who, a year later, had his second wife executed, as well as his son from his first marriage, allegedly for having had an affair.[101]

Constantine was baptised on his deathbed.[102] For centuries thereafter, the laws of Church and State guaranteed religious freedom, and forbade forced conversion of non-Christian religious minorities.[103]

Blaming the Sack of Rome on Female Sexuality

As the Western Roman Empire weakened, orthodoxy increased in response to a series of military crises. Four decades after the death of Constantine, heretical bishops were expelled by the Christian Emperor Theodosius[104] after ten thousand soldiers were killed by the Goths in the Battle of Adrianople in 378.[105] Like the pagan Emperor Diocletian, the orthodox Christian Emperor Theodosius blamed the profanity of heretics and religious minorities for the loss of divine favour.

The archeological record shows that pagan shrines were defaced with Christian symbols across the Empire, from Rome to Alexandria.[106] Income which had been used to maintain pagan temples was redirected to the Nicene church, and public cult-worship was suppressed.[107] The last ancient Olympic Games were held in 395.[108] Christianity became the official state religion, but other religions remained popular.

Then the unthinkable happened: after eight centuries of resilience, Rome, the symbolic epicentre of the Empire, was sacked by the Visigoths in 410. Pagans blamed the Sack of Rome on the wrath of the gods, who were rejected by Christians. Christians blamed the cataclysmic event on paganism, but also put female sexuality front and centre, particularly in the writings of Augustine, especially *The City of God*, his theological response to the Sack of Rome.[109]

In *The City of God*, Augustine offered a bleak view of the iniquity of mankind, in which the fear of damnation was as prominent as hope in a loving God, and – speaking from his own experience, which included fathering a child out of wedlock – sexuality was suspect. Augustine argued that humanity had been inherently sinful since the fall of Adam. The youngest infant was contaminated with Original Sin.[110] "Nothing is so powerful in drawing the spirit of a man downwards," Augustine wrote, "as the caresses of a woman."

Not everyone agreed with him. His contemporary, Jovinian, wrote in praise of marriage, and believed that there was nothing intrinsically superior about remaining a virgin. He questioned the moral benefit of celibacy and abnegation, and saw a link between the obsession with chastity and "the present distress".[111]

Religious celibacy became increasingly important for men and women. For women, by side-stepping patriarchal gender roles as wives and mothers, communities of nuns acquired autonomy and power in Buddhism, Hinduism and Christianity.

An Idealistic Philosopher in Alexandria

For both pagan and Christian women, virginity helped open the doors to some of the most prestigious academic positions in the ancient world. The mathematician Hypatia is the prime example of this phenomenon.[112]

Hypatia taught philosophy and astronomy as the head of the Neoplatonist school in Alexandria, Egypt. She was famed for her wisdom and teaching, for editing the works of Euclid and Ptolemy, and for co-authoring some of the commentaries attributed to her father, Theon, as well as writing commentaries in her own right.

Although she was a pagan, all the pupils we know to have been taught by her were Christians, and around the time of the Sack of Rome she became an advisor to Orestes, the Roman prefect, or governor, of

Alexandria. But the manner of her death was to eclipse all of her own achievements.

In 412, two years after the Sack of Rome, a new bishop of Alexandria was appointed after a bitter contest. Cyril removed his opponents from clerical office, and then expelled all the Jews from Alexandria. When the prefect, Orestes, wrote a letter denouncing Cyril to the emperor, Cyril's followers tried to kill him. Orestes had the man who led the mob tortured to death.

After a brief truce, Hypatia was killed in the power-struggle between Orestes and Cyril, having been asked to intervene by the bishop of Ptolemais, her former pupil Synesius of Cyrene. Followers of Cyril dragged her from a carriage into a church, stripped her naked, murdered her, dismembered her, and then set her on fire.[113]

Her murder shocked the entire Roman world. Killing a philosopher during a political squabble was taboo. She died a pagan in a fight between Christians, but her death was appropriated by everyone. A woman admired for wisdom and dignity, who wanted to bring the highest moral standards to political office for the benefit of everyone, was held up as a martyr by adversaries of every creed and none.[114]

Two centuries later, apologists for Cyril accused Hypatia of using magic to beguile Orestes, prompting some historians to argue that Hypatia was the first woman to be executed by Christians for witchcraft. But throughout the Dark Ages, the Church taught that belief in witchcraft was superstitious, and secular courts levied the death-penalty for witch-hunting.[115]

Church and State stopped lynch-mobs in their tracks in times of famine, disease or water contamination, and dismissed sorcery as absurd superstition, until the printing press spread fake news about women and witchcraft – and ushered in centuries of misogynistic persecution during the Renaissance.

Fake News about Women and Witchcraft in The Hammer of the Witches

People have been scapegoated for causing sickness and other natural disasters since records began. The law-codes of Babylon, Egypt and Rome laid down the death-penalty for causing illness or crop-failure; along with bullying, sorcery is the most common reason recorded by anthropologists for capital punishment among non-segmented hunter-gatherer societies.[116] But around 1500 years ago, under the influence of Augustine, Church and State halted the witch-hunts.[117]

Under the worldview of the early Christian Church, if God was loving and all-powerful, then sorcerers were powerless, and should not be blamed for causing natural phenomena. At most, they could be excommunicated or ordered to do penance.[118] The Lombard Code of 643 states that witchcraft "ought not to be believed by Christian minds".[119] We could set aside the torch and pitchfork.

Pope John XXII authorised inquisitors to investigate sorcery as a form of heresy in the 1320s, but the Church was unequivocal[120]: the idea that mortals had supernatural agency over the weather, could cast spells on other people, fly at night, change into animals or have sex with demons was absurd.[121]

As late as 1431, when the nineteen-year-old Joan of Arc was captured by the Burgundian allies of England during the Hundred Years War between England and France, they needed a reason to kill her that would tarnish her reputation as a visionary. She had led an army armed only with her banner, lifting a key English siege at Orléans to restore the region to the King of France. After her capture, seventy trumped-up charges, including smears about witchcraft, were laid against her, but it was her heretical proclivity for repeatedly cross-dressing – as a soldier – that was used to light the pyre.

It was not until 1484, around the same time that Leonardo da Vinci was sketching plans for flying-machines, that Pope Innocent VIII, at the behest of a Dominican inquisitor and academic called Heinrich Kramer, issued a papal bull authorising the correction and punishment of devil-worshippers.[122]

Kramer had been expelled from Innsbruck after becoming obsessed with the sexual habits of a defendant, Helena Scheuberin, during the first Church-led trial for witchcraft in a thousand years. Kramer's methods were quickly seen as illegal and unethical, even by the miserable standards of the fifteenth century, and the prosecution was halted. The bishop who expelled Kramer described him as senile and crazy.

But Kramer was also an eloquent speaker, with a brilliant mind. After becoming prior of his local Dominican house at a young age, he was appointed Professor of Theology at the University of Salzburg. Before the Innsbruck debacle, his efforts as an inquisitor had brought him recognition in Rome.

Having persuaded the pope that witchcraft was not only real, but presented a clear and present danger, he spent three years writing a masterpiece of confabulation called *The Hammer of the Witches*, or *Malleus Maleficarum*. Citing in the preamble not only the authority of the pope, but his own expertise as a witch-hunter, Kramer spun the disastrous experience at Innsbruck into an endorsement of his methods of finding, torturing and terminating witches.

Winning over a sophisticated secular audience, which had been schooled to believe that witchcraft was mere superstition, was not easy. With the scholarly imprimatur of the pope, *The Hammer of the Witches* reads like an FBI behavioural-science journal for the Renaissance: it stated, with the same assurance that FBI profilers use when asserting that serial-killers hunt within their own ethnic groups, that most witches were women.

The Hammer of the Witches provided a legal, theological and practical justification for Kramer's ideas. It was also a manual explaining how to identify and interrogate witches – a sort of *Witch-hunting for Dummies*.

The fact that witch-hunts were expressly forbidden by Canon Law was brushed aside. Kramer said that church law did not refer to "modern" witches, who were clearly more malevolent than their predecessors. If Kramer could convince you that witchcraft was real, then it became a small step to see the need to torture witches into revealing the identities of their confederates, and then to kill them in self-defence, before they could spoil crops, spread disease, contaminate water or lure you to the dark side.

Within three years of its publication, the Catholic Church had condemned the book, and the practices and procedures detailed within it, but it had no means to suppress it at a time when censorship was still in its infancy. There was no index of prohibited books, and printing presses were not licensed. *Malleus Maleficarum* became a template for secular courts throughout Europe, and the book went through thirteen editions between 1487 and 1520.

The printing press has been a symbol of progress and enlightenment for so long that it is easy to forget just how much rubbish has been published. From the beginning, along with the Gutenberg Bibles and hymnals, the philosophy journals and scientific tomes, there were folksy almanacs, terrible poems, sentimental ballads, and chapbooks of romance and chivalry. Ladies learnt the finer points of etiquette, including the correct way to walk together around a garden, as their societies collapsed around them in war.

Communications technology has been a force-multiplier for fake news ever since the printing press was invented. Pamphlets and woodcuts fulfilled the same purpose as clickbait today. As with fake news on social media, the repetition of superstitious fears via the printed page lent an aura of scholarly "truthiness" to claims that weather, famine and disease were being manipulated by witches, with diabolic intent.

What differentiated the European witch-hunts of the Renaissance from the ancient crime of sorcery was their obsession with the satanic sexual wiles of women, who were allegedly more easily seduced by Satan than men. Even when witch-hunters were not personally misogynistic, they expected witches to be women, thanks to *Malleus Maleficarum*. To a large extent, they institutionalised the sexual obsessions of Heinrich Kramer, and illustrated the enduring power of fake news.

In the marketplace of ideas, the only mechanism open to the Church was to denounce the book using facts and logic. Initially, it looked as though they would succeed. A tract by Ulrich Molitor, *De Laniis et Phitonicus Mulieribus*, demolished Kramer's ideas and reiterated traditional Church teaching that witchcraft was not real. Molitor's book was even more widely circulated than *Malleus Maleficarum* in the first decade after it was published, and led some commentators to suggest that the witchcraft hysteria had gone for good.

Unfortunately, reasoned argument was no defence against bad weather. Europe experienced anomalous weather-patterns, severe crop-failures, plagues and civil wars in an era of climate cooling which culminated in the Little Ice Age. Secular courts in need of a morally cathartic scapegoat dusted off Kramer's work.

Malleus Maleficarum went through sixteen more editions between 1574 and 1669.[123] It was the best-selling book after the Bible for a hundred and fifty years. Tabloid-style broadsheets and woodcuts with lurid images turned witch-trials into what we would now call media sensations. The rapid dissemination of populist ideas facilitated a witch-hunt without precedent in the history of Europe. An ancient fear of magic, ridiculed by the secular elite during the Dark Ages, became the conventional wisdom of the Renaissance.

Persecution was spasmodic, and particularly acute at times of crisis, when state forces were at their weakest. Thirty years after the first performance of *Macbeth*, more people were allegedly killed by the self-styled Witchfinder General, Matthew Hopkins, during three years of the English Civil War, than had been executed for witchcraft in England in the previous, relatively peaceful, hundred years.

An unusual weather-pattern or harvest-failure could also trigger a wave of trials. In Scotland, hundreds of people were burnt as witches in Edinburgh after the Danish fiancee of King James VI was blown off course to Norway by unusual storms on the way to her wedding. The numbers accused and convicted rose sharply in areas where torture was permitted, as victims sought relief by denouncing others.

On the fringes of northern Europe, in places like Iceland, Estonia and Lithuania, where traditional shamanism had been strong, the majority of victims were male, but in most areas eight out of ten victims were female. Interrogators sought lascivious details of demonic congress, exhibiting an interest which was more prurient than professional. If a suspect was identified, she was often invited (under torture) to denounce the other witches in her circle.

Some occupations were more vulnerable than others. Landladies had three strikes against them: they were more affluent, dealt with strangers, and might handle contaminated food and drink. They were more likely to be accused than midwives.

Accusations of witchcraft could be levelled at rich and poor alike, roping in those suspected of profiteering from rising prices during food-shortages. There were many risk-factors for denunciation, including what we would regard as mental illness, having a limited social network, or being disliked as a scold or a gossip. Many were guilty of nothing more than being unpopular.

The witchcraft hysteria coincided with the Reformation and Counter-Reformation, but even at the height of the Wars of Religion (roughly 8 million people died during the Thirty Years War), Catholic and Protestant witch-hunters in Germany still exchanged information onsuspects.[124]

As in other wars, mysterious deaths were caused by collateral damage, as mercenaries pillaged crops and spread disease. Your best friend was often your worst enemy, with a lethal threat coming from allied armies diffusing plague. The sudden increase in famine and pestilence led to a huge spike in German witchcraft-trials in the 1620s.

The precise nature of an auto-da-fé militated against the kind of death-toll seen in warfare or war-induced famine (the population of France probably halved in the Hundred Years War, for instance), but based on modern research, it is estimated that around sixty thousand people were executed for witchcraft before the persecutions abated during the eighteenth century.[125] At least forty-five thousand of those murdered – or three out of every four victims – were women. The Renaissance witch-hunts continue to generate fake news today, with claims that up to nine million women were murdered being bandied around in popular media, roughly 150 times more than the true figure.These estimates of gynecide have been traced to an eighteenth-century anti-clericalist called Gottfried Christian Voigt.[126]

His estimate was used by anti-Catholic authors during the German Kulturkampf of the nineteenth century, and by Nazi neo-pagans in the twentieth, before percolating through feminist literature after the Second World War.

Only one region rejected the fake news about witchcraft. When seven thousand men, women and children were accused of withcraft in the Basque country in 1609, and after a dozen had been burnt at the stake, a young man named Alonso Salazar Frias was sent to investigate. Soon, 1,800 victims had retracted denunciations, often claiming that they had been made under torture.

"The real question," Frias concluded, "is: are we to believe that witchcraft occurred in a given situation simply because of what the witches claim? No: it is clear that the witches are not to be believed, and the judges should not pass sentence on anyone, unless the case can be proven with external and objective evidence sufficient to convince everyone who hears it."

Despite objections from some senior colleagues, who claimed that Frias was "in league with the devil", all cases were dismissed, and rules of evidence were introduced to prevent any recurrence.[127] Frias was part of an institution founded by Queen Isabella of Castile – of whom more below. The suspects were saved by the rational skepticism of the Spanish Inquisition.

Isabella, Queen of Castile, Founds the Spanish Inquisition

Isabella did not expect to become Queen of Castile. For most of her childhood, her destiny was to create a dynastic alliance on behalf of her half-brother, Henry IV, by marrying a suitor of his choosing.

The duty of a royal princess was to strengthen her family through marriage and child-bearing, but in the absence of a suitable male heir, some patriarchies let women wield real authority. At the intersection between absolute power and perceived weakness, Renaissance Queens were often both victims and perpetrators of oppression.

Isabella's early life was like an implausible plot-line from a *telenovela* soap opera. Like many royal princesses, her future marriage was influenced by shifting alliances and intrigue. At the age of six, she was betrothed to her second cousin, Ferdinand of Aragon, followed by his elder brother, Charles of Viana. When she was fourteen, she was betrothed to King Alfonso V of Portugal, then to a noble called Pedro Giron Acuna Acheco, who died on his way to meet her, then back to Alfonso V of Portugal, then to Charles, Duke of Berry, the brother of the French King Louis XI. Finally, at the age of eighteen, she eloped to marry her first suitor, Ferdinand of Aragon.

Isabella's half-brother, Henry IV, was twenty-six years old when Isabella was born. He was nicknamed "Henry the Impotent" because of his inability to consummate his first marriage with Blanche II of Navarre. His attempts to hawk Isabella to the most powerful bidder were part of an effort to shore up his unpopular regime.

Isabella and her brother Alfonso did not attend court in Segovia until Henry's second wife, Joan of Portugal, finally gave birth to a daughter, Joanna. Henry's opponents claimed that Joanna was the illegitimate daughter of a courtier called Beltran de la Cueva, and gave her the nickname "Joanna la Beltraneja".

Under pressure from rebellious nobles, Henry agreed to nominate his half-brother Alfonso as his heir, so long as Alfonso married his niece, Henry's daughter Joanna; Alfonso died of plague, and the rebels demanded that Isabella be named in his stead. Henry agreed, provided that Isabella did not marry without his consent.

A year later, when she eloped with Ferdinand, a succession crisis ensued. After Henry IV died, his brother-in-law Alfonso V of Portugal married Henry's daughter Joanna la Beltraneja, who was also his niece. Alfonso V then tried to make his new wife the Queen of Castile. After a year of warfare, Isabella's claim to the throne was secured.

This incestuous family dispute had an extraordinary impact on world history. If Isabella's brother Alfonso had not died of plague, or if Isabella hadn't decided to elope with Ferdinand, or if the rebellious nobles of Castile had believed the prostitutes who testified that Henry IV was virile, things could have been very different. Without the alliance of Ferdinand and Isabella, Christopher Columbus might never have set sail for the New World, their troops might never have conquered the Muslim state of Granada, their grandson Charles V would not have inherited a vast European empire, and thousands of Jews would not have been killed by the Spanish Inquisition.

The region that Ferdinand and Isabella governed was a plural society, with Christians and Sephardic Jews mingling in the cities of peninsular Spain, and with the Muslims of Andalucia in the south of the country. Sephardic Jews may have fled to Iberia after the Roman destruction of the Temple in Jerusalem in the year 70, and Muslims had been living there for nearly eight hundred years by the time Granada was defeated.[128]

When the Spanish Inquisition was set up in 1477, there were approximately eighty thousand practising Jews living in Spain, as well as two hundred thousand Jewish *conversos*, many of them devout Christians descended from families which had converted in earlier pogroms triggered by political crises.[129] Initially, the Inquisition focused on preventing the *converso* population from sliding back into the "heresy" of Judaism, but under Canon Law, practising Jews could not be coerced to convert.[130] They were beyond the scope of the Inquisition.

The Spanish Inquisition was founded just two years after Isabella's victory over King Alfonso V and Joanna la Beltraneja in the Battle of Toro, and four years before she and Ferdinand went to war with the Muslim state of Granada. Although the two monarchs protected Jews from attack, and both Jews and *conversos* served them as advisors, officials, financiers and physicians, they ultimately gave way to sectarian paranoia, convincing themselves that clandestine groups of *conversos* across Spain were practicing Judaism in secret.[131]

Operating almost exclusively in towns, with a handful of staff who did not receive government funding, the Spanish Inquisition relied on familiars and private citizens who were willing to denounce their *converso* neighbors anonymously for secretly following the faith of their fathers.

Eventually, the Spanish Inquisition persuaded Ferdinand and Isabella that *conversos* were "endangered by contact and communication with the Jews". Despite the funds they received from the Jewish community, three months after the fall of Granada in 1492 they issued the Alhambra Decree, giving Jews four months to leave "all our realms and territories . . . despite the great harm to ourselves, seeking and preferring the salvation of souls above our own profit".[132]

Faced with exile or conversion, forty thousand Jews left the country. The remainder converted before the deadline. Vulnerable to denunciation by their neighbours, they felt the full force of skeptical inquisitors, who were given the job of monitoring the sincerity of their new Christian faith.

Conversos suspected of practicing Judaism were called *Marranos*. They might be questioned about not lighting fires on the Sabbath, or buying meat from a formerly kosher butcher. Those found guilty might do penance and have property confiscated for a first offence; recidivists could be "relaxed" to the secular authorities, to be burnt at the stake.

Roughly two thousand people were executed at the behest of the Spanish Inquisition between 1480 and 1530. More than 90 percent of them were Jewish – equivalent to one in twenty of those who had converted in the four months before the Alhambra Decree took effect.[133]

Many of the innovations of the Spanish Inquisition were heavily criticised in Spain. Forcing victims to wear the penitent robes of a San Benito in a public walk of shame and atonement, the inability to cross-examine witnesses, the proliferation of spying, the confiscation of property, and the death-penalty for repeated "Judaising" were particularly unpopular.[134] In an era of sectarian war, Juan Mariana, an apologist for the Spanish Inquisition, argued that "the ancient customs of the Church should be changed in conformity with the needs of the times."[135] In other words, scapegoating minorities could sweep aside the rule of law in times of crisis.

The persecution of the Jewish minority was met with indifference across Europe. Jews had already been expelled from England, France and parts of Germany by the time the Spanish Inquisition was founded. One of the few leaders to protest was one of the most notorious popes in history. Nine thousand Jewish exiles were welcomed into Italy following the Alhambra decree by the Spanish-born Pope Alexander VI, better known to posterity as Rodrigo Borgia.[136]

Lurid tales of bloodthirsty inquisitors did not circulate until decades later, during the Wars of Religion, when Spanish troops were marching across Flanders.[137] By that stage, persecution had declined precipitously, with one thousand to two thousand people being executed for heresy between 1530 and 1700.[138]

A handful of hapless victims were burnt at the stake each year – or strangled if they recanted, just in case they changed their minds again before they could be dispatched to their heavenly reward.[139] Its procedures were rigorous enough for some defendants to avoid the secular courts by deliberately blaspheming, so that their case would fall under the jurisdiction of the Spanish Inquisition.[140]

The Spanish Inquisition may have killed fewer Jews over the centuries of its operation than were taken in a single day by the gas-chambers of Treblinka during the Grosse Aktion, when 265,040 Jews died between 23 July 1942 and 21 September 1942. But its purpose was different[141]: it wasn't set up to generate a massive body-count, but to enforce conformity.[142]

Totalitarian states followed the Spanish Inquisition's play-book for years to come. The public walk of moral atonement in San Benito robes presaged the farcical Soviet show-trials of the twentieth century, and the humiliation of Jews during Kristallnacht.[143]

A religious court set up by Isabella at a time of crisis was not wound up until 1834, by which time the pluralistic society of Spain had been destroyed. It was not just the *limpieza* rules or autos-da-fé which so sickened the diplomats of France and Italy, but the ethnic cleansing of "enemy races" from the only homes they had known. A group supposedly inspired by love of God and neighbour had developed a psychopathic definition of charity.

Queen Mother Catherine de Medici Agrees to the St Bartholomew's Day Massacre

Nearly a century after Isabella secured power through her marriage to Ferdinand, Catherine de Medici acquired power through widowhood. She was excluded from affairs of state while her husband, King Henri II of France, lived, but after both Henri and her sixteen-year-old son Francis II died within a year of each other, Catherine de Medici's nine-year-old son was crowned King Charles IX of France in 1560.

As his regent, she had to juggle the competing claims for influence of the Catholic House of Guise and the Protestant House of Bourbon. This fissure plunged the kingdom into the French Wars of Religion.

In 1572, in a twist worthy of *Game of Thrones*, her attempt at reconciliation through the marriage of her Catholic daughter Margaret, who was in love with Henri de Guise, to Margaret's Huguenot cousin Henri de Bourbon of Navarre, was sabotaged by an assassination attempt on the Protestant Admiral Coligny while he was in Paris for the wedding.

This led to a revenge attack on Catherine de Medici, followed by the murder of many thousands of Protestants in Paris and other cities, including Coligny.[144] After coming under attack, it is likely that Catherine agreed to eliminate leading Huguenots in the Saint Bartholomew's Day Massacre, but she continued to try to make peace between the warring factions.

Twenty-five more years of civil war followed. Before she died, Catherine had buried three of her four sons; she was no longer on speaking terms with her daughter after Margaret had left her husband.

Her last son, Henri III, outlived her by only a few months: he was assassinated for murdering the Duke of Guise.

Henri III's cousin Henri de Bourbon of Navarre had already made a strategic conversion to Catholicism, allegedly saying: "Paris is well worth a Mass." After securing his claim to the throne as Henri IV, he signed the Edict of Nantes to protect the Protestant Huguenot minority. Between the accession of Charles IX in 1560 and the Edict of Nantes less than forty years later, roughly 3 million people had been killed.[145]

Henri IV is said to have paid tribute to Catherine. "I ask you, what could a woman do, left by the death of her husband with five little children on her arms, and two families of France who were thinking of grasping the crown: our own and the Guises? Was she not compelled to play strange parts to deceive first one and then the other, in order to guard, as she did, her sons, who successively reigned through the wise conduct of that shrewd woman? I am surprised that she never did worse."

Queen Elizabeth I Sanctions a Scorched-earth Campaign in Northern Ireland

By the time Elizabeth Tudor was three years old, in 1536, her mother had been decapitated, and she had been declared illegitimate by her father, Henry VIII. Her half-sister Mary, seventeen years her senior, had rarely been allowed to see her mother, Catherine of Aragon, who had been exiled from court after Henry divorced her.

Her half-brother Edward was born by the time Elizabeth was four, but his mother died in childbirth. Henry VIII married three more times, but died less than a decade later, in 1547. This placed a sickly Protestant nine-year-old boy on the throne of England.

As Edward VI turned fifteen, it was clear that he was dying, probably of tuberculosis. His Catholic half-sister Mary, who was thirty-seven, was next in line of succession.[146] Mary became queen with her sister by her side, but Elizabeth was an object of intrigue for Protestant courtiers hoping to replace her Catholic sister. She was put under house-arrest for a year by Mary.[147]

Mary set about restoring Catholicism in England, insisting that her Protestant sister Elizabeth attend Mass. The year after becoming queen, she married Philip of Spain. The match proved to be deeply unpopular. Mary burnt 283 leading Protestants for heresy, including the Archbishop of Canterbury, Thomas Cranmer; the Bishop of London, Nicholas Ridley; and Hugh Latimer, chaplain to her brother Edward VI. She was soon nicknamed "Bloody Mary".

Elizabeth's exile ended when Mary suspected she was pregnant. She was recalled to assume power if her sister died in childbirth, but it was a phantom pregnancy.[148] Following a second phantom pregnancy, and suffering pain caused by cysts or ovarian cancer, Mary died during an influenza epidemic in 1558. Two years before Catherine de Medici became regent of France, Elizabeth became Queen of England and Ireland at the age of twenty-five.

Elizabeth was soon acknowledged as Queen by Mary's widower, now King Phillip II of Spain, and her first few years were spent trying to consolidate her reign and restore harmony to England. Phillip was one of many suitors who tried to woo her, but she was reluctant to get married, especially after a bout of smallpox at the age of twenty-nine led to the loss of half her hair and exacerbated her tooth-decay.

Elizabeth opted to plot a middle course.[149] She had no interest in prying into matters of conscience, and no desire to anoint a successor whose religious sympathies could foment rebellion by the fundamentalists on either side. Despite her moderation, she was excommunicated by the Pope in 1570. Seventeen years later, after Elizabeth executed Mary, Queen of Scots for plotting to assassinate her, her former brother-in-law, Philip II, sent an Armada to invade England. It was scattered by storms and English fire-ships, but it took time for this deliverance to become known.

Rallying her troops in the belief that invasion was imminent, and might be supported by English Catholics, Elizabeth showed moxie in a speech in 1588: "My loving people, we have been persuaded by some that are careful of our safety, to take heed how we commit ourselves to armed multitudes for fear of treachery; but I assure you, I do not desire to live to distrust my faithful and loving people. . . . I know I have the body of a weak and feeble woman, but I have the heart and stomach of a king, and of a King of England too, and think foul scorn that Parma or Spain, or any Prince of Europe should dare to invade the borders of my realm." It was her finest hour.

*

But a victim of oppression could also be an oppressor. Elizabeth also had the stomach to send expeditions to fight in the European Wars of Religion, and to suppress rebellion in predominantly Catholic Ireland. They used scorched-earth tactics to prevail. The destruction of crops may have killed around one in three people in the southern Irish province of Munster in the 1580s.[150]

The poet Edmund Spenser, who witnessed the campaign, wrote that civilians "were brought to such wretchedness as that any stony heart would have rued the same. . . . Out of every corner of the wood and glens they came creeping forth upon their hands, for their legs could not bear them; they looked Anatomies [of] death, they spoke like ghosts crying out of their graves; they did eat of the carrions, happy where they could find them, yea, and one another soon after, in so much as the very carcasses they spared not to scrape out of their graves."[151]

Another rebellion broke out in the 1590s, this time in the northern Irish province of Ulster. Having lost thirty thousand troops and £2 million fighting Irish rebels, the Nine Years War bankrupted Elizabeth. She turned to a ruthless commander, Charles Blount, the

Eighth Lord Mountjoy, whose destruction of food-supplies in 1602 and 1603 left the rebellion in stalemate – at a cost of tens of thousands of mostly civilian lives.

Mountjoy was not a two-dimensional villain. He was an officer fighting in hostile territory, whose main strategic advantage was that he could maintain his supply-lines while eliminating those of his foe, using the kind of scorched-earth tactics which would destroy one in three German towns in the Thirty Years War, decades later.

He expressed fulsome remorse at the collateral damage caused to civilians. "We do now continually hunt all their woods, spoil their corn, burn their houses, and kill so many churls, as it grieveth me to think that it is necessary to do this."[152] Senior English officers witnessed children eating the corpse of their mother;[153] in an attempt to restore law and order out of the chaos they had wrought, a Captain Trevor executed a group of old women for kidnapping and eating children.[154]

The scorched-earth tactics prevented Elizabeth from losing the war, but they were not sufficient for her to win it. Rather than placing the heads of the rebel leaders on spikes as an example to others, they were pardoned and restored to their estates. Elizabeth died as they signed the Treaty of Mellifont.[155] Within four years, the pardoned rebel leaders had all fled, leaving her successor, James I, to colonise northern Ireland ("for want of people unmanured") with Protestant settlers from Scotland and England.[156]

Francis Bacon was thrilled at the living space opening up in northern Ireland, and the potential to ease over-population and discontent in Scotland and England.[157] English and Scottish "undertakers" were forbidden to have any native tenants on their lands. Not even Elizabeth had been that ambitious. Her Catholic sister Mary had approved a small plantation in the Irish midlands to punish rebellious chieftains, but the removal of the churls as well as the chiefs was rejected by her advisors as a "marvelous sumptuous charge".[158]

The Orders and Conditions approving the plan began with the familiar pieties about "His Majesty . . . not respecting his own profit", but the King was advised that "the well planting of this colony" in northern Ireland with Anglican settlers would bring more good than "the planting of ten times as much land in Virginia", where Jamestown had been founded a few months before.[159]

The Ulster Plantation would "extirpe the very root of rebellion . . . increase the public revenue, and reward the public servitors".[160] What could possibly go wrong?

Four centuries after the Ulster Plantation, another woman, Prime Minister Theresa May, would be left to pick up the pieces when David Cameron resigned after the Brexit referendum that took the United Kingdom out of the European Union. Her efforts to leave the European Union without creating a "hard" border on the island of Ireland would suffer the heaviest parliamentary defeat in British history.

Despite the rise of patriarchy, for thousands of years women fought for freedom and tolerance. Many, like Helena, succeeded in using soft power in ways which are hardly appreciated today. Others, such as Isabella, Catherine and Elizabeth, were thrust into ruling positions and acted ruthlessly, for *raisons d'état,* or their personal safety. The struggle for a more open and plural society, where people can simply be themselves, without fear of discrimination, continues.

II
The Dark Side

Chapter Five

The Paradox of Cruelty

"A people are as healthy and confident as the stories they tell themselves. Sick storytellers can make nations sick."

BEN OKRI

OK, so you have a dark side. We all do. That doesn't mean you're a bad person. Whatever your beliefs and values, you're wired to be nice. But then, so were most participants in the worst atrocities ever recorded.

Waves of bigotry and persecution follow eras of prosperity and peace throughout human history. We repeatedly ask ourselves how a species predisposed to kindness can inflict so much suffering, exploitation and cruelty – especially when the perpetrators are convinced that they are righteous people.

Since the beginning of recorded history, we have told stories to explain our dark side. In the Hebrew Bible's Book of Creation, God made the heavens and the earth, then on the sixth day He said: "Let us make man in our own image . . . male and female he created them . . . God blessed them, saying, 'Be fruitful, multiply, fill the earth and subdue it.'" And on the seventh day, God rested. Job done. Except that the Book of Genesis doesn't stop there. Instead, in Chapter Two, it tells a story about a man and a woman who lived in Eden.

The story of Adam and Eve, written in an Iron Age society on the edge of the Fertile Crescent, is insightful. It posits that our species began with an abundance of food sources, that child-bearing became increasingly difficult over time, and that we lived under constant threat of attack by wild animals, especially snakes. It also suggests that, at some point after we became self-aware, we were forced to develop agriculture: "by the sweat of your face will you earn your food". With the murder by the first farmer, Cain, of his brother Abel, the first shepherd, things really started to hit the fan.

Living with Our Own Cruelty

For 95 percent of the time Homo sapiens has been on earth, kindness was the key to our survival as a species. But then populations exploded, and we were forced to compete for scarce resources. Having a conscience attuned to collaboration was a hindrance, until we manipulated our moral sensibilities to our advantage. Our inner moral voice inhibits cruel behaviour by generating severe emotional distress. Convincing ourselves that we are good makes it so much easier to be bad.

Most of us are not sociopaths, but we are natural-born narrators. Before we take arms against a sea of troubles, we try to make sense of the disasters that befall us. If a plausible explanation bobs to the surface, we cling to it tenaciously, discounting evidence to the contrary. We seek a culprit in every crisis, scapegoating out-groups. We cast ourselves as victims, and exploit our moral instinct to punish wrongdoing. In other words, we tell ourselves good, strong lies.

Some of these lies are conscious and deliberate. Plato said that a philosopher-king must be willing "to administer a great many lies and deceptions", but these are useful "only as a medicine . . . for the benefit of the state".[161] For Plato, this included lies about the innate virtues of the ruling class, which legitimised their rule.[162]

Hegel said that the Great Man "is he who expresses the will of his time, who tells his time what it wills; and who carries it out". Greatness could not be achieved without learning to "despise public opinion".[163] This was not deceitful, as "great achievements are certain to be subsequently recognized and accepted".[164]

Sometimes we lie without realising it. Remorse triggers facial tells, including involuntary blush-responses, which act as a natural lie-detector. The biologist Robert Trivers has suggested that we avoid betraying our underlying motives through self-deception, evading attempts to smoke out wilful mendacity. Once we persuade ourselves that we are doing the right thing, we dismiss any evidence that challenges our narrative, no matter how obvious it may be.

Our beliefs and values are a crucial bulwark against psychological distress. The more passionately we believe something, the harder it is to accept evidence to the contrary. This is why jurisprudence and science take such pains to avoid assertions that are not based on evidence. Without that structure and discipline, whenever our worldview was undermined we merely swapped one set of bloodthirsty myths for another.

Not that science offers a panacea against prejudice. Higher education and intelligence can reinforce biases, as we curate evidence in our favour. The smartest people are often lured to the dark side. A disproportionate number of ISIS volunteers are college-educated engineers. Nobel laureates and celebrated philosophers were enthusiastic supporters of the Nazi Party. Over 60 percent of the fanatical Nazi Einsatzgruppen killing-squad leaders had PhDs.

Rather than reasoning dispassionately, we rationalise our passions. Hegel said: "Nothing great in the world has been accomplished without passion. . . . This may be called the cunning of reason – that it sets the passions to work for itself."[165] We find it easier to see passion swaying our antagonists than ourselves, but we cannot combat the dark side in society without acknowledging our own prejudices and biases – taking the planks out of our own eyes before removing the specks from the eyes of others.

Seeing only evidence which reinforces our opinions is known as "my-side" or confirmation bias. We may be right, but it will not be because we are giving alternative perspectives a fair hearing. By definition, we are not aware of our own biases, but we can identify where we are vulnerable by acknowledging when we are at our most passionate, and we can challenge ourselves to check our bias and listen to a diverse range of opinions.

To understand the psychological mechanisms behind the paradox of cruelty, we need to explore our cognitive biases in more depth, in order to see how our moral instinct to punish wrongdoing underpins homicide statistics, and how easily reciprocal altruism can turn into a game of them versus us, where we collectively scapegoat out-groups. We need to show the lengths to which we will go in order to distance ourselves from the distressing cognitive dissonance caused by our cruelty, and how a kind and collaborative species deploys a warped moral sense when our biases go unchallenged.

The Power of Bias

It is not hard to see why confirmation bias could be a useful trait. Once you have made your mind up on a course of action, it is important to back your judgement. Repeated second-guessing and dithering can turn Henry V into Hamlet.

Adapting the facts to suit your own beliefs is also helpful in negotiations. Without being consciously aware of what we are doing, we act as advocates rather than judges in assessing evidence, assembling the picture that favours our interests and values.[166]

In an experiment published in 1997 by Linda Babcock and George Loewenstein of Carnegie Mellon University in Pittsburgh, people had to guess at damages awarded by a judge in a real traffic accident, having reviewed twenty-seven pages of evidence, and then act as a plaintiff or defendant to negotiate a settlement with another participant.

Participants were incentivised to make as fair an assessment as possible.

They were much more likely to make an accurate estimate of the damages if they did not know which side they would take in the subsequent negotiations. If they knew in advance whether they were acting for the plaintiff or the defendant, their view of the evidence was subconsciously skewed in favor of their side.[167]

We can construct sophisticated arguments to support our prejudices, especially if there is a legitimate grievance or plausible rationale. Something destroyed our crops; perhaps it was some*one*?

One of the most important areas of cognitive bias is the belief that we are the good guys. Even the bad guys will seize on evidence that they are the good guys – which, perversely, makes it easier to be bad.

A ten-year study of 716 teenagers in Peterborough, led by Per-Olof Wikström of the University of Cambridge, found that 4 percent of the group accounted for nearly half of the sixteen thousand crimes in the study – more than 280 offences each – including nearly all serious crimes involving violence and robbery.

The delinquents were highly impulsive, and unlike the majority of teenagers, showed little aversion to breaking the law. They had often grown up in disadvantaged areas with little social cohesion or moral education.[168] That does not mean that they saw themselves as bad people.

In a separate study by Constantine Sedikides, conducted on slightly older offenders, seventy-nine English prisoners aged between eighteen and thirty-four, serving sentences for violence and robbery, were asked to rank themselves on nine different character-traits. The prisoners believed that they were more generous, honest, moral, self-controlled, kind, compassionate, honest, dependable, trustworthy and law-abiding than a typical member of the prison population. On eight of the traits they gave themselves a higher score than an average member of the general public, and when it came to being law-abiding, put themselves at par or only marginally below. Maintaining a positive self-image in the face of evidence to the contrary helped them commit crimes with minimal remorse.[169]

We can easily believe that others are delusional about their level of kindness, but it is harder to accept that we suffer from the same problem. If we are being blamed for something, it helps if we can say that it is not our fault, or that we were just obeying orders. Likewise, knowing that someone else is around to help a person in need, lets us off the hook psychologically when we should be showing initiative.

The psychologists Richard Nisbett and Eugene Borgida told their students at the University of Michigan about a "helping experiment" which had been run in New York. Participants sat in separate booths and spoke about their personal lives. One was an actor who pretended to be prone to seizures. As the others listened, he choked, said he was dying, and gasped for help. The experiment was run three times. Only four out of fifteen participants immediately left their booths to help. Knowing that others might take responsibility, six subjects never got out of their booths at all.

The psychologists then showed their Michigan students footage of two people who had allegedly taken part in the New York study, and asked them to predict how they had behaved. Despite knowing that less than one in three subjects had taken the initiative, and more than one in three had done nothing, the students thought that both interviewees had rushed to help. We are all convinced that we are good, even though less than one in three of us will jump up to help a person in convulsions if someone else is there. Challenging this conviction takes more cognitive effort than we are willing to put in.

The psychologist and Nobel laureate Daniel Kahneman argues that our minds are lazy. Organ-donation rates in culturally similar neighbouring states range from 4 percent to nearly 100 percent, depending on whether the state operates an opt-in or opt-out system.

We substitute easy questions in order to avoid hard ones: "Do I like company X?" instead of "Is it accurately valued?" Even if our beliefs are modified in the light of new evidence, the curse of hindsight persuades us that we knew the truth all along.[170]

Our capacity to rationalise our motivations retrospectively survives severe cognitive impairment, as shown in experiments which literally messed with the heads of people who had had the hemispheres of their brains surgically separated.

People who were shown a sign saying "WALK" on their right side used the left side of their brain to explain that they got up to get a soda. A permanent hospital resident who was convinced she was at home, told doctors she had spent a fortune to put an elevator in. We have, in Steven Pinker's phrase, a built-in "baloney generator".

Manipulating Our Instincts
To Punish Wrongdoing

The punishment of wrongdoing is an intrinsic component of a collaborative moral sense.[171] Avenging wrongs sends endorphins to the pleasure-centres of the brain. Movies play on this response. We cheer when the bad guy gets his just deserts or the good guy takes the law into his own hands. Trained soldiers report an adrenalin rush and a feeling of euphoria in close-quarters combat.

According to Donald Black, up to 90 percent of homicides are rationalised by the perpetrators as a punitive response to a slight or injustice on the part of the victim. This helps explain why violent crime is linked more closely to endemic deprivation and insecurity over status than the cyclical booms and busts of the economy.[172]

Generally, those taking the law into their own hands are men. Excluding infanticide, 92 percent of homicides are committed by men, mostly between the ages of twenty and forty.[173] Where there are disproportionately high numbers of single men, homicide rates are also likely to be high. A slight triggers a violent response to preserve status, especially where the forces of law and order are weak or have broken down, as in America's Wild West.

When our incentives changed from collaboration to competition, we have told stories to justify our response. Righteous anger has been used to salve our consciences as we made the shift from kindness to cruelty.

The Dark Side of Reciprocal Altruism

As the Groningen broken-window experiments have shown, we are very influenced by the behaviour of our peers and the moral norms within groups. It makes sense to identify with in-group collaborators in order to strengthen reciprocal altruism. We are usually indifferent to out-groups, but animosity can develop rapidly.[174]

Henry Tajfel showed that bias within in-groups could develop in boys who thought they preferred the same artist. They were told they belonged to a group which liked the works of either Paul Klee or Wassily Kandinsky, although in fact they were assigned at random. When they were given money to share, they consistently gave more to boys from their own group. In-group bias occurred even when boys were not assigned to a group which ostensibly had a common interest, and were simply assigned to group X or group Y.

The psychologist Jay Van Bavel randomly assigned adult subjects to different teams and showed them images of team-mates and rivals while they were in an fMRI scanner. When they saw team members, parts of the brain associated with recognising value and distinguishing important stimuli were activated, but not when they saw rivals.

A study involving children between the ages of four and six assigned them to groups that wore red or blue T-shirts. When they were shown photographs of other children, they preferred images of kids who wore a T-shirt of the same colour, and when they were told stories about the kids in the photographs, they remembered good behaviour from children who wore a T-shirt of the same colour, and bad behavior from children who wore the other colour.

The psychologist Muzafer Sherif ran a famous set of experiments in the 1950s on groups of twelve-year-old boys at a camp in Robber's Cave State Park in Oklahoma. As they competed for prizes, verbal sparring was followed by vandalism and fighting. The gangs had very negative views of each other until they had to work together to get the water supply operating and fix a broken-down truck.

One of the most famous and controversial studies of inter-group dynamics occurred in 1971, when Dr Philip Zimbardo of Stanford University recruited male students from Palo Alto for role-play in a mock penitentiary. The Stanford Prison Experiment was stopped after six days. Warders were applying increasingly harsh punishments, including shooting fire extinguishers at prisoners, the use of solitary confinement, punishment press-ups, and denial of toilet facilities, to the point where some prisoners had breakdowns and one went on hunger strike.[175] Zimbardo subsequently wrote a paper called "The Lucifer Effect", in which he argued that "Good people can be induced, seduced, and initiated into behaving in evil ways."

Our ability to categorise people into "them" and "us" is facilitated by our hard-wired ability to scan for familiar faces – an ability we developed when we didn't have noticeably different skin- or hair-colouring. Newborns do not differentiate between faces from different races, but experiments conducted by Paul Bloom have shown that infants as young as three months old prefer to look at faces from their own racial-group. If we do not grow up in ethnically diverse environments, the category of people like "us" can quickly become racial.

Blame-storming and Appeasement
in Times of Crisis

People have always sought a scapegoat when things go wrong, especially if intangible forces are at work. Apart from bullying, the other key reason for capital punishment among hunter-gatherers is for sorcery: placing others under a curse that causes illness or death.

In agricultural societies, the trifecta of famine, disease and the contamination of water supplies were typically attributed to malign sorcery or the wrath of the gods. If we couldn't explain how they happened, we took the easy route of blaming minorities: Jews, witches, or, in ninth-century France, Magonians.

Prefiguring alien invasion movies by nearly twelve hundred years, Magonia was a mythical cloud-kingdom whose inhabitants used sorcery to steal crops during hail and thunder. After hail-storms in 816 destroyed the harvest, Agobard, the Archbishop of Lyons, had to restrain a mob from killing three foreigners, supposedly from the magical land of Magonia. We know about this incident because Agobard was moved to write a book about the fears of the peasants, called *Contra Insulsam Vulgi Opinionem de Grandine et Tonitruis* ("Against the Foolish Belief of the Vulgar Concerning Hail and Thunder").Deities were demonstrably wrathful in agricultural societies, and had to be appeased. In times of acute environmental pressure, especially related to crop-failure, this could involve special forms of sacrifice to atone for behaviour that displeased them.

In Ireland, for example, high-born, well-fed and pomaded aristocrats were ritually sacrificed at liminal interfaces between the physical and spiritual worlds. Ned Kelly of the National Museum of Ireland has suggested that these Iron Age bog bodies were tortured kings, ritually executed for failing to ensure the fertility of the harvest.[176]

Mesoamerican art shows children being sacrificed at the start of different cycles in their calendar, a practice used by Conquistadores to justify their conquest and greed.[177] Evidence of child-sacrifice has been documented in a number of pre-Columbian cultures.[178] According to Spanish chroniclers, the victims were chosen precisely because they were the purest sacrifice their societies could give to the gods: their parents believed that the children were destined for a better future in the afterlife as a result. So denial of the gods not only imperilled the fertility of the harvest on which your entire family depended, it also meant denying your child a wonderful afterlife throughout eternity. The only way to challenge this conclusion was to challenge the fundamental narrative that society held about the gods and the afterlife: in other words, blasphemy. Questioning or modifying vile customs became taboo, suppressing the feedback loop between our cultural norms and our individual moral intuitions.

Supernatural agency made sense of natural disasters which were otherwise inexplicable. For Voltaire, the Great Lisbon Earthquake and tsunami of 1755, which spared the bordellos but buried the churches on All Saints' Day, challenged faith in a benign and loving God.[179]

It would have been much less perplexing to an ancient Greek. A bio-geochemist can point to the importance of plate-tectonics in regulating our biosphere, but in classical Greece, earthquakes were a manifestation of Poseidon.[180]

We no longer blame people for destroying crops or poisoning wells, but we still have knee-jerk reactions to threats, and a readiness to behave irrationally. Fear of pandemic disease leads to a run on bathroom tissue rather than better personal hygiene. When President Trump announced a travel ban to prevent contagion by a "foreign" virus, the only things that seemed to be spreading faster than Covid-19 were images of home-made haz-mat suits and empty supermarket shelves. One journalist wrote: "Is it not mind-boggling that we need experts to advise us to cover our mouths, wash our hands and refrain from touching our faces as if it were some bewildering new technology?"[181]

A populist imperative for action overwhelms wiser counsel, as shown by the panic-stricken state-by-state response to an epidemic in West Africa in 2014. After a doctor in New York City tested positive for ebola, Governors Andrew Cuomo and Chris Christie introduced mandatory quarantines for all US medical personnel coming back from the fight to contain the virus, defying President Obama's scientific advisors.[182] Doctor Anthony Fauci, the director of the National Institute of Allergy and Infectious Diseases, told ABC News that the governor's actions would undermine efforts to halt the disease: "The best way to stop this epidemic and protect America is to stop it in Africa."[183]

We enact environmental laws with no basis in science following media scares. In the UK, unfounded fears of side-effects published in 1998 led to a sharp reduction in the number of parents giving their children the MMR vaccine against measles, mumps and rubella.

We no longer burn witches for causing thunder, but panic-buying empties the shelves of the local Stop'n'Shop in advance of the latest Stormpocalypse. Despite the fact that global warming is measured over decades rather than seasons, every unusual weather event is used as a salvo in the war over climate change.

In times of crisis, we still seek out the easy target, ignoring evidence which challenges our prejudices – like the gay men who were pilloried as communists during the Cold War, in what became known as the Lavender Scare. Hundreds of men were forced to resign with no probable cause or due process, just on the suspicion of being gay.

As Islamist terrorists commit atrocities around the world, the toxic vitriol of keyboard-warriors on social media has created a virtual lynch-mob, seething at the apparent assault on Western values, and willing to disregard platitudes and social niceties when it comes to tarring all their Muslim neighbours with the same brush. According to the Pew Research Center, terrorism was the number one priority for Americans in 2017, beating the economy, to be cited by 76 percent of respondents, even though in 2017 more people in America were killed by lawnmowers or toddlers with household guns than by Islamist terrorists.

Radicalisation is lesson number one in the insurgency handbook. IRA leaders were happy to see British soldiers kick down doors in house-to-house searches in west Belfast in the 1970s, because they knew it would alienate and galvanise civilians to rally to their cause.

The Islamist strategy is reliant on our backlash. Terrorists hope that our response to their atrocities will provoke heinous behaviour towards peaceful, law-abiding Muslim-Americans, as they become "them" rather than "us", and we ignore all evidence to the contrary.

Cruelty, Glory and Cognitive Dissonance

Thomas Hobbes lists three principal causes for warfare: "First, competition; secondly, diffidence; thirdly, glory. The first maketh men invade for gain; the second for safety; and the third for reputation. The first use violence, to make themselves masters of other men's persons, wives, children and cattle; the second, to defend them; the third, for trifles, as a word, a smile, a different opinion, and any other sign of undervalue, either direct in their persons or by reflection in their kindred, their friends, their nation, their profession, or their name."

But crossing the moral Rubicon from homicide among hunter-gatherers to open warfare between bands required a significant psychological shift. Instead of punishing individual transgressors, warfare involves mortal combat between people who have no personal axe to grind. We have to overcome our instinctive moral aversion to harming others, and our fear of being harmed.

Brigadier General S. L. A. Marshall speculated that up to 75 percent of soldiers in the Second World War avoided shooting accurately at the enemy, prompting the US army to desensitise recruits in rapid-fire drills by using man-shaped silhouettes instead of bulls'-eyes, as well as shifting responsibility up the chain of command and dispersing responsibility across the platoon.[184] This difference in training and responsibility resulted in soldiers in Vietnam firing accurately almost 90 percent of the time, according to Lieutenant Colonel Dave Grossman.[185]

Fostering camaraderie and trust among platoon-members gave an additional moral imperative for selflessness in combat. When Medal of Honor winner Audie Murphy, one of the most decorated soldiers of the Second World War, was asked why he single-handedly engaged a company of German troops for an hour with a machine-gun mounted on a burning tank, he said: "They were killing my friends." Murphy would later become a famous Hollywood actor, but his heroism came at a heavy psychological price. He endured post-traumatic stress disorder for the rest of his life, sleeping with a gun under his pillow.[186]

We all like to believe we're the good guys; it's very important to our well-being. Cognitive dissonance causes psychological distress when people have to reconcile conflicting moral values, such as obeying orders from an authority figure which will cause harm to others.[187]

In the Milgram experiments held in Yale in 1961, participants believed they were giving increasingly severe electric shocks to an actor in another room if he gave the wrong answers in a fictitious memory-trial. After a few rounds, the actor was screaming and banging on the wall, and all the participants asked if they could stop.

After a psychologist told them that the other person would not suffer any lasting harm, that they bore no responsibility, and that they had no choice but to continue, more than six out of ten went on to deliver 450-volt shocks to the now-silent actor.

Psychologists are no longer allowed to replicate the Milgram experiments, because the stress imposed on participants is seen as unethical. Subjects were weeping, groaning, trembling, stuttering, sweating, laughing, biting their lips and digging their nails into their bodies.

Echoing Joshua Greene's findings about our aversion to "prototypical violence", the experiments showed that obedience plummeted if subjects had to make contact with the actor, or when the psychologist was not standing over them. Compliance halved if they had to touch the actor in order to administer the shock, and dropped to just over 20 percent if the psychologist was not in the same room.

People were also influenced by dissenting voices. Only one in ten gave the maximum 450-volt shock if they had seen another subject refuse to do so, and no-one did so if another psychologist in the room openly disagreed about administering further shocks.

Rationalising

While Shakespeare's Henry V used peer pressure to rally his band of brothers at Agincourt, chieftains could not rely on brilliant motivational speeches to their happy few. We need our actions to be morally legitimate, even praiseworthy.

One of the oldest moral justifications for war is the obverse of the Golden Rule: "Do unto others before they do unto you" – what Hobbes called diffidence. Self-defence is sanctioned in moral and legal codes around the world. If you can assign responsibility to the enemy not only for prior atrocities, but also for hypothetical future misdeeds, where no evidence of culpability is required, then pre-emptive murder, even of the very young, is just getting your retaliation in first.

We have also devised ingenious propaganda on another of Hobbes' causes of conflict: the righteousness of gain. One of the earliest recorded wars was motivated by the opportunity to plunder. The legendary Sumerian king Gilgamesh of Uruk fought to acquire cedar wood. The accounts of his victorious pillaging are careful to point out the moral imperative: Gilgamesh needed cedar to enhance his ziggurat, a massive wooden structure built to honour the gods.[188] Sumerian kings – like all royal families – were keen to legitimise their hold on power by claiming that their rule was divinely ordained.

It was harder to rationalise conflict on the basis of Hobbes' third category of glory. The Roman poet Horace characterised patriotism as an act of selfless love in his ode *Dulce et Decorum est pro Patria Mori* ("It Is Sweet and Glorious To Die for One's Country") – which was still an inspiration in the blood-sacrifice of the First World War nearly two thousand years later.

One of the most potent ways to combine gain and glory was the lure of destiny. Even if this inexorable providence was not clear in the beginning, with the curse of hindsight it was sanctified by success on the field of battle. More than three thousand years ago, the retrospective "mandate of heaven" legitimised the Zhou rulers who deposed the Shang dynasty in China. An appeal to tribal greatness gave a providential sense of purpose, whether it was the Israelites as God's Chosen People or the Americans who embraced their Manifest Destiny from sea to shining sea.

Dehumanising

If we couldn't come up with a compelling rationale for our actions towards our fellow human beings, we could always depict them as not-quite-human instead. In *Survival of the Friendliest*, Brian Hare and Vanessa Woods describe how the "hug hormone" oxytocin can also inhibit empathetic responses from the medial pre-frontal cortex when we feel threatened, making it easier for us to de-humanise others.[189]

In 1864, seven hundred Colorado militia under Colonel John Chivington murdered and mutilated over a hundred peaceful Cheyenne and Arapaho in the Sand Creek Massacre. Two-thirds of those killed were women and children. An officer who ordered his troops not to participate was murdered after giving evidence against his fellow soldiers. Chivington defended his actions, saying: "Kill and scalp all, big and little; nits make lice."

In Rwanda 130 years later, a crisis engineered by the assassination of President Habyarimana along with President Ntaryamira of Burundi led to the genocide of the minority Tutsi at the hands of the majority Hutu. Propaganda broadcasts on the radio invoked the psychology of disgust, representing the Tutsi as filth, vermin and – particularly frequently – as inyenzi, or cockroaches.

Over half a million men, women and children were murdered in the genocide, accounting for around two thirds of Tutsis and nearly one in three pygmy Batwas living in Rwanda at the time, as well as any Hutus who had the courage to try to shelter them.

In Myanmar twenty years later, fake news spread on Facebook by a Buddhist monk about a rape and jihadist plot led to pogroms against the minority Muslim population. In 2016, amidst the rape, murder and ethnic cleansing of the Rohingya people, a non-profit organisation called C_4ADS identified a Burmese-language "campaign of hate speech that actively dehumanises Muslims". C_4ADS's efforts prompted Facebook to hire more native Burmese speakers, and build systems to flag and remove the dehumanising content.[190]

Distancing

Our intuitive moral mode is activated when sensory contact is involved. By the same token, the more distance we can put between ourselves and the suffering which is inflicted, the more willing we are to cause pain.

In the Milgram experiments, when subjects were asked to read out the instructions to administer shocks to a third party, rather than deliver the shocks directly, more than nine out of ten agreed to do so – a 50 percent increase over the standard experiment.

The use of scorched-earth tactics to destroy the food of civilians and subversives alike, enabled armies to annihilate populations with minimal remorse. By the time people had died from starvation and disease, the perpetrators were often well over the horizon, and lamenting the mysterious quirks of Providence which could cause such suffering.

Oliver Cromwell, Lord Protector of the short-lived Commonwealth of England, Scotland and beyond, is remembered in Ireland for his massacre of three thousand souls in the 1649 Siege of Drogheda – which, for Cromwell, was a "righteous judgement of God" that deterred further bloodshed. [191] His Parliament also seized the lands of aristocratic Catholics in Ireland who fought for God, King and Country. They were pejoratively nicknamed "Tories", from Tóraí, the Irish word for "outlaws".

Apologists point out that Cromwell's New Model Army was relatively disciplined in battle by the standards of the time, but often fail to mention that Cromwell's son-in-law, Henry Ireton, destroyed crops to starve rebels into submission, killing more than two hundred thousand people, or somewhere between one in ten and one in three of the Irish population. [192]

Research into casualties in the Second World War has shown that 90 percent of soldiers were killed by remote means such as artillery, bombs, land-mines or booby-traps, rather than aimed bullets or anti-tank weapons. [193] In modern drone warfare, where the sensory experience of harming others, or the fear of being harmed, is diminished, our ability to kill others without raising intuitive moral red flags has increased.

Where Unfettered Cognitive Biases Lead

In the twentieth century, the ability to convince yourself that you were the good guy, acting in self-defence, overcame the most extreme cognitive dissonance.

Bruno Muller, an Einsatzkommando Nazi leader and mass murderer of Poles and Jews, told a two-year-old Jewish girl he was holding: "You must die so that we can live."[194]

An Austrian soldier, asked to murder Jewish women and children in Belarus, wrote of his transition from cognitive dissonance to firm resolution in a letter home: "During the first try, my hand trembled a bit as I shot, but one gets used to it. By the tenth try, I aimed calmly and shot surely at the many women, children and infants. I kept in mind that I have two infants at home, whom these hordes would treat just the same, if not ten times worse. The death that we gave them was a beautiful quick death, compared to the hellish torments of thousands and thousands in the jails of the GPU. Infants flew in great arcs through the air, and we shot them to pieces in flight, before their bodies fell into the pit and into the water."[195]

German soldiers were not punished if they asked not to participate in the shooting, although some feared that they would be re-assigned to hazardous tasks such as mine-sweeping if they didn't follow orders. Despite many reports of moral qualms, most succumbed to peer pressure. In one German infantry company of five hundred soldiers, less than one in forty refused to participate.

As the latter half of the twentieth century progressed, our willingness to tell good strong lies to ourselves remained undimmed. The Soviet Union downplayed personality cults following the death of Stalin, but let the tanks roll into Hungary in the same year that Khrushchev denounced his dictatorship – and into Czechoslovakia twelve years later, to suppress democratic reforms. An authoritarian regime could not tolerate dissenting voices in the room, and in the absence of laws which protected fundamental human rights, there were no cultural norms to stop them.

Two years after Soviet tanks crushed the Hungarian Uprising, Mao Tse-Tung launched the Great Leap Forward, a peerless folly that may have killed more people than the Second World War, in an attempt to industrialise China.[196] Crop-yields collapsed after the Great Sparrow Campaign denuded the countryside of the key predator to the locust. China continued to export grain rather than admit that millions were starving.

Two and a half million revolting peasants may have been murdered, out of a total death-toll of between 18 million and 55 million people, making the Great Leap Forward one of the worst acts of governmental mass-murder in the history of the world.[197] Mao then purged the Communist Party of political rivals in the Cultural Revolution, galvanising young cadres of the Red Guard to destroy old habits, old customs, old ideas and old culture. In a facsimile of the Great Terror in the Soviet Union, hundreds of thousands of "capitalist roadsters" were murdered on the flimsiest of pretexts, and swaths of China's cultural artefacts were destroyed, in a process which continued until Mao died in 1976.

A silver lining of the Cultural Revolution was that rural literacy soared. Mao had said that revolution began in the village, and millions of educated urban youths spent time working in the countryside.[198] By the time of Mao's death, the Khmer Rouge in Cambodia had decided that revolution ended in the village as well, emptying the cities of all their inhabitants. In the Year Zero, child-soldiers were trained to murder intellectuals who might challenge the Revolution, "for the purification of the populace".[199] In their utopian zeal, they used the same tactics the Nazis had adopted in the Hunger Plan, to destroy the culture and civilisation of Eastern Europe.

Less than four years later, more than 2 million men, women and children, out of a population of 7 million people, had been killed through murder and famine.[200] The crisis did not end until the persecution of an ethnically Vietnamese minority, and ongoing border skirmishes, led to an invasion by their neighbours in 1979.

As Cambodia was in the Chinese sphere of influence, China retaliated by invading northern Vietnam. The Soviet-sponsored Vietnamese responded by scapegoating the wealthy, ethnically Chinese Hoa minority, leading to the exodus of eight hundred thousand Boat People across south-east Asia.[201]

After being dragged belatedly into two global conflicts in the space of twenty-five years, American statesmen accepted after the Second World War that containing communist expansion around the world, while defending democracy and human rights, was in the national interest.[202]

This was bound to lead to dilemmas. US-backed groups in places such as Iran, Iraq, Chile, Guatemala, Nicaragua, El Salvador and Bangladesh committed appalling human-rights violations.[203] The moral confusion of the Vietnam war was epitomised by the shelling of Ben Tré during the first few days of the Tet Offensive, in February 1968. A US officer said: "It became necessary to destroy the town to save it."[204]

This was followed by the My Lai massacre five weeks later, when hundreds of men, women and children were rounded up and murdered by US soldiers.[205] By the end of the American phase of the war, 58,318 US soldiers were dead, and 1,626 were missing in action. More than 1 million Vietnamese had perished.[206]

Weaponising Reason

Dissidents of the counter-culture argued that the cold-warriors of the USSR and the US were morally equivalent, without dwelling on the fact that in the West dissent was a right, not a privilege. The US had to address their criticism precisely because there was a greater good at stake.[207]

In peace and prosperity, scapegoats fade away – only to be revived in times of crisis, to assuage our wrath. A Roman pagan living under freedom of worship in the era of Constantine would hardly have believed that his descendants would be persecuted for heresy in the time of Justinian. An African-American farmer like Anthony Johnson in Virginia, who successfully took legal action in the 1650s to secure the return of his slave, would hardly have believed that his family would be run out of the state a few decades later.[208] A cosmopolitan, urbane German Jew in the early twentieth century would hardly have believed that the land of Goethe was about to descend into darkness.

High intelligence is no defence against our deep-seated beliefs. If we are passionate in relation to our values, then we cannot be dispassionate in assessing evidence or arguments to the contrary. This makes it easier to demonise those we disagree with, and dismiss their valid concerns in times of crisis. Reason must be weaponised in order to counter our biases, and consider other narratives.

We have relied on confirmation bias to convince ourselves that we were doing the right thing, the moral thing. The techniques we pioneered to justify and play down atrocities would be adopted in the twentieth century on an industrial scale. As we shall see, the strategic use of famine was deployed in the Nazi Hunger Plan to minimise dissonance, by distancing the perpetrators from their crimes.

You may not care much for our sorry history of lies and excuses: arcane and abstruse reasons for our cruel behaviour might make your eyes glaze over. But if you want to see how cognitive bias can skew a moral compass, it helps not to be emotionally invested.

The paradox of cruelty is that a species wired for kindness has repeatedly committed atrocities which contradict the very values it claims to be defending. By understanding the lies we used to tell ourselves, we gain an insight into how and why we turn to demagoguery and intolerance in times of crisis.

Chapter Six

From Passion to Persecution

"It is only about things that do not interest one that one can give a really unbiased opinion, which is no doubt the reason why an unbiased opinion is always absolutely valueless."

OSCAR WILDE

In 2017, Janan Ganesh, a political columnist for the *Financial Times*, predicted that the liberal cause would eventually triumph over what he called the "forces of reaction". In the wake of Brexit, at the level of electoral politics, liberalism and "the Enlightenment itself" seemed to be under serious threat, but there was reason for "long-term exuberance".

In a British Social Attitudes survey, more than seven out of ten eighteen-to twenty-four-year-olds said that they had no religion. Ganesh is not the only commentator to herald the "eventual death of God on British shores" as a sign of progress that is closely linked to open-mindedness, tolerance and "cultural exposure to the outside world". Perhaps our failure to listen to other voices is due to specific belief-systems and tribal affiliations, rather than human nature itself.

We'll see. Certainly, it is undeniable that the moral sanction of Christianity has been sought to justify persecution, war, extortion, oppression and scapegoating on an epic scale. Eight million died in the Thirty Years War between Catholics, Calvinists and Lutherans,[209] and one in three German towns was destroyed.[210] But religious strife is little more than a rounding error in our catalogue of violence and bloodshed. Throughout history, according to *The Encyclopedia of Wars*, for every battle-death in religious wars there have been forty-nine battle-deaths for other reasons.[211] Sadly, the Thirty Years War wasn't even the deadliest conflict that began in 1618. That dubious accolade goes to the conquest of Ming China by the Qing, where between 12 million and 25 million people were killed without a religious pretext.

The end of religion does not sound the death-knell for cognitive bias. Secularism does not necessarily lead to less scapegoating or cruelty. In living memory, avowedly atheist movements, trying to build a "kingdom of freedom", created dictatorships which killed tens of millions.

The late Christopher Hitchens, who made an eloquent and compelling argument for pluralism in his book *god is not Great*, believed that the moral zeal to perfect the species in secular, totalitarian states should be thought of as a religious impulse, rather than a rationalist one.[212] As a way to displace responsibility for rationalist failings, this approach is quite creative; as an insight into human nature, it misses the point spectacularly. By conflating passion with religion, Hitchens made it easier for rationalists to dismiss secular ideologies as religious cults, without addressing the inconvenient truth that their own secular humanist ideals are inevitably fraught with biases, blind-spots and evasions.

We start with the best of intentions. We want to be kind. It is not the intrinsic merit of our beliefs and affiliations which is the problem, but our willingness to use these differences to categorise people into a dehumanised "them" – a basket of deplorables – and a virtuous "us".

We have seen that discrimination between in-groups and out-groups can be triggered by something as trivial as role-play in a mock penitentiary, a preference for Klee over Kandinsky, having red or blue T-shirts, or simply being assigned to Group X rather than Group Y.[213] A group of like-minded people can rationalise acts which are diametrically opposed to the values they profess to be defending.

Christians obeyed the commandment of Christ to love their enemies by killing them. Enlightenment revolutionaries who believed that all men are created equal enslaved them. Utopian rationalists unleashed terror in order to impose the despotism of liberty. Nice people voted Nazi.

Throughout history, minorities have been more likely to shelter the victims of persecution, and to be at the vanguard of social reform. Listening to the views of minorities, who are less likely to be swayed by our cultural norms, is crucial if we want to stay out of the echo-chamber. When the tyranny of the majority in an open society prohibits religious, cultural or linguistic expression, it diminishes us all.

The more passionately we cherish our ideals and values, whether progressive new atheism or old-time religion, the harder it is for us to be objective. When we dismiss dissenting voices because of their beliefs and values, because of what they stand for rather than what they say to us, it does nothing to encourage a healthy skepticism about our own ideals and motivations.

George Santayana said that those who do not remember the past are condemned to repeat it. If we are to understand the present, we need to see how easily progress can flip to persecution. It's not about them; it's about us.

Christians Loving their Enemies by Killing for God

More than eight out of ten people alive today maintain some kind of religious affiliation, and that ratio may be rising. Religion is pervasive in recorded history.

We can only speculate about what the world would be like if Christianity had never existed. We are wired to be nice, but as the Groningen and Milgram experiments have shown, the behaviour of our peers influences our choices. We need cultural norms which nurture kindness. Religion has not always provided them. The historical existence of Jesus is not seriously questioned in scholarly circles nowadays, but moral objections to the teachings of Christianity remain.[214]

Christopher Hitchens argued that the New Testament threat of eternal damnation was worse than the atrocities recounted in the Hebrew Bible. Gibbon saw the decline and fall of the Roman Empire in "the specious demands of charity", which meant that "the last remains of [Roman] military spirit were buried in the cloister".[215] Humanists who see Judeo-Christianity as having a positive impact on their values also see clerical hostility to freedom of thought, especially in the Inquisition of Galileo. Others think it monstrous that an all-powerful God of Love would allow His children to suffer.

The moral authority of the Catholic Church in particular has been shredded by the revelation of the yawning gap between what they practised and what they preached. Senior prelates described blatant lies as mental reservations, moved pedophiles to new parishes, and swore children to secrecy over horrific sexual and physical abuse. Serial offenders were enabled by the Church to cause enormous devastation over decades.

We do not know what the world would have been like without religion, but we do know what happened when Christianity pivoted from condemning bloodshed (for more than a millennium) to sanctifying it. The endorsement of Holy War in the First Crusade was followed by centuries of anti-Semitic pogroms, the Inquisition, censorship, and numerous wars of religion.

In one of the great ironies of history, the Jewish seer Jesus, who had a profound intuitive insight into bias and hypocrisy, has been invoked for millennia to legitimise acts which were utterly at variance with his actual teachings.

From Love to Penitence and Pilgrimage

For the most part, Jesus the ethicist is admired by atheist and apostle alike.[216] Richard Dawkins called Jesus "one of the great ethical innovators of history".[217] Gandhi said: "If then I had to face only the Sermon on the Mount and my own interpretation of it, I would not hesitate to say, 'Oh yes, I am a Christian.'"[218]

A large collection of the sayings of Jesus and the reflections of his followers were in circulation within living memory of the crucifixion, and form the basis of Christian faith.[219] In most modern translations of the New Testament, the word "love" appears hundreds of times – nearly twice as often as the word "sin".[220]

Early Christians had a shared understanding of faith, not as belief without evidence, but as belief in what they hoped for[221]: that God is love,[222] offering forgiveness, redemption and eternal life to people everywhere. Paul said that faith, hope and love endure, but the greatest of these is love (1 Corinthians 13).[223] Jesus rejected the tit-for-tat vengeance of an eye for an eye, urging his followers to go the extra mile by loving their enemies, turning the other cheek to those who struck them, and praying for their persecutors.[224]

Jesus spoke to the marginalised, including prostitutes and tax-collectors.[225] He favored compassion over condemnation, telling his listeners not to judge other people, and to address their own shortcomings before correcting those of their brothers.[226] Good deeds were more important than rituals.[227]

He was hostile to the hypocrisy of the elites, especially the rich families who held Temple positions and collaborated with the Romans.[228] He acknowledged that his views would divide opinion in Jewish society: "I have not come to bring peace but a sword."[229]

Jesus tells a scribe that the greatest commandment of Judaism is to "love the Lord your God with all your heart, with all your soul, with all your mind and with all your strength. . . . You must love your neighbour as yourself" (Mark 12).[230] In the Gospel of Luke, Jesus follows this up with the story of the Good Samaritan – but not in the Gospel of Mark. Instead, the scribe who asks Jesus about the greatest commandment of Judaism goes on to say that loving God and loving your neighbour are far more important than any burnt-offering or sacrifice. "You are not far from the Kingdom of God," Jesus tells him.

This was a direct challenge to the moral and political authority of the rich dynasties which presided over Temple rites. In case anyone had missed the point, Jesus drove the money-changers, who exchanged Roman currency for the Jewish coins required for sacrificial offerings, out of the Temple (Matthew 21).[231]

Jesus was not alone in criticising the Temple authorities, who were regarded by some as quislings, administering a Vichy-style regime for their Roman masters. In the year 56 the High Priest, Jonathan son of Ananus, would be assassinated on the Temple Mount,[232] and less than twenty years later a full-scale Jewish insurrection would lead to the destruction of the Second Temple by Rome.[233]

At the time of Jesus' crucifixion, day-to-day control of Jerusalem was in the hands of a Jewish council, the Sanhedrin, presided over by the High Priest, Caiaphas, and an assembly of Sadducees. They were keen to maintain order during the fractious days of Passover, when diaspora Jews flooded into the city to sacrifice at the Temple. Although Pontius Pilate was in Jerusalem for Passover, most of the Roman garrison was stationed on the coast, at Caesarea, with a larger military force based in Syria.[234]

According to the Gospels, the Sanhedrin made repeated attempts to arrest or entrap Jesus, finally seizing him at Gethsemane and bringing him before Annas, the father-in-law of Caiaphas – and High Priest before him. Jesus is then questioned by Caiaphas, who seems to see Jesus as a disruptive political adversary, a threat to the Pax Romana.

Caiaphas argues that it is better that one man should die so that the nation will not perish (John 11 and 18). Stating that he serves no king but Caesar (Matthew 19), he hands Jesus over to Pontius Pilate for crucifixion on the grounds of sedition.

The Gospels record dissent over this decision among the Jewish authorities. Instead of being left on the cross to rot, *pour encourager les autres*, Joseph of Arimethea, a member of the Sanhedrin, receives permission from Pilate to place Jesus in a tomb (Luke 23). Three days later, Jesus' followers discover that the tomb is empty. They had enough faith in his resurrection to suffer brutal martyrdom in the years to come.

One reason why biblical scholars think the crucifixion is authentic is because it caused so many problems for Christianity.[235] No Jewish tradition had anticipated a crucified Messiah. In the chaos, confusion and fear that followed the execution of Jesus, a familiar doctrine was dusted off to make sense of what had happened: Jesus was sacrificed to appease the wrath of God. Our profound imperfections made it impossible for us to redeem ourselves: we needed a blameless person to be our scapegoat and return us to paradise. All we had to do was believe, and our souls would be healed.

A being who would rather avoid the cognitive effort required to take the plank out of his own eye before taking the speck out of his brother's eye was only too willing to embrace justification-by-faith. For the pre-destined Elect of God, myriad flaws could be dismissed in a warm fug of narcissistic moral torpor. Humility in the face of human frailty morphed into complacency and sectarianism. The faith that our souls would be healed when Jesus disappeared from the tomb was a sign of things to come.

Church elders became alarmed. Christians who did not lead a saintly life were warned that faith without actions was dead.[236] Evangelists fanned out across the Empire to spread the good news, or gospel, of Jesus Christ – at first among the Jewish diaspora, and then as a distinct religion.[237] It was a religion that encouraged people to follow their conscience. Showing love to others was the way to love God.[238]

Initially, Christianity stayed close to its roots in Judaism.[239] The brother of Jesus, James the Just, was admired for his observance of the Torah and his love of the poor. James led the church until the year 62, when the new High Priest, Ananus, exploited a power-vacuum between the death of the Roman Governor Festus and the arrival of his replacement, Albinus, to have James killed for blasphemy. Within eight years, all that remained of the Second Temple was the Western Wall.[240]

After the failure of the Jewish rebellion in the year 70 and the Bar Kokhba revolt in 136, Christianity's roots in Judaism were played down.[241] It had always been politic to minimise the role of the Romans in the killing of Jesus.[242] Anti-Semitism was given an added impetus by accusations of collective responsibility for the crucifixion, as well as fears that Christians were fraternising too closely with Jews.[243]

Jews had had to rebut allegations of poisoning wells and sacrificing Greeks in Temple rituals since Flavius Josephus wrote *Against Apion*.[244] But thanks to Helena, as we've seen, other religions were protected from the time that Christianity was adopted by the Emperor Constantine. Through centuries of warfare, water contamination, famine and plague, the censure of Church and State was a powerful brake on lynch-mobs seeking scapegoats.

Even when the Western Roman Empire collapsed into what we might now describe as a failed state, rival Christian warlords ignored Church teaching on persecution at their peril.[245] In the absence of imperial authority, the Bishop of Rome, Leo the Great, had had to negotiate with Attila the Hun and Gaiseric the Vandal. The Roman Catholic Church which emerged from the ashes of the Latin Empire prized obedience and orthodoxy, but was dragged into laying the foundations for the separation of Church and State, as well as freedom of conscience.[246]

The Church was ambivalent about spilling blood even in self-defence. [247] Christianity did not stamp out murdering, pillaging and betrayal, but it encouraged warlords to feel very, very bad about it. Their cognitive dissonance led them to a morbid fascination with the torments awaiting them in hell. Inferno literature was popular for centuries before Dante lifted his quill, with the visions of an Irish knight, Visio Tnugdali, translated forty-three times into fifteen languages, including ten separate German versions.[248]

To expiate their guilt and smooth the path to salvation, the nobility sought atonement for their sins in penitence, in pilgrimage and in repudiation of their wealth, as a form of after-life insurance. To make up for years of skulduggery, many sought to buy their way into heaven through ecclesiastical gifts. More than a quarter of the land in England alone was in the hands of the Church by the time the Normans invaded in 1066.[249]

The Crusades: Absolution through Holy War

Then in 1095, Alexius I Komnenus, Emperor of Byzantium, wrote to Pope Urban II seeking his help against the Sunni Seljuk Turks. The Byzantine Empire had lost nearly half its territory to the Seljuks in 1071, including most of Anatolia and Syria.[250]

Alexius I probably expected no more than a few hundred knights to come to his aid, but Urban II was offering a new form of absolution: the forgiveness of sins through Holy War. After drumming up support throughout France and Italy, at the Council of Clermont Pope Urban II launched the First Crusade.[251]

Robert the Monk wrote down a version of his speech some years later.[252] The speech provided a rationale for revenge, as well as dehumanising a "race absolutely alien to God", but its major innovation was to sanctify acts of violence. A religion which taught people to love their enemies and turn the other cheek, framed the Crusade as an armed pilgrimage to bind east and west together, re-take Jerusalem, and purge the knights-errant of their sins by killing for God. Cognitive dissonance evaporated.

The response to Urban's speech was without precedent in western history. Tancred of Hauteville, a key knight of the First Crusade, was elated. His biographer noted that Tancred had "burned with anxiety because the warfare he engaged in as a knight seemed contrary to the Lord's commands . . . these contradictions deprived him of courage . . . After the judgement of Pope Urban granted remission of all their sins to all Christians going out to fight the gentiles, then at last, as if previously asleep, Tancred's vigor was aroused, his powers grew, his eyes opened, his courage was born."[253] More than seven thousand knights and thirty-five thousand trained infantry joined Tancred on the three thousand-kilometre trek to Jerusalem, including wealthy princes such as Robert of Normandy, Stephen of Blois and Robert of Flanders, and well-known opponents of the papacy, such as Godfrey of Bouillon.[254]

Alexius was almost as wary of his Latin allies from the West as he was of his Seljuq enemies to the East. His daughter Anna wrote that the Court was shocked by the scale of the crusading army, distrusted Franks, and loathed Normans from Italy like Bohemond of Taranto, who had attacked Byzantine territory in the Balkans.[255]

But if Urban was delighted by the reaction of knights and nobles, he rapidly became disturbed by the enthusiasm and zeal of the peasantry, who also responded to his call to arms. Inspired by itinerant preachers such as Peter the Hermit, between forty thousand and sixty thousand men, women and children took the cross, with little or no military training or financial means, swelling the ranks of those making their way to Jerusalem.[256]

Urban exhorted bishops to prevent their parishioners from leaving without seeking their advice beforehand, and suggested that husbands should not "rashly set out on such a long journey without the agreement of their wives". Soon Urban was telling religious in Spain and Italy that they could not go on Crusade without the permission of their bishops or abbots, and telling knights of the Reconquista that they would receive the same absolution if they stayed and fought in Spain.

Seljuk harassment of pilgrims had upset eons of tolerance. Jerusalem had been in Muslim hands for centuries, mostly without incident.[257] But the desecration of holy sites in Jerusalem had led to the scapegoating of minorities in Christendom in the past. When Caliph Al-Hakim the Mad damaged the Church of the Holy Sepulchre in 1009, thousands of kilometres away in western France, the Jews of Limoges were expelled as "habitual allies of the devil".[258]

The proclamation of Holy War unleashed pandemonium. Crusader sermons sparked anti-Semitic riots in Rouen and Lorraine, prompting Jewish communities to send warnings to their family and friends in Germany. Putative Crusaders attacked local minorities along the line of march to Byzantium. Count Emicho of Flonheim targeted Rhineland Jews in Speyer, Trier, Metz, Regensburg, Cologne, Worms and Mainz, despite accepting large bribes to leave them in peace.[259]

Overall, roughly five thousand Jews died, eight hundred in Worms alone, with some deciding to take the lives of their families rather than be murdered or tortured to convert. Emicho's mob pillaged their way along the Danube until they were comprehensively defeated by the Hungarians, and Emicho fled homewards.[260]

Meanwhile, the cohorts of the First Crusade slouched towards Jerusalem, to be reborn in legend. Riven by hunger, disease and infighting, their capture of the city in 1099 seemed a miracle – the first time Jerusalem had been under Christian control in 461 years.

The Crusaders seized Jerusalem from the Shiite Fatimids of Egypt, who had re-taken it from the Sunni Seljuq Turks a year before.[261] Corpses were stripped and sliced open in case they had swallowed jewels. Jewish defenders of the city burnt to death when their synagogue was torched. Modern estimates place the number of Jews and Muslims killed in Jerusalem at somewhere between three thousand and five thousand people.[262] After the massacre was over, by all accounts, the Crusaders went to the Church of the Holy Sepulchre and gave thanks to God.

A Second Crusade was launched in 1147, accompanied by further pogroms against Jews in western Europe, in a failed attempt to recapture the County of Edessa from Seljuk Turks. The alliance between Latin and Byzantine eventually unravelled less than a century after Jerusalem was captured, when Italian merchants in Constantinople were killed in the Massacre of the Latins in 1182.[263] Saladin took Jerusalem five years later. A Third Crusade was launched in 1189 after Jerusalem was taken by Saladin. When the Kings of France, England and Germany failed to recapture the city, Pope Innocent III launched the Fourth Crusade in 1202. Led by Venetians, whose clergy described the Greek Byzantines as "worse than Jews", they sacked Constantinople and allegedly placed a prostitute on the Patriarch's throne in Hagia Sophia as they raped, murdered and pillaged.[264]

Despite the debacle of the Sack of Constantinople, five years later Innocent III decided to unleash Holy War against heretical Cathars in southern France.[265] The Albigensian Crusade stormed the town of Beziers, massacring twenty thousand citizens after they refused to hand over a few hundred Cathars. The legend grew that Arnaud-Amauary, the papal legate, urged the troops on. "Kill them all," he supposedly said. "God will know His own!"[266]

Tactically, the massacre had a salutary effect. Strategically, it was a disaster for a Pope seeking conformity, not carnage. The Church needed a surgical approach to heresy within Christendom.[267] In 1234, the Papal Inquisition was established in southern France, and in 1252 Innocent IV authorised the use of torture to obtain evidence.[268]

Inquisitors preferred imprisonment, pilgrimage, or the wearing of a penitent cross to executing heretics.[269] Bernard Gui of Carcassone, a notorious Inquisitor, executed less than one in twenty of those he found guilty.[270] But after sanctioning Holy War in the Crusades, the Church turned a blind eye to punitive lynch-mobs.

In 1076, Pope Gregory VII excommunicated the entire town of Cambrai for burning Ramihrdus, a priest accused of heresy.[271] In 1244, hundreds of Cathars were burnt in Montségur by royalists who were avenging the murder of two inquisitors and their retinue, without suffering any sanction.[272]

Martin Luther and Reform as the Instrument of Conquest

Anti-Semitism increased across Western Europe after the First Crusade, despite efforts by secular and religious leaders to suppress it.[273] Blood-libels pre-dated Christianity, but after the First Crusade, unsolved child-murders were attributed to the need for Christian blood to make unleavened matzo bread.[274] Pope Innocent IV condemned these blood-libels in 1247, as did Pope Gregory X in 1272.[275]

Blood-libels triggered pogroms in times of crisis, as state authority was weakened.[276] Five thousand Jews in 146 locations were killed in the Rintfleisch Massacres during the German Civil War of 1298, twelve years after the murder of Werner of Oberwesel.[277]

As the Black Death wrought havoc in 1348, the old saw about poisoning wells and spreading disease was used to justify the destruction of Jewish communities in hundreds of locations, including the Strasbourg Massacre.[278] Jews were eventually expelled from France, England, Lithuania, Austria, Hungary, Spain, Portugal and some Italian and German principalities. Refugees flocked into Poland, which grew to have the largest Jewish population in Europe.[279]

Anti-Semitism persisted in Martin Luther's Reformation. It was intended as a protest against corruption and a return to the authenticity of early Christianity.[280] It became a viral sensation which used nationalist instincts to reject Rome. Two months after issuing his Ninety-five Theses in 1517, they were printed across Europe in vernacular languages. By 1530, 10 million copies of ten thousand Protestant works were in circulation.[281]

Having initially urged his followers to convert Jews through Christian love in his pamphlet *That Jesus Christ Was Born a Jew*, Luther became disillusioned by what he saw as the obstinate refusal of Jews to embrace Reformed Christianity. By 1543, he had regressed to an atavistic attitude, and in *On the Jews and Their Lies* he described them as "base, whoring people", wallowing in the "devil's faeces". He wrote: "If we wish to wash our hands of the Jews' blasphemy and not share in their guilt, we have to part company with them. They must be driven from our country . . . we must drive them out like mad dogs . . . we are at fault for not slaying them."

As with the Spanish Inquisition, there was no room in Luther's Germany for a plural state which protected minorities. Luther advocated setting fire to Jewish schools and synagogues, razing Jewish houses, and forbidding rabbis to teach, on pain of death. Following his advice, Jews were expelled from Saxony in 1536.[282]

Luther had initially rejected the use of violence, but sectarianism ultimately prevailed, despite the Habsburg Holy Roman Emperor Charles V describing the Reformation as an "argument between monks". Luther translated the New Testament into German, cultivating princes who disliked the remote Habsburgs and coveted the wealth of the Church. Many converted to the slogan "German money for a German church".[283]

Soon all authority was questioned. If believers could defrock venal priests, surely they could depose corrupt princes as well? A Knights'

Revolt in the Rhineland in 1522 was followed by a Peasants' War in 1524. The Peasants' War was the largest popular uprising in Europe prior to the French Revolution in 1789, and the threat to the secular elite imperiled the Reformation almost as soon as it had begun. Up to a hundred thousand peasants may have been slaughtered before the revolt was suppressed.[284]

The Peasants' War exemplified the importance for secular rulers of taking control of the narrative. The medieval Church had prevented dissent by having a monopoly on literacy, administration and education. In an era of radical populist printing, it was not easy to suppress a book when copies could be distributed so quickly. Elite sanction to question taboo subjects like papal authority were taken in unexpected directions, and with lightning speed. Ideas metastasised. Everyone was playing catch-up.

Although he had wanted believers to nominate their ministers, Luther was now bound to link Church and State together, even if that meant that he had to turn a blind eye to the moral infractions of his patrons.

When Philip I of Hesse formalised his bigamous relationship with one of his wife's ladies-in-waiting, citing the customs of the Patriarchs in the Hebrew Bible, Luther advised him to marry in secret. When the marriage was exposed, Luther told him to deny it with a "good, strong lie".[285]

The Censorship Wars

Attempts at censorship followed in the wake of tensions in the Habsburg Empire. An Index of forbidden books was compiled in the Netherlands in 1529, a few decades before the Eighty Years War, which ended in Dutch independence. A second Index was published in Venice in 1543, during the Habsburg-Valois Wars in Italy, as the French formed an alliance with the Muslim Ottoman Turks. France issued an

Index in 1551, eleven years before the French Wars of Religion.

A Papal Index approved by the Counter-Reformation Catholic Church was not published until 1564, when the complete works of hundreds of authors were prohibited entirely, along with bans on specific titles and partial redaction of other works.[286] That same year, one of the most celebrated victims of the Papal Inquisition, Galileo Galilei, was born in Pisa.

Galileo defended his ideas with dazzling polemic, and a complete absence of political nous. By the time he was censured for his heliocentric belief that the earth orbited the sun, rather than the geocentric view that the sun orbited the earth, Copernicus' *De Revolutionibus* had been in circulation for nearly three quarters of a century, and used in the creation of the Gregorian calendar by Pope Gregory XIII.[287]

Tycho Brahe had advanced astronomical arguments against heliocentrism, pointing out that if the earth orbited the sun, the distance to the stars should be calculable by measuring the apparent shift in position of stars, or stellar parallax, as the earth moved around the sun. The lack of a discernible stellar parallax meant that either heliocentrism was wrong, or the stars were an unimaginably vast distance away, and far larger than the earth.[288] The necessary speed of the earth's rotation on its axis under heliocentrism was also seen as counter-intuitive.

Technology to measure a stellar parallax would not be developed for another two hundred years, and although stars outside the Milky Way were seen by Boyle in the nineteenth century, they were not shown to be other galaxies until the observations made by Hubble in the 1920s.[289]

Plagiarising Tycho Brahe extensively, the Papal Inquisition concluded in 1615 that heliocentrism was "foolish and absurd in philosophy". Discussion of heliocentrism as a mathematical hypothesis was permissible, provided that Galileo did not argue that the hypethesis was true.

Jesuits remained sympathetic until Galileo published *The Assayer* in 1623, a polemical broadside which humiliated Father Orazio Grazzi. Pope Urban VIII supported Galileo until 1632, encouraging him to publish a *Discourse Concerning the Two Chief World Systems*, with the imprimatur of the Papal Inquisition.

The Pope's only proviso was that Galileo include the pros and cons of heliocentrism, as well as the Pope's publicly known personal views on the matter. Galileo used a character named "Simplicio", Italian for "Simpleton", as the mouthpiece of the Pope.

A fascinating discourse was suppressed, and Galileo was shown the instruments of torture. He was deemed to be "vehemently suspect of heresy" and placed under house-arrest, where he wrote *Two New Sciences,* one of his most important works.[290]

The *Index Librorum Prohibitorum* was an object of ridicule in England. Thomas James called it "an invaluable reference work" in deciding which books to collect for the Bodleian Library in Oxford.[291] His subtext, that Anglican England was a beacon of enlightenment and liberty when set against the folly of Popery, projected an aura of moral superiority which was at odds with reality, ignoring the exodus of English subjects to America to secure religious freedom.

Censorship was not exclusive to the Catholic Church. The Crown had taken control by founding the Stationer's Company in 1557, licensing fifty-three printing presses during the reign of Mary Tudor, and censoring suspect publications under her sister Elizabeth. Works which were seen as subversive, heretical or obscene were suppressed in England just as they were elsewhere, with bans on literary and theatrical productions surviving into the 1960s. Most notably, *Lady Chatterley's Lover* sold 3 million copies after Penguin won an obscenity trial in 1960, and became the subject of the Philip Larkin poem "Annus Mirabilis". At a time when religious dissent ineluctably led to political dissent, a Puritan who attacked the Popish tendencies of the Anglican

Church in 1630 not only had his property confiscated, but had the letters "SS", for "Sower of Sedition", branded on his forehead.[292] As late as 1696, John Toland's book *Christianity Not Mysterious* was burnt at the stake by the public hangman in Dublin on the orders of Parliament.

Toland, who coined the term "pantheist", and was the first person ever to be described as a free-thinker, was prosecuted by a grand jury in London, but avoided the death-penalty. He likened the exclusively Protestant Irish Parliament in Dublin to "Popish Inquisitors who performed that Execution on the Book, when they could not seize the Author, whom they had destined to the Flames".[293]

Over the previous 150 years, 12 million people had been killed in the Wars of Religion. Luther did not begin by advocating violence. In the Invocavit Sermons in 1522, he said that Christians should rely on the word of God rather than physical force.[294]

"Do you know what the Devil thinks when he sees men use violence to propagate the gospel? He sits with folded arms behind the fire of hell, and says with malignant looks and frightful grin: 'Ah, how wise these madmen are to play my game! Let them go on; I shall reap the benefit. I delight in it.'" After the moral sanction of Holy War, including by Luther himself, there were plenty of madmen willing to play "the Devil's game".

The Hypocrisy of Enlightenment Slaveholders

There was a time when the election of a black President of the United States was seen as a watershed, inflating hopes that a benighted dialogue on race and discrimination, in a country where black men were still five times more likely to be incarcerated than white men, and black minors were eighteen times more likely to be sentenced as adults than white minors, might soon be consigned to the dustbin of history.[295] Cell-phone footage of police brutality, and the atavistic scenes in Charlottesville, soon punctured that balloon.

The legacy of slavery continues to haunt civic discourse. Unlike witch-hunts and lynch-mobs which scapegoat minorities in crisis-driven spasms, the systematic development of slavery in America was a response to prosperity, not pestilence, and built a scaffold of lies and euphemisms to justify permanent bondage on the basis of race.

The institution of slavery in what became the United States of America emerged after centuries of opposition to slavery in Europe, among Christian sects whose founders had condemned the practice in trenchant and unambigious terms, as well as in the southern colony of Georgia, whose founder, James Oglethorpe, had initially imposed a ban on all forms of slavery – a ban which had lasted for decades.[296] Plantation slavery would force white America to turn its moral code upside down in order to grasp the opportunity presented by soaring demand for commodities, in a democracy founded on the premise that all men are created equal.

The United States was one of the most highly educated and homogenous nations in the world, sharing a language, legal system, revolutionary heritage and Christian faith, yet the level of ambivalence about slavery could be traced with astonishing accuracy based on the mix of crops grown in each area. The reluctance to extend the "moral circle" to the enslaved in areas where the economy was most reliant on slavery was striking.[297]

Slavery survived the development of light-speed communications, the foundation of the National Academy of Sciences, and the beginning of the trans-continental railroad. It might have lumbered into the twentieth century, if rebel shells hadn't fallen on Fort Sumter.

Because America was inspired by the Age of Reason, with 80 percent voter participation among the white, male electorate, as well as an array of civil and religious liberties, a free press, and First Amendment protection for the right of free speech, the excuses used to sustain slavery had to be articulated, defended and recorded.[298]

It remains a case-study in confirmation bias without parallel, perpetuated by progressive scions of the Enlightenment, like Thomas Jefferson, whose cognitive dissonance can be seen in how awkward his various rationales for slavery became. We can read the laws which established hereditary lifetime indentured service, as well as the Slave Codes which suppressed evidence of equality and made it a crime to teach a black person to read or write. We can quantify the mortality rates which led the Founding Fathers to believe that slavery would wither away if the international slave trade was ended, and the population rebound among slaves born in the United States which was used to re-frame slavery as a positive good, even as families in the Upper South were broken up and sold "down the river" to meet demand for slaves in the Lower South. It took a series of good strong lies to solidify the barrier between black and white America, and to maintain those lies after the Revolution. It would take more lies to end slavery in the Civil War, and to embed inequality in Jim Crow Reconstruction.

*

It is tempting to think it was always thus, but it wasn't.[299] A judicial ruling that a man who had not committed a crime could be held in servitude for life did not occur in the Thirteen Colonies until 1655. The black man who lost his freedom for life in that case was John Casor.

The court in Northampton County, Virginia, ruled in favor of his master, Antonio, an illiterate migrant from a Portuguese colony, who anglicised his name to "Anthony" after working his way out of indentured service. He soon became a prosperous farmer who was well regarded by the court for his "hard labour and known service".[300]

Antonio eventually moved his family to Maryland, where his grandson named his farm in honour of the "old country": Angola. The man who had enslaved John Casor in Virginia was known to the court as "Anthony Johnson, negro".[301]

In seventeenth-century Virginia, black and white indentured servants worked side by side in the tobacco fields. Both groups received food and lodging from their masters, and were entitled to Sunday, and half of Saturday, off work.

White indentured servants ended their terms of labour and became freeholders in the colony. Africans such as Francisco Payne and John Graweere also worked their way to freedom for themselves and their families. Black men used the courts to secure their rights – including the right to own slaves in the case of Anthony Johnson, who was one of the first people in Virginia to have his right to own a slave legally recognised.

The moral case against slavery had already been made by the sixteenth century, [302] when less than 3 percent of all African slaves had been trafficked to the New World.[303] These arguments had had a profound influence on some early American colonists.

James Oglethorpe founded Georgia in 1730 on the principle of "agrarian equality", in the hope that it would be divided into fifty-acre family farms. Farmers were allowed to finance the passage of indentured servants, but there was an absolute ban on all forms of slavery.[304] But restrictions on slavery could not withstand the lucrative demands of sugar, cotton and rice production. As Native Americans died in their millions from pestilence and over-work, demand for labour in mining and sugar came from the Caribbean Islands and Latin America.[305]

Estimates of the number of Africans transported as slaves to the New World between the sixteenth and nineteenth centuries range from 10 million to 20 million. Patrick Manning estimated that 12 million souls were supplied from West Africa, with 1.5 million dying on board ship during the notorious Middle Passage.[306] Countless more died in the raids and battles which led to their capture and enslavement, while waiting to embark, and on forced marches to the coast.

From the late seventeenth century, slaves were shipped to Charleston from the West Indies, as demand for "Carolina Gold" rice led to soaring profits on coastal plantations. Twenty years after the foundation of Georgia, the ban on slavery was rescinded, as the mass production of cotton using plantation labour led the colonists to become "stark Mad after Negroes".[307]

In a pattern repeated when sugar plantations arrived in Barbados, Martinique, Saint Domingue and Guadeloupe, the racial barriers between slave and free solidified as demand for plantation goods increased. As the number of enslaved Native American prisoners in South Carolina dwindled, the ethnicity of the remainder was expunged, and they were reclassified as "black" in plantation records.

The fate of slavery hung in the balance in the Upper South, where freeholders grew tobacco efficiently on a relatively small scale. The boundaries between black and white remained fluid in Virginia until 1676, when planters defeated a rebellion by black and white servants, and introduced a Slave Code.[308] Any suggestion that Africans could be prosperous, free and active citizens had to be stifled. This way of thinking undermined the racist case for enslaving them, and stoked fears of insurrection.

After 1676, free Africans were forbidden from hiring white indentured servants. They lost the right to vote, to bear arms, to serve in the militia, to hold public office, or to strike a white person in self-defence. Private liberation of slaves was forbidden in 1691, with slaveholders required to pay for the removal of freed slaves from the state. Slaves were forbidden to travel or earn money in their free time.

Although racism against African-Americans was pervasive in the North as well as the South, the creation of a plantation economy dependent on forced labour required a Slave Code which removed all sources of cognitive dissonance. In South Carolina, legislators railed against the finery of urban slaves who dressed like white people, passing the "Law for Preventing the Excessive and Costly Apparel of Negroes".

Legal sanctions were used to prevent miscegenation, the intermarriage of white and black. A 1705 law arrogated absolute power over life and death: "If any slave resist his master . . . correcting such slave, and shall happen to be killed in such correction . . . the master shall be free of all punishment . . . as if such accident never happened."[309]

One of the great propagandists of the Revolution, Tom Paine, author of *The Rights of Man*, argued that America should "discontinue and renounce" slavery in 1775, but he avoided abolitionism in his key polemic, *Common Sense*.[310] Up to seventy-five thousand copies of *Common Sense* circulated among a population of about 2.5 million Americans during the Revolutionary War.[311]

Readers were inspired by the idea that Independence would provide "freedom and security", but Paine's only reference to African-Americans was designed to trigger fears of insurrection, after British offers to emancipate the slaves of rebels. "The cruelty hath a double guilt: it is dealing brutally by us, and treacherously by them."[312]

A series of compromises enacted by the Constitutional Convention of 1787 declared that for purposes of representation in Congress, enslaved blacks in a state would be counted as three-fifths of the number of white inhabitants. According to the Virginia Constitutional Convention delegate and future President James Madison, these compromises were required because "the States were divided into different interests not by their . . . size . . . but principally from their having or not having slaves".

The Declaration of Independence is cited as the inspiration for the gradual abolition of slavery in the North, where slaves were less than

1 percent of the population by 1810; but it was also an inspiration in the South, where slaves were 37 percent of the population, and slavery was retained.[313]

Jefferson wrote in the Declaration of Independence "that all men are created equal, that they are endowed by their Creator with certain unalienable Rights, that among these are Life, Liberty and the pursuit of Happiness." Benjamin Franklin, who held these truths to be self-evident, continued to own slaves until 1781.

Except for John Adams and his son John Quincy Adams, every President prior to Lincoln had owned slaves, and most continued to own them while in office.[314] The glaring contradiction was not lost on contemporaries. "How is it that we hear the loudest yelps for liberty among the drivers of negroes?"[315] Samuel Johnson, the English moralist and essayist, asked.

Jefferson tried to shift responsibility for slavery and the international slave trade onto King George III.[316] According to his notes of the discussion on the draft Declaration of Independence, the clause "reprobating the enslaving of the inhabitants of Africa" was struck out "in compliance to to South Carolina and Georgia, who had never attempted to restrain the importation of slaves, and who, on the contrary, still wished to continue it.[317] Our northern brethren, also, I believe, felt a little tender under those censures; for, though their people have very few slaves themselves, yet they had been pretty considerable carriers of them to others."[318]

That tenderness extended to avoiding use of the terms "slave" or "slavery" in the Constitution.[319] Slaves were "such" or "other Persons."[320] This did not mean that slaves, or former slaves, were Persons in the legal sense, with citizenship protected under the Constitution, as the Supreme Court confirmed in the Dred Scott case seventy years later.[321]

In his *Notes on the State of Virginia*, Jefferson argued that slavery degraded master and slave alike. "The man must be a prodigy who can restrain his manners and morals undepraved by such circumstances."[322] He knew what he was talking about.

Jefferson relied on his slaves as collateral for his substantial debts, and for sex. His father-in-law had also slept with his slaves, and his slave daughter Sally Hemings bore a striking resemblance to Jefferson's wife Martha, her half-sister. After Martha died, Jefferson fathered five children with Sally Hemings, beginning when she was about fifteen years old. Hemings refused to return from Europe, where Jefferson was Ambassador to France, until he promised to set their children free.[323]

Jefferson was compromised by his dependence on slavery, and his racist belief in the inferiority of African-American reason and imagination: "I think one could scarcely be found capable of tracing and comprehending the investigations of Euclid; and that in imagination they are dull, tasteless, and anomalous."[324]

There is no evidence that Jefferson ever educated one of his slaves to the point where they could tackle Euclidean geometry, or that he sought ways to test their imagination objectively, but he did suppress evidence of racial equality before the Revolution by lobbying the House of Burgesses (in effect the Virginia parliament) to prevent free African-Americans from entering or living in Virginia.[325]

Despite his biases, Jefferson wrestled with the fact that the Declaration of Independence and the persistence of slavery were at odds: "We lay it down as a fundamental, that laws, to be just, must give a reciprocation of right; that without this, they are mere arbitrary rules of conduct, founded in force, and not in conscience. . . . That a change in the relations in which a man is placed should change his ideas of moral right or wrong, is neither new nor peculiar to the colour of the blacks."[326]

Jefferson tried to prevent the expansion of slavery in western territories, and to prevent the importation of further slaves. He persuaded the Virginia Assembly in 1778 to ban the importation of slaves into the state.[327] A 1782 Act to Authorize the Manumission of Slaves lifted the proscription on freeing people by will or deed, and obliged masters to provide for former slaves over the age of forty-five and under the age of twenty-one. From 1790 to 1810, the free population of Virginia increased seven-fold.[328]

Jefferson never advocated the immediate emancipation of slaves in America. He favoured expulsion to African colonies instead. "If a slave can have a country in this world, it must be any other in preference to that in which he is born to live and labor for another."[329] He was even vaguer when it came to when precisely this working of Providence was to happen.[330]

George Washington was the only Plantation Founding Father who provided for the freedom of his slaves.[331] In his will, he directed that all his slaves be freed upon the death of his wife. She wisely decided to free them all at once instead.

Qualms about the morality of slavery could be plotted with remarkable accuracy based on the level of economic dependence on the "peculiar institution". In the North, every state had set emancipation in motion by 1804.[332]

In the Upper South, where plantation farming was marginal, the "inalienable Rights of Mankind" and the command of Christ not to "keep fellow creatures in bondage" were cited in enthusiastic waves of liberation, particularly in areas where wheat replaced tobacco as the main crop.[333] More than 90 percent of the black population in Delaware and 49 percent of the black population in Maryland were already free by 1860, before the onset of the Civil War.[334] In the Lower South, where the production of sugar in Mississippi, rice in South Carolina and cotton in Georgia were heavily dependent on plantation slave-labour, no attempt was made to abolish slavery, and freeing African-Americans was forbidden by Slave Codes.

By the end of the eighteenth century, roughly 8 million Africans had been shipped as slaves to the New World. Britain profited more than any other nation from the triangular trade in slaves, commodities and manufactured goods, but resistance was growing, especially among minority groups who challenged the confirmation-bias of the status quo. Here as in other eras, educated minorities had a disproportionate influence on social reform.

As a tightly knit religious minority which expelled those who married out, including the First Lady, Dolley Madison, Quakers had been forbidden from entering the ranks of the gentry and, before the Great Fire of London, risked censure for supposedly spreading plague when they refused to take part in body counts organized by the Anglican church.[335] Quakers founded two of the biggest banks in the UK, Barclays and Lloyds, as well as many manufacturing concerns during the Industrial Revolution.

In 1787, the Society for Effecting the Abolition of the Slave Trade was founded in London by a dozen men, nine Quakers and three evangelical Anglicans. They felt a personal moral obligation to do everything in their power to end the slave trade. Through the Society they were in a position to influence the evangelical Anglican William Wilberforce, the leader of the parliamentary anti-slavery campaign until the passage of the Slave Trade Act of 1807.

By 1808, both the United Kingdom and the United States had officially banned the international slave trade, although it took decades before all loopholes were closed – initially slave traders who sighted a Royal Navy vessel would throw their "cargo" overboard to drown, since the traders could not be legally detained if no contraband slaves were found on their ships.[336] More than 3 million slaves would be sent to the New World in the nineteenth century, but the Royal Navy West Africa Squadron became increasingly effective in obstructing them.[337]

Many of the Founding Fathers hoped that the end of the international slave trade would lead slavery to wither away. Benjamin Franklin, who became a leading abolitionist in the 1780s after a lifetime of slave ownership, thought slavery required a "continual Supply from Africa" for its survival. He had some hard data to back this up.

The black population of Philadelphia had seen deaths outnumber births by six to one in the decade before the Revolution. In plantations where up to three quarters of the slaves were male, gruelling conditions, and appalling infant mortality, meant that deaths outstripped births. Replenishment required four times as many Africans to be shipped to the New World as Europeans by 1820. Slave populations fell by 5 percent per annum where there was no influx of new slave labour.[338] Premature weaning and low birth-weights led to mortality rates for African-American infants which were double those for Europeans. Half of the children born into slavery would die before their first birthday. Washington thought that gradual emancipation would create the "agrarian equality" envisaged by James Oglethorpe, with land-prices increasing as small farmers bought lots in former plantations.[339] He was wrong. Despite appalling rates of infant mortality, and the prohibition on further imports of slaves, the slave population of the United States tripled between 1810 and 1860.[340] By 1860, African-Americans accounted for one in four of all slaves in the New World.

When Congress banned the international slave trade, the economics of slavery in the Upper South were marginal, but in the absence of foreign competition, demand in the Lower South for domestically bred slaves became a lucrative tonic for troubled consciences.

After the Revolution, there was a flurry of evangelical missionary activity among the African-American population of the Upper South, but black members were soon cast out from white congregations.[341] In 1806, the Virginia Assembly passed a law to re-enslave any freed African-American who was still resident in the state twelve months after his manumission.[342]

A slave-owning South might have continued below the Missouri Compromise line from the free North, had the slaveocracy not heard the siren-call of Manifest Destiny. As Native Americans were expelled from their homelands in the 1830s, with 25 to 50 percent dying on the Trail of Tears from hypothermia, starvation and disease, planters eyed westward expansion in the lands opening up in their wake.[343]

In 1837, Abolitionists petitioned the government to end the slave trade between states and prohibit slavery in the federal capital. J. C. Calhoun of South Carolina delivered a famous speech to the Senate on the virtues of slavery.[344] Slave Codes stipulated that slaves could not be dumped onto the mercies of the state when they were too old to work. Calhoun painted a sentimental picture of life for the retired slave, arguing that slavery was morally superior to the Dickensian suffering in industrialising nations.[345]

"I appeal to facts," Calhoun said. "Never before has the black race of Central Africa, from the dawn of history to the present day, attained a condition so civilized and so improved, not only physically, but morally and intellectually. It came among us in a low, degraded, and savage condition, and in the course of a few generations it has grown up under the fostering care of our institutions, reviled as they have been, to its present comparatively civilized condition. This, with the rapid increase of numbers, is conclusive proof of the general happiness of the race, in spite of all the exaggerated tales to the contrary. . . . I hold that in the present state of civilization, where two races of different origin, and distinguished by color, and other physical differences, as well as intellectual, are brought together, the relation now existing in the slaveholding States between the two, is, instead of an evil, a good – a positive good."

Never trust a man who rhetorically appeals to facts. Calhoun's influential speech was a textbook case of confirmation bias, selectively using data on population growth, and creating a false equivalence between the urban poor in the Industrial Revolution and the rural idyll of the elderly slave.

Calhoun was less articulate about the inter-state slave trade. A sophisticated market linked the tobacco fields of Virginia with the sugar, cotton and rice plantations of the Lower South. Roughly 1 million people would be sold down the river, leading to massive social displacement as slave families were broken up.[346] The most valuable slaves were men in their twenties, but women of child-bearing age followed close behind.

"I consider that a woman who brings a child every two years," Thomas Jefferson said in 1820, "as more profitable than the best man on the farm. What she produces is an addition to the capital, while his labors disappear in mere consumption."[347]

Jefferson never reconciled his economic needs with his moral qualms. Reflecting on slavery in the South, he wrote: "I tremble for my country when I reflect that God is just." He trembled before his creditors more. When he died, 130 slaves were sold to pay his debts.

Soon after Calhoun's Senate speech in 1837, his fears of division between North and South proved to be prescient.[348] Congress passed the Fugitive Slave Act in 1850, obliging Northern states to send escaped slaves back to the South. Slavery dominated federal politics over the next decade. The Whig Party sank due to the Kansas-Nebraska Act of 1854, which allowed states north of the Missouri Compromise line to establish slavery by an Assembly vote, a doctrine known as Popular Sovereignty.[349]

Into the breach stepped the American, or Know Nothing, Party, which ran on a populist, anti-immigrant platform which was distrustful of experts and suspicious of the political elite. It had a million members by 1855. Hostile to slavery on principle and to Papists in practice, it channelled the anger of white, working-class Protestant Nativists, who burnt down Catholic churches on the East Coast, and fought against Chinese immigration on the West Coast.

The party won eight gubernatorial races and eighty-eight Congressional seats in Maine, Indiana, Pennsylvania, California, Ohio and Illinois, but in Massachusetts their star dimmed after it was discovered that a Know Nothing member of the state Assembly Committee Investigating Sexual Impropriety in Convents had been spending the committee's funds on prostitutes, causing a lurid media scandal.[350]

In 1857, the Supreme Court decided that the federal government could not regulate slavery in the Dred Scott case. Fears rose that slaves might compete with free labour across the country, and Nativists were co-opted into the new Republican Party later that year.

As the battle against the expansion of slavery intensified, most Northern politicians favored containment of slavery within its existing borders, or letting local legislatures decide on the question, rather than radical Abolitionism.[351] Persuading them to change their minds required the skills of a master politician.

How Abraham Lincoln Became the Great Emancipator

Abraham Lincoln came to national attention through his bid to become a Senator for Illinois in 1858, pitting him against the incumbent Stephen Douglas, a leading Democrat, former presidential nominee and author of the Kansas-Nebraska Act. The two men made stump speeches on the same platform, and the partisan reaction of their audience was noted by reporters and circulated throughout the United States. Their campaigns were not just about the Senate seat, but about framing the debate for the next presidential election.[352]

For Lincoln and the Republicans, the debates presented an opportunity to split the Democrats into northern and southern factions. Douglas professed indifference as to whether slavery was voted up or down in local assemblies, but Popular Sovereignty was regarded with suspicion by Southern Democrats. Plantation owners sought cast-iron guarantees that the westward expansion of slavery would continue.[353]

For Douglas, the debate would paint Republicans in general and Lincoln in particular as radical fanatics. Nativists might be opposed to slavery, but that did not mean social and racial equality. It would require a great deal of legerdemain to make a coherent case for the end of slavery based on the natural rights of African-Americans, without taking those rights to their logical, and unpopular, conclusion. Lincoln would toy with the idea of creating colonies of freed slaves in Africa to avoid the racial tensions which would come with Emancipation, but that did not address the civil rights he expected freedmen to have in America. Douglas put him on the spot.

Illinois did not allow African-Americans to become citizens, and Douglas exploited fears that Emancipation would lead to equality. "Do you desire to turn this . . . State into a free negro colony, ('no, no,') in order that when Missouri abolishes slavery she can send one hundred thousand emancipated slaves into Illinois, to become citizens and voters, on an equality with yourselves? ('Never,' 'no.') . . . I believe this Government was made on the white basis. ('Good.') I believe it was made by white men for the benefit of white men and their posterity forever, and I am in favor of confining citizenship to white men . . . instead of conferring it upon negroes, Indians, and other inferior races. ('Good for you.' 'Douglas forever.')."[354]

Lincoln never put himself too far ahead of the public.[355] Privately, he detested Nativism. He wrote: "When the Know-Nothings get control, it [the Declaration of Independence] will read 'all men are created equals, except negroes and foreigners and Catholics.' When it comes to that I should prefer emigrating to some country where they make no pretense of loving liberty – to Russia, for instance, where despotism can be taken pure, and without the base alloy of hypocrisy."[356] But publicly, Lincoln had to lie.

The African-American activist Frederick Douglass remarked on Lincoln's "entire freedom from popular prejudice against the colored race"[357] but Lincoln pandered to the bigotry of his audience in Illinois: "I am not, nor ever have been, in favor of bringing about in any way the social and political equality of the white and black races . . . I am not nor ever have been in favor of making voters or jurors of negroes, nor of qualifying them to hold office, nor to intermarry with white people; . . . there is a physical difference between the white and black races which I believe will forever forbid the two races living together on terms of social and political equality."[358]

At the same time, the meaning of the Declaration of Independence was defined with "tolerable distinctness in what they did consider all men created equal – equal in certain inalienable rights, among which are life, liberty, and the pursuit of happiness." A black man was "not my equal in many respects – certainly not in color, perhaps not in moral or intellectual endowment. But in the right to eat the bread, without the leave of anybody else, which his own hand earns, he is my equal and the equal of Judge Douglas, and the equal of every living man."[359]

Lincoln hated Douglas' attitude to slavery for the impact it had on moral norms.[360] Despite winning the popular vote in Illinois, Lincoln lost the Senate election in the state legislature. It was a pyrrhic victory for Douglas, who alienated the South in the debate by articulating the Freeport Doctrine, which described how the anti-slavery Kansas Assembly could subvert the Supreme Court decision in Dred Scott by refusing to enact a Slave Code.[361]

Douglas became the Democratic candidate for President, but his stance on Popular Sovereignty split the Democrats into Northern and Southern factions, helping the Republicans win the 1860 election with less than 40 percent of the popular vote.

Lincoln was assiduous in publicising the Lincoln-Douglas debates before making his own bid to become a presidential contender. "Public sentiment is everything," he said. "With public sentiment, nothing can fail; without it nothing can succeed."[362]

Lincoln secured the Republican nomination as the compromise candidate, having divided his own party into rival blocs, thereby denying the Convention favorite, Governor William Seward of New York, the chance to become President. His administration combined high principle with deep political guile.

As President, Lincoln had extraordinary control over federal patronage – which in the era before civil-service reform was used to reward party cronies.[363] Lincoln was no exception. His administration replaced 1,457 out of 1,639 federal officials – nearly 90 percent of all available positions.[364] As Lincoln's first Secretary of War, Simon Cameron, said, an honest politician was "one who, when he is bought, will stay bought".

The Lower South believed that they had the right to secede rather than see Lincoln put slavery "in the course of ultimate extinction", as they outlined in their Declaration of Causes for secession.[365] Rebels blockaded the federal Fort Sumter in Charleston Harbor, South Carolina.

Lincoln was at pains to reassure the listeners to his Inaugural Address, especially in the wavering border states of the Upper South which had not yet seceded, that he would not abuse his powers.[366] Despite his eloquence, Confederate forces shelled Fort Sumter until the garrison capitulated. Lincoln announced that he was mobilizing an army of seventy-five thousand men.

Virginia, Arkansas, North Carolina and Tennessee seceded after Lincoln mobilised. Tribal loyalty dragged many officers into fighting against a Union they had pledged to defend. One was a Colonel who said he could "anticipate no greater calamity for the country than a dissolution of the Union. . . . Secession is nothing but revolution."[367]

Lincoln promoted the Colonel to Major General and offered him command of the United States Army, but when Virginia seceded, he felt he had to fight for his state. His name was Robert E. Lee. With his pro-Union friend Thomas "Stonewall" Jackson, they became two of the most famous Confederate generals of the Civil War.

Ambivalence about secession in the Upper South was strongest where slavery was weakest, and the level of manumission before the war was highest. Four border states where slavery was legal never seceded, and when Virginia left the Union to join the Confederacy, it prompted the pro-Union western Appalachian hill-country to split away from the east, creating the modern US state of West Virginia.

The Civil War death-toll was staggering. If soldiers were not dying from disease in camps and trenches, or being mown down by repeating carbines or several early Gatling guns which had been purchased personally by Union commanders, they were being killed by artillery and long-range rifles. Officers eschewed flamboyant uniforms as snipers picked them off. At Bloody Angle in Spotsylvania in Virginia, an oak tree was sliced in two after twenty hours of close-quarter infantry cross-fire from single-shot muskets which took twenty seconds to muzzle-load. More than one in four soldiers never made it home.[368] By the end of the Civil War, 760,000 soldiers were dead or dying – more than in all other wars fought by America, from Independence to Vietnam, put together.[369]

Lincoln did not argue for abolition and the enrolment of African-American troops until he could frame it as an "indispensable necessity" to save the Union.[370] As the death-toll soared, attitudes changed. Emancipation would hasten the end of the war and act as a fitting punishment on the South for starting it in the first place. When two congressmen, James Wilson of Iowa and Isaac Arnold of Illinois, proposed a Thirteenth Amendment to the Constitution, which would emancipate the slaves, Lincoln supported it by arguing that passage would undermine the morale of the Confederacy and weaken their military. After months of conflict, the Amendment was finally passed on 31 January 1865 by a two-vote margin.

Eventually, 185,000 black men enlisted in the Union Army; 134,000 of them were from slave-holding states.

Less than three months after the passage of the Thirteenth Amendment, Lincoln was assassinated. As white Democrats reclaimed State Houses after Reconstruction, a series of Jim Crow laws limited the rights of poor Southern black and white citizens.

In Louisiana, 99.5 percent of black men were not registered to vote by 1910, despite being in the majority.[371] Racial segregation was enforced on buses and trains, and in bathrooms and public schools, under the Separate but Equal policy, with the blessing of the Supreme Court in 1896 in Plessy v. Ferguson.[372] Miscegenation, or the right of black and white people to marry each other, remained illegal in Virginia until 1967.[373]

What is shocking, when sifting through newspaper articles and editorials, is just how normal the concept of slavery was in the North as well as the South. Getting an educated, progressive and advanced society to end slavery after it had become an entrenched norm had required extraordinary political dexterity. Lincoln reflected on the moral certitude of his adversaries. Both belligerents "read the same Bible and pray to the same God, and each invokes His aid against the other". For Lincoln, where North and South diverged was in their definition of liberty.[374]

We now know that white skin has proliferated only in the last eight thousand years, in order to absorb sunlight, as we followed the melting glaciers to northerly latitudes, but racism and bigotry persist.[375] The meaning of liberty in what Lincoln called the "wolf's dictionary" – the freedom to exploit others – has yet to be fully repudiated.

Using Terror To Impose the "Despotism of Liberty"

In the autumn of 2018, the Foreign Secretary of the United Kingdom, Jeremy Hunt, was addressing his fractious and divided party-conference on the vexing question of Brexit negotiations about the British withdrawal from the European Union. Seeking a populist metaphor which would guarantee column-inches ahead of any leadership coup, he likened the European Union to one of the most brutal and repressive regimes in human history, that of the the USSR.[376]

The remarks were widely condemned in Britain. The Latvian Ambassador said that after invading in 1940, the USSR "killed, deported, exiled and imprisoned hundreds of thousands of Latvia's inhabitants", and had ruined the lives of three generations. Her opposite number from Estonia tweeted: "Soviet régime was brutal, I lived under it, comparison is insulting." A European Commission spokesman was no less damning, if more measured: "I would say respectfully that we would all benefit – and in particular foreign affairs ministers – from opening a history book from time to time."

Brexiteers hope that Britain will be better off when it sloughs off the shackles of the EU, even if it takes fifty years for all the benefits to be realised. Bolsheviks hoped that they would form a "kingdom of freedom" on Russian soil. Nationalist Britons share one thing in common with atheist Soviets: they passionately believe in what they hope for. They have faith.

The idea that rationalists can rigidly adhere to secular shibboleths is deeply unsettling for some prominent "New Atheists", who have come up with alternative definitions of faith which keep religion front and centre. But belief in what you hope for is not just a religious formulation. It is also the popular definition of faith. George Michael was not singing "You gotta have *belief without evidence*", and no one would ever swear fealty in their wedding vows on that basis.[377]

Steven Pinker, a brilliant advocate for the Enlightenment, defines faith as "belief without 'good' reason", and concludes that since there is no good reason to believe in supernatural entities, religious faith is inimical to reason "by definition".[378]

We cannot champion Enlightenment ideals without being mindful of our passion, and checking the bias that comes with it. It is not that there is anything objectionable about reason, science and humanism, other than the idea that professing fealty to them ipso facto makes someone kinder, smarter, more tolerant, more progressive, more self-aware and more sensitive to our unacknowledged proclivity towards group-think and prejudice.[379]

Belief in Reason has not made people reasonable. Dismissing the *philosophes* who lent cerebral heft to the French Revolution as "intellectual lightweights" does not explain how the Third Estate concluded that appalling violence in the name of Reason and Liberty was justified; how Jefferson wrote that all men are created equal whilst lamenting his own role in human bondage; or how an affluent, educated Germany could spawn genocide from the Social Darwinist ideology of Adolf Hitler.[380] [381]

David Hume was an intellectual colossus of the Enlightenment. He was also a racist. "I am apt to suspect," he wrote in his book *Of National Characters*, "the negroes to be naturally inferior to the whites."

Voltaire repudiated all non-Deist belief, but when it came to Judaism, he was profoundly anti-Semitic: "They are, all of them, born with raging fanaticism in their hearts . . . I would not be in the least bit surprised if these people would not someday become deadly to the human race."[382]

Of course, these samples of reactionary, illiberal and irrational prose were not penned by modern humanists. Steven Pinker acknowledges that our forebears were "morally retarded", but despite the keyboard-warriors who troll religious forums making pejorative remarks about sky-fairies, he notes a significant increase in progress in recent decades, which he ascribes to the triumph of Enlightenment values.[383]

A similar trajectory could have been described before the Great Depression, before Stalin connived in the Ukrainian Famine, or Hitler launched the Holocaust. There are fewer crises nowadays which could rile a lynch-mob in the affluent West, but cognitive bias has not gone away. We cannot rely on the hope that this time will be different.

The proclivity of utopian rationalist states to descend into totalitarianism was noted by Karl Popper in 1945, in his book *The Open Society and Its Enemies*. He criticised their teleological historicism, the belief that history progresses by deterministic laws to an ineluctable goal, the same lure of destiny which has been used to rationalise conflict since records began.[384]

With the confirmation-bias inherent in our species, contrary evidence was discounted, dismissed or rationalised away: a necessary struggle before the triumph of the master-race, or proof that the corrupt capitalist *ancien régime* was "digging its own grave".

Those who disagreed were suffering from "false consciousness."[385] Rather than guaranteeing human rights, dissent was silenced. Utopian rationalists were on a moral crusade to save mankind – whether mankind wanted salvation or not.

One of the first, and most influential, utopian states started as an expedient response to a crisis. A succession of bad harvests, as well as enthusiastic support for the American War of Independence, had bankrupted King Louis XVI of France, forcing him to call the Estates General for the first time in 170 years.[386]

Playing catch-up with two centuries of reform in the Anglosphere, Commoners convened as the National Assembly, dis-established all religious orders, seized the assets of the Church and ended the tax exemptions of clergy and nobles. Remaining clergy were obliged to swear an oath of loyalty to the state or face expulsion. With the help of Ambassador Thomas Jefferson, a Declaration of the Rights of Man and of the Citizen was drafted.

Article IV states: "Liberty consists in doing anything which does not harm others." Under the banner of "Liberty, Equality and Fraternity", revolutionaries abolished feudalism, sanctioned divorce, guaranteed freedom of worship, decriminalised same-sex liaisons, and extended civil rights to Jews and Africans. But fears about enemies, both foreign and domestic, meant that personal liberties were always subordinate to safeguarding the Revolution.[387]

Concerned by the machinations of aristocratic exiles abroad, France was soon at war with Austria, Prussia and Great Britain. After the execution of the King in 1793, a Jacobin clique led by Jacques Hébert and Joseph Fouché replaced religion with the Cult of Reason.[388] Crosses, statuary and icons were removed; cemetery entrances bore the phrase "Death is an eternal sleep"; former churches, including the Cathedral of Notre Dame in Paris, were converted into Temples of Reason, and a national Festival of Reason was proclaimed.

Roughly 170,000 people died in civil war in the Vendée following the killing of the King and the proscription of the Church.[389] A Committee of Public Safety was set up by Georges Danton, and eventually led by Maximillien Robespierre, a Deist who was inspired by the writings of Jean-Jacques Rousseau. He called the Festival of Reason "a farce", and replaced the Cult of Reason with the Cult of the Supreme Being.[390]

As the revolutionaries fragmented into factions, fear of what *They* might do to *Us* led to bloodshed. Soon the zealous, such as Hébert, and the moderate, such as Danton, were guillotined in the Reign of Terror. Seventeen thousand were executed as enemies of the state, along with another twenty thousand victims of extra-judicial killings, as counter-revolutionary paranoia gripped France.

For Robespierre, the liberty to do no harm in Article IV of the Declaration of the Rights of Man and of the Citizen was subordinate to the Law, "the expression of the general will", in Article VI.

In his Report on the Principles of Political Morality, he defended the Reign of Terror: "If virtue be the spring of a popular government in times of peace, the spring of that government during a revolution is virtue combined with terror: virtue, without which terror is destructive; terror, without which virtue is impotent. Terror is only justice prompt, severe and inflexible; it is then an emanation of virtue; it is less a distinct principle than a natural consequence of the general principle of democracy, applied to the most pressing wants of the country. . . . The government in a revolution is the despotism of liberty against tyranny."

It takes an extraordinary level of cognitive-bias to swallow an oxymoron like "the despotism of liberty", but Robespierre went further. In a revolution, justice had to be swift, at the expense of due process: "slowness of judgments is equal to impunity . . . uncertainty of punishment encourages all the guilty."[391]

Six months later, Robespierre was guillotined. A million more people would die in the Revolutionary Wars, as well as 4.5 million in the Napoleonic Wars which followed.[392] Apologists argued that the body-count was a necessary evil. Critics argued that using force to uphold the "general will" of the people against dissenting voices led to the tyranny of the majority, or the tyranny of the one.[393] Thomas Jefferson's initial enthusiasm for the French Revolution waned, but he nevertheless continued to defend it, arguing, essentially, that the end justifies the means.

"Was ever such a prize won with so little innocent blood?" Thomas Jefferson wrote in a letter to a friend. "My own affections have been deeply wounded by some of the martyrs to this cause, but rather than it should have failed, I would have seen half the earth desolated. Were there but an Adam and Eve left in every country, left free, it would be better than as it now is."[394]

The French Revolution had a profound effect on later political movements, including the European Revolutions of 1848, which demanded reforms akin to the Bill of Rights adopted in the United States sixty years before.[395]

Karl Marx and Revolutionary Terror

In February 1848, a twenty-eight-page pamphlet by Karl Marx and Friedrich Engels called *The Communist Manifesto* was published. Observing the transition of power and wealth which had occurred from the gentry to industrial entrepreneurs, it formulated a materialist conception of history, whose defining characteristic was the conflict between the haves and the have-nots: "The history of all hitherto existing society is the history of class struggles."[396]

A feudal land-owning class had been displaced by a capitalist, industrial bourgeoisie as the means of production evolved. The capitalists, in turn, would inevitably be replaced by the oppressed proletarian majority. The *Manifesto* ended with this phrase: "Workers of the world, unite!"

But Marx believed that the triumph of the proletariat might have to be given a nudge into existence, and later in 1848 he wrote: "There is only one way in which the murderous death agonies of the old society and the bloody birth throes of the new society can be shortened, simplified and concentrated, and that way is revolutionary terror."[397]

After the Revolutions of 1848, communism sank into obscurity until the defeat of France in the Franco-Prussian War of 1870. Radicalised by months of siege and hunger, the Paris Commune refused to recognise the new National Assembly in Versailles, until it was crushed in La Semaine Sanglante.[398] The Commune electrified Marx and Engels.[399]

In Russia, Vladimir Ilyich Ulyanov, better known as Lenin, was born months before the Communards came to power. He agreed that it was the first true dictatorship of the proletariat, but he drew another lesson: the destruction of the class enemy must not be inhibited by "excessive magnanimity".[400]

Chronic food-shortages, industrial unrest, and the appalling carnage of the Great War gave Lenin a political crisis *par excellence*. Hoping that further destabilisation would remove Tsarist forces from the field of battle, the German High Command provided a sealed train in April 1917 to take Lenin from exile in Zurich to revolution in Russia.

On 25 October, the Winter Palace was stormed and power was handed over to the local Workers' Council, or Soviet, under Leon Trotsky. In the Assembly elections which followed, Bolsheviks won 25 percent of the vote.[401] When the Assembly rejected Soviet decrees on peace and land-reform, it was promptly dissolved by the self-styled vanguard of the proletariat.

Private property was seized, businesses were nationalised, and the Soviet government signed the Treaty of Brest-Litovsk at the beginning of March 1918, taking Russia out of the war. Under the terms of the Treaty, Russia lost 90 percent of her coal-mines and 25 percent of her territory – almost all of it along her western frontier.[402] Poland reappeared on the map of Europe, as did Finland, Latvia, Lithuania, Estonia, Belarus and Ukraine.

By the end of the Russian Civil War that followed, 750,000 soldiers and roughly 7 million civilians had died from war, disease, famine, and reprisals by Red and White forces.[403] Roughly one in ten Cossacks, or 300,000 to 500,000 people, were killed or deported East to Siberia.[404]

The Red Army re-captured Ukraine and Belarus, but hopes of exporting revolution to Germany and the rest of Europe were dashed when they were defeated by the Polish army at the gates of Warsaw. Lenin became the Chairman of the Council of People's Commissars of the Union of Soviet Socialist Republics, and remained in that post until his death in 1924.

After Lenin died, and socialist protests in Germany and Hungary failed to trigger communist coups, the appetite to follow Trotsky's lead on global revolution faded. The USSR focused on implementing Socialism in One Country under an ethnic Georgian called Iosif Vissarionovich Dzhugashvili – better known by his *nom de guerre*, Joseph Stalin, and for decades on the Left as "Uncle Joe".[405]

The Mass Murders of Joseph Stalin

It was not until the Soviet archives were opened in the 1990s that Stalin's full culpability for mass-murder became known.[406] He managed to retain an avuncular image while setting quotas for executions of "enemies of the people".[407] The enduring legacy of Karl Marx's revolution was the creation of a totalitarian state.

More than 18 million people passed through the 476 Soviet Gulags before they were closed. Between 1.5 million and 3 million died there from hunger, disease, hypothermia and forced labour.[408] In the absence of any credible legal code or Bill of Rights to prevent the abuse of civil liberties, consent for persecution was a given.

The political crises that Stalin confronted, engineered or just stumbled into required a series of excuses to justify the murder of millions of Soviet citizens. Stalin identified a host of enemies, both foreign and domestic, to scapegoat.

The Russian Civil War put millions on the wrong side of national frontiers: ethnic Ukrainians, Belarussians and Germans in Poland, as well as Poles and other minorities in Ukraine and Belarus. After defeating the Red Army at the Battle of Warsaw, Poland fomented unrest in Ukraine and Belarus, providing military training to Ukrainians in Poland as well as a group of covert operatives called the Polish Military Organizations in the Soviet Union.[409]

To the East, Japan was mulling over how to build on victory in the Russo-Japanese War of 1905, whether by invading the Soviet Union, or occupying China and other Pacific nations. Soviet intelligence intercepted a message to Tokyo from the Japanese Ambassador to Moscow in 1931, advocating an invasion of Siberia, and believed, incorrectly, that Japan and Poland had agreed to attack from East and West.[410]

Domestically the scapegoats were peasants, Party officials and members of the Secret Police, who were accused variously of hoarding food, deliberately mismanaging the Five-Year Plan, and demonstrating excessive zeal in the Terrors that Stalin ordered.

The recovery of Soviet industry and agriculture after the Civil War encouraged Stalin to press on with reform. In 1929 he declared that wealthier Kulak peasants had to be "liquidated as a class."[411] A local Troika of Party, Procurator and Police decided which peasants should be exiled to the Gulags. Land was to be collectivised to feed the urban industrial workers.

At every level of the Party, efforts were made to exceed targets. Collectivisation quotas that were expected to take twelve months were shortened to twelve weeks, encouraging peasants to revolt. In 1930 the Secret Police counted a million acts of resistance in the Ukraine, including deliberate hoarding of food and grain.[412]

Stalin beat a tactical retreat. In a pamphlet entitled "Dizzy With Success", he said that collectivisation had been carried out with too much zeal, leading to excesses that had to be addressed.[413] He temporarily halted collectivisation while purging the Party ranks of those who complained about unrealistic production targets, allowing collectives to seize seed grain from private farmers who were taxed into oblivion.

A bumper harvest in 1930 became the baseline for 1931, when pest infestation and bad weather reduced yields. To make quota, collectives were forced to sacrifice seed grain needed for the following year, guaranteeing a poorer harvest. The Soviet Union exported grain in 1932 while 1 million people starved to death in Kazakhstan (the fault of the local Party boss, according to Stalin).[414]

As the death-toll mounted, Stalin saw portents of victory. Evidence of acute suffering was selectively interpreted as an indicator that reactionary elements were in their last death throes of resistance.

Failure to achieve target grain quotas was due to sabotage, according to Stalin's head of security in Ukraine, Vsevolod Balytski,.[415] He claimed to have identified over a thousand illegal organizations, including a Ukrainian Military Organization and Polish nationalists, some of whom had infiltrated the Ukrainian Communist Party.

Military spending in Poland had been reined in as the economy hit the doldrums in the Great Depression, and agitation in Ukraine had ceased following the agreement of a Polish-Soviet Nonaggression Pact in July 1932, but the NKVD did not trust Polish bromides, and Stalin feared that he could lose the Ukraine to nationalist uprisings as a result of the food shortages.

Stalin turned Ukraine into a "fortress." He maintained targets. Collectives which failed to return the required amount were blacklisted, liable to fines of 15 times the monthly quota. Party officials who objected were liable to denunciation as saboteurs. Peasants who couldn't provide enough grain had to slaughter their livestock instead, in a special meat tax, and any peasant found with hoarded grain could be executed.

Stalin refused all offers of outside assistance, and did not distribute the 3 million tonnes of Soviet grain reserves as famine relief. Instead, borders were sealed in January 1933 to stop Ukrainians fleeing West in a "counter-revolutionary plot."[416]

Of the 5.5 million who starved to death in 1932 and 1933, 3.3 million were from the Ukraine.[417] As parents died, some told their children to eat their remains. More than 2,500 Ukrainians were found guilty of cannibalism. Polish intelligence reported that whole villages were deserted, and cannibalism had become "something of a habit", albeit one met with abhorrence.

Despite the obvious suffering, attempts to highlight the scale of the devastation by western journalists such as Gareth Jones were met with denial and obfuscation by Party apparatchiks, as well as foreign admirers of the regime, who maintained their confirmation bias despite being aware that people were "dropping like flies."

Arthur Koestler, who did not repudiate Stalin until the Great Terror in 1938, believed the victims "were enemies of the people who preferred begging to work."[418] The Moscow correspondent of the *New York Times*, the Pulitzer Prize winner Walter Duranty, called Jones' reportage "a big scare story", arguing there was no "actual starvation," only "widespread mortality from diseases related to malnutrition."[419] Since disease carries away debilitated famine victims, it was a distinction without a difference. Duranty said you couldn't make an omelet without breaking a few eggs.

Despite all his talk of counter-revolutionary conspiracies, the famine was hard to explain even for a master of Newspeak.[420] Stalin's image as the seer of communism was dented. At the 17th Congress, he narrowly avoided being deposed. Officials claimed that he had tied with the most popular candidate, Sergei Kirov, the Party Secretary in Leningrad, and the negative vote tally against him was suppressed.[421]

Party officials approached Kirov to replace Stalin as General Secretary. He reported their approach to Stalin. He was killed months later in suspicious circumstances. Old foes of Stalin such as Zinoviev and Kamenev were deemed "morally complicit" in his murder, and were jailed, tortured and executed after a series of show trials in 1936. Of the 139 Central Committee members elected with Stalin in 1934, 70 percent were executed within four years in the Great Terror that followed.[422]

The justification for the Great Terror began when the Commissar for Internal Affairs and Chief of the NKVD, Nikolai Yeshov, said he had evidence of a vast conspiracy to restore capitalism and destroy the Soviet Union, spanning the army, the Communist Party and the NKVD. Agents of the "Center of Centers" were committing acts of sabotage, including the castration of prize sheep.[423]

Within a few months more than half the General Officers of the Red Army were dead, as well as 50,000 police, military and party functionaries. Stalin and Yezhov ordered the "direct physical liquidation of the entire counter-revolution."

In late July 1937, they approved Order 00447, to "Repress Former Kulaks, Criminals and Other Anti-Soviet Elements". Order 00447 set a quota of 79,950 executions and a further 193,000 deportations to the Gulag. As local NKVD officers sought to exceed the targets handed down from Moscow, the Gulags quickly filled up; 386,798 people were executed under Order 00447 within eighteen months. A further 144,000 were accused of spying for Poland, of which 111,091 were executed – making a Soviet Pole forty times more likely to die in the Great Terror than the average Soviet citizen.[424]

A total of 681,692 people were killed in the Great Terror, mostly at night, in sound-proofed rooms or in distant forests. Victims were killed by pistol, with two NKVD officers holding their arms while a third shot into the base of the skull, followed by a coup de grace into the temple. They were then buried in pits.

In Butovo, near Moscow, only twelve NKVD officers sufficed to kill 20,761 people by the end of 1938.[425] Troikas reviewed each case before passing sentence. This lent a semblance of due process to the Terror – but the average amount of time spent on each fatal decision was about sixty seconds.

Demand for victims outstripped the supply of suspects the NKVD had on file, leading to arbitrary arrests on spurious grounds. Victims could be sentenced to ten years in the Gulag for owning a set of rosary beads.[426] NKVD officers such as Vsevelod Balytski invented cabals of counter-revolutionaries, often linked to the moribund Polish Military Organisation, before being hoisted by their own petard, and executed for negligence for not identifying and eliminating these threats sooner.

The upper echelons of the NKVD were purged of all ethnic minorities, leaving Russians and Georgians over-represented. The coda to the Great Terror saw Stalin torture and execute the leading executioners, including the former Commissar for Internal Affairs who had initiated the witch-hunts, Nikolai Yeshov.[427]

In the Soviet Union, exploiting Stalin's paranoia was the path to advancement. Exceeding quotas for deportation and murder was a way to curry favour – at least until Stalin cleaned house by eliminating his most zealous henchmen.

After twenty years of revolution, deportation and re-education, the 1937 census revealed a Soviet Union which was still religious, with 8 million fewer citizens than expected.[428] Stalin suppressed the results of the census.[429] The demographers were either deported or shot.

By "Russifying" the NKVD and persecuting Soviet Poles, Stalin conceded the failure of class-struggle to blur the lines of ethnicity, as well as the failure of "Socialism In One Country". The Union of Soviet Socialist Republics was a *res publica* in name only. The utopian Marxist "kingdom of freedom" was nowhere to be found.

How Nice People Voted Nazi

In 1951, the secular Jewish émigré Hannah Arendt wrote the pioneering *Origins of Totalitarianism*. In an attempt to make sense of the horrors of communism and fascism, she argued that the masses who followed Hitler and Stalin suffered from "spiritual and social homelessness", in an atomised society where they lacked status. This was, of course, with the curse of hindsight.

In 1928, the Nazi Party had been on its knees. Despite terrible suffering in the Great War, including half a million civilian deaths from malnutrition, hyper-inflation, and the fear of "Judeo-Bolshevik" revolt, they received just 2.6 percent of the national vote.[430] They might have just withered away as a fringe group.

Then Wall Street crashed. Scarred by the experience of hyper-inflation, the Weimar government adopted austerity measures, which made things worse.[431] Thirty percent of the manual working class were unemployed within months. Bankers were prime targets for scapegoating – often with an anti-Semitic twist.[432]

The success of the Nazi Party was driven by the crisis of the Great Depression. In 1928, a little over one in forty of the population had voted for them. Four years later, their vote had risen fourteen-fold to 37.3 percent – easily the highest share of the vote of any party in the Reichstag.[433]

Far from feeling homeless, the 17.3 million Germans who voted Nazi in 1933 were more likely to identify with traditional cultural norms. Nazis polled badly in diverse, cosmopolitan cities where the Communists and the SPD had strong roots. Only 13 perecent of the urban unemployed poor voted for them, making them nearly three times less likely to vote Nazi than average.

The Nazi heartland was the small provincial city or rural village, where senior citizens, working-class "tories", self-made entrepreneurs, doctors, teachers, engineers and civil servants voted heavily for the one party which was willing to tackle immigration and "Judeo-Bolshevism" head-on. The demographics were similar to those of Leave voters in the Brexit referendum.[434] The vast majority of people who voted for Brexit are neither racists nor fanatics. But then, neither were millions of those who voted for the NSDAP. Less than one in twenty Nazi voters were members of the party.

At a time when 95 percent of Germans had registered as tithe-paying church-goers, Protestants were nearly twice as likely to vote Nazi as Catholics. This had more to do with the embattled-minority status of Catholics, who voted for the Catholic Centre Party after attempts to assert the authority of the state over the church in the nineteenth-century Kulturkampf, but minorities often challenge mainstream confirmation-bias.[435] In Catholic-majority France and Italy, Protestants were more likely to shelter Jews from the Nazis, and vice-versa in majority-Protestant regions of the Netherlands.

The subtext of the Nazi rise to power was the fear of immigrants during economic austerity. Seventeen of the twenty-five points in the Nazi Party programme, first promulgated in February 1920, focus on the rights and obligations of German citizens, and the corresponding limits on foreign immigrants.

Some of the points in the plan are downright contradictory. The plan starts by calling for the unification of all Germans in a greater Germany, based on the principle of self-determination, and rejects onerous post-war treaties, citing the equality of Germany with other nations. Addressing the fear of starvation following the Great War, point three proceeds to demand land and territory, or colonies, "for the sustenance of our people", rejecting the principles of self-determination and equality invoked in the first two points.

The bulk of the programme was a populist list of promises to German citizens, at the expense of foreign immigrants. Point four stipulates that citizenship is for those of German blood – the German race – only. Point five states that non-citizens can only have guest-status in the country. Point six demands that every public office is held by a German citizen. Point seven says that foreigners will be deported if the German population cannot be supported, and point eight calls for the deportation of migrants who arrived after March 1914, as well as the imposition of a total ban on further immigration.

All German citizens will have equal rights and obligations (point nine), which entails the duty to work productively (point 10), a right to higher education for all capable Germans (point 20), a greatly expanded welfare programme for senior citizens (point 15), state support for small firms and the middle classes (point 16), the criminalisation of war-profiteering (point 12), an end to unearned income (point 11) and land speculation (point 17), the nationalisation of big trusts (point 13) and heavy industry (point 14), and an end to child labour (point 21).

To deliver this program, the Nazis set out to form a German standing army (22), replace the legal system with a new German common law (19), and increase the powers of central government (25). Accusing the mainstream media of spreading fake news, point 23 of the programme decreed that all writers and employees at German-language newspapers must be German citizens, with no "foreign" ownership of German media, and no foreign-language publication in Germany without the permission of the state.

In contrast with immigration and the privileges of citizenship, the blatantly anti-Semitic passages of the Nazi programme almost appear to be an afterthought. Point four states that since citizenship was reserved for "one who is of German blood . . . no Jew can be a member of the race". Point 18 of the programme levied the death-penalty for usurers and profiteers, without mentioning Jews explicitly.

Point 24 guaranteed freedom of religion for all, "so long as they do not endanger its existence or oppose the moral senses of the Germanic race". In case anyone thought that freedom of religion was more than a sop to Catholics after the Kulturkampf, it went on to say: "The Party as such advocates the standpoint of a positive Chris tianity . . . . It combats the Jewish-materialistic spirit within and around us."

Even if it meant trampling on civil liberties, or cultural norms of tolerance and human rights, a populist party which put Germans first, and protected ordinary, hard-working citizens from the "Jewish kleptocracy" which had supposedly caused the Great Depression, as well as the "Judeo-Bolshevist" Communists who exploited it, was always going to get a hearing.[436] Within eighteen months of assuming office, Hitler became the dictator of Germany, having invoked emergency powers after a Dutch communist was arrested for an arson attack on the Reichstag – an attack which, some historians believe, was planned by the Nazi leadership as an excuse to seize complete control.

The millions who voted Nazi in 1933, especially the 719,446 Nazi Party members, are too easily dismissed as stupid, confused, corrupt or brainwashed, rather than ordinary people caught up in a crisis, whose fear and scapegoating of "Them" overwhelmed any cognitive-dissonance they had.

If the rise of the Nazis proves anything, it is that intellectuals are as susceptible to confirmation-bias as anyone else, and that rapid, rational, cognitive processing is no guarantee of empathy, wisdom or moral insight. Among the thousands of Nazi Party members was Martin Heidegger, erstwhile lover of Hannah Arendt, and one of the most celebrated Existentialist philosophers of the century.[437]

The academic brilliance of two Nobel laureates, Phillip Lenard and Johannes Stark, did not preclude them from petty begrudgery, poor judgement and political folly. Even the Nazis ignored them when their attempts to get the party to condemn the "Jewish physics" of Einstein, which had eclipsed their own theories of space-time, led to attacks on Werner Heisenberg, a school-friend of the SS head Heinrich Himmler. Heisenberg would go on to use the "Jewish physics" of Einstein and Bohr to develop the German nuclear-fission program.[438]

The Einsatzgruppen leaders who murdered the Polish cultural elite in Operation Tannenberg at the start of the Second World War were themselves, as we have seen, part of the German intellectual elite. Over 60 percent of them held PhDs.[439]

In 1932, it was still almost conceivable that a German could vote Nazi without being personally hostile to Judaism. The Jewish minority, roughly

505,000 people, were less than 0.75 percent of the population. They were a highly educated and assimilated group, many of whom spoke elegant German.[440] As Himmler said, there were many Nazis who disliked Jews in principle, but made exceptions in practice for their particular Jewish friends, physicians or, in the case of Magda Goebbels, lovers.

Magda, who eventually became the wife of Joseph Goebbels, Hitler's Propaganda Minister, had a first marriage, and affairs, with many men throughout her life, including the Zionist Chaim Arlosoroff – with whom she planned to emigrate to Palestine, long before the founding of Israel. As the Soviets closed in on the *Führerbunker*, she and Goebbels would poison their six children and shoot themselves.

*

Shorn of anti-Semitism, the fascist message of populist, authoritarian, right-wing nationalism appealed broadly. Mussolini railed against Jewish banking families, which he scapegoated for ruinous speculation, but more than 4 percent of the founders of the Fasci Italiani da Combattimento in 1919 were Jewish – thirty-five times the relative proportion of Jews in the population.[441] Hundreds of Jews joined Mussolini's March on Rome in 1922.[442]

Mussolini did not introduce profoundly anti-Semitic laws in his first sixteen years in office. When he did so in 1938, under pressure from Hitler, it cost him his Jewish mistress, biographer and Director of Propaganda, Margherita Sarfatti.[443]

Much of what became fascist ideology and policy was championed by the utopian rationalism of intellectuals, from the eugenicists who pursued forced-sterilisation programmes in Sweden, to Fabian socialists like Bertrand Russell and George Bernard Shaw, or the founders of Planned Parenthood on both sides of the Atlantic, Margaret Sanger and Marie Stopes.[444] In 1912, Winston Churchill attended the International Eugenics Conference, chaired by Charles Darwin's son

Leonard, who lobbied for scientists to arrest and sterilise the "unfit" disabled and "feeble-minded".[445]

The logical corollary was that there was no merit in keeping the lame and the halt alive. On utilitarian grounds, this placed an unjustifiable burden on the state. With the publication in 1920 of *Die Freigabe der Vernichtung Lebensunwerten Lebens* ("The Destruction of Those Unworthy of Life"), the psychiatrist Alfred Hoche and the jurist Karl Binding argued that the worth of an individual was contingent on her utility to the nation. Termination of "defectives" improved "racial hygiene". They dismissed the idea of a right to life as "unscientific" and "sentimental".[446]

Nazi propaganda films highlighted that the number of severely handicapped people alive in the Reich had risen by 450 percent in fifty years due to medical advances, compared to a 50 percent increase in the general population. Spuriously extrapolating these trends for fifty more years, they claimed that one in five Germans would be disabled by the 1980s. Writing in the *Journal of the German Medical Association*, Doctor Karl Hannelmann said "rats, bugs and fleas also occur naturally, just like the Jews and Roma. All life is a struggle, that is why we must biologically eradicate all these pests, and today that means so fundamentally changing their living conditions through preventive detention and sterilisation laws, that all these enemies of our people are slowly but surely eradicated".[447]

The first victims of the gas-chambers were not Jewish, but mentally and physically handicapped Germans. The Aktion T4 programme was approved by Hitler a month after the invasion of Poland. From October 1939 to August 1941, five thousand disabled children were euthanised by lethal injection, usually of phenol. Many of the sixty-five thousand disabled adults terminated under Aktion T4 were killed in fake showers or specially adapted vans by carbon monoxide – all for the rational, utilitarian good of the nation.[448]

Hitler wanted a post-Darwinian moral code for the Aryan *Herrenvolk* which would replace Christianity with a scientifically coherent value system.[449] "Science cannot lie", Hitler was quoted as saying by Martin Boorman in 1941, "for it's always striving, according to the momentary state of knowledge, to deduce what is true. When it makes a mistake, it does so in good faith. It's Christianity that's the liar. It's in perpetual conflict with itself . . . . The dogma of Christianity gets worn away before the advances of science. Religion will have to make more and more concessions. Gradually the myths crumble. All that's left is to prove that in nature there is no frontier between the organic and the inorganic. When understanding of the universe has become widespread, when the majority of men know that the stars are not sources of light but worlds, perhaps inhabited worlds like ours, then the Christian doctrine will be convicted of absurdity."

Hitler spoke frequently of an active Creative Power and his narcissistic destiny as the instrument of Providence, but by his own lights he was a stone-cold rationalist. If the only biological law was survival of the fittest, then a strong leader had to accept that the moral imperative was to strengthen your race in the struggle.[450] "If I can accept a divine commandment, it's this one: Thou shalt preserve thespecies."[451]

To improve biological fitness required the elimination of weaker members of your own race and the elimination of inferior foreigners whose living space your people needed. Judeo-Christian values of justice, mercy and love were not only absurd, they were a contagion which denied the natural order of things.[452] Jews were not so much a people as "a pestilence . . . worse than the Black Death", corrupting stronger races with their values.[453]

"For the future of the world," he wrote in *Mein Kampf*, "it does not matter which . . . triumphs over the other, the Catholic or the Protestant. But it does matter whether Aryan humanity survives or perishes." Hitler wasn't just going to war for living-space. He was fighting hard-wired human nature.

This presented a problem. Hitler recognised that exterminating millions of Slavs could trigger wholesale cognitive-dissonance. He had to eliminate them without offending the moral sensibilities of the *Herrenvolk*, who were still tainted with the teachings of Judeo-Christianity, and reluctant to get their hands dirty.[454]

He could hardly present his war of conquest as an act of self-defence, but memories of malnutrition and starvation in the Great War were still fresh in the mind. Reviving the ancient fear of famine, and therefore framing the drive for Lebensraum as a them-versus-us fight for survival, held some possibilities. Still, the German electorate had not signed up for mass murder.

Hitler had to distance the public from what was required. He had to minimise sensory contact which could trigger an intuitive moral reaction. The Nazi leadership would be surprised by the readiness of soldiers, civilians and policemen to participate in the most heinous atrocities of the war, but they never stopped worrying about the moral strain this imposed. Inspired by the treatment of Native Americans in the West, and of Armenians at the end of the Great War, the Slavs, quite simply, had to disappear.[455]

In tandem with Generalplan Ost, which outlined the post-war occupation of eastern Europe, Hitler's lieutenant Hermann Goering signed off on the Hunger Plan.[456] Long before the Nazis improvised the Holocaust to exterminate the Jews, they envisaged starving 50 percent of the population of Eastern Europe, or 30 million people, to death.[457]

Nearly 3 million Soviet prisoners of war were deliberately starved to death in their camps, experiencing a greater death-toll than Jews in the early stages of the Holocaust, until German labour-shortages prompted a temporary reprieve. Throughout the war, life and death in

Nazi labour or eastern prisoner-of-war camps would be determined by the exigencies of the conflict, and whether the contribution to the war effort justified the extra calories which were temporarily expended on the prisoners. It was a ruthless calculus that set no intrinsic value on human life.[458]

The German plan for the Polish state was pithily summarised by Hitler as a "massive extermination of the Polish intelligentsia". The "liquidation of leading Poles" was approved by Reinhard Heydrich, who ordered Einsatzgruppen units to kill 61,000 people.[459] By detaching the civilised "bearers" of Polish culture from the labouring class, the Nazis aimed to suppress resistance, and minimise the cognitive-dissonance associated with the enslavement of their European neighbours.

Of the remaining population, 85 percent would be superfluous within thirty years under the Hunger Plan, having withered away through starvation, exile and sterilisation.[460] In the meantime, Polish children in the Warthegau would be taught an ungrammatical form of pidgin German, so that they could understand their masters but still be easily distinguishable from them.[461] As in the Slave Codes of the American South, the idea that a German and a Pole could be the equal of each other in humanity and culture had to be suppressed.

The elimination of Polish Jewry was important, but not urgent. Unlike German Jews, more than 90 percent of Polish Jews were unassimilated, speaking Yiddish rather than Polish, attending Jewish schools, reading Jewish newspapers, voting for Jewish parties, and living in Jewish neighbourhoods. Leading Jewish intellectuals were included on the Tannenberg death-lists, but Jews as a group were not prioritised. Yiddish sounded like a reassuringly primitive German dialect to Nazi ears, and Polish Jews seemed closer to the favoured stereotypes of Nazi propaganda than their German co-religionists. Jews were rounded up and placed in urban ghettos, where rural deportees suffered a heavy death-toll from malnutrition in the first months of German occupation. For the remainder, ghettoisation was merely a stay of execution.

Up until the Second World War, Hitler killed fewer Jews than Stalin had in the Great Terror, and the Final Solution for the Jews was deferred until military victory had been achieved. Only as the tide of war turned against him did he modify his objectives. If he could not win the war militarily, he would win the war of ideas by eliminating their source.

"The rumour has spread among the population," a writer from the official Nazi newspaper, *Volkischer Beobachter*, noted in April 1942, "that it is the task of the Security Police to exterminate the Jews in the occupied territories. The Jews were assembled in their thousands and shot; beforehand they had to dig their own graves. At times the execution of the Jews reached such proportions that even members of the Einsatzgruppen suffered nervous breakdowns."[462]

Ten months before the article in the *Volkischer Beobachter*, on 22 June 1941, 3,050,000 German soldiers, police and auxiliary forces stood poised to invade the Soviet Union, the eastern half of Poland and the Baltic states of Lithuania, Latvia and Estonia, along a thirteen-hundred-mile front. Swift victory, in a matter of weeks, was assured by Der Führer, who predicted that the Soviet Union would collapse like a "house of cards" once the "Judeo-Bolshevik" leadership had been crushed.[463]

As in Poland, elite Einsatzgruppen units were dispatched behind the vanguard, to eliminate the *Nomenklatura*, in this case Jewish men and Communists (the two were believed to be synonymous), or any intellectuals who had been missed by Stalin during the Great Terror three years before. The task was summarised by Erich Koch, a Nazi Party Gauleiter: "If I find a Ukrainian who is worthy to sit with me at table, I must have him shot."[464]

Up until the invasion of the Soviet Union and its satellites, the prosecution of the war had gone relatively smoothly. But as with

Napoleon's attempt to conquer Russia more than a century before, it quickly became clear that all was not well. Between June and August 1941, more German soldiers would be killed in action than in the previous twenty-one months of the war put together.[465]

Despite seeing thousands of Soviet troops overrun in the first few days, and killing half his General Officers in the Great Terror, Stalin had massive military reserves to draw upon, especially in the Pacific, as well as troops who fought ferociously to slow down and eventually halt the German advance. By the end of December 1941, a quarter of the German army had been killed or wounded on the Eastern Front, the United States had entered the war, and the Wehrmacht still had not reached the centre of Moscow.

The Nazi leadership became agitated. A scapegoat was required. If Judeo-Bolshevism had not collapsed as predicted, the fault had to lie with the Jews. In Germany, all Jews over the age of six were forced to wear the Star of David by mid-September 1941 – less than three months after the invasion had been launched.[466] In Latvia and Lithuania, Einsatzgruppen units were briefed that the defence of the Fatherland required anti-Partisan operations to be stepped up a month after they had begun, since the Jews intended to exterminate all Germans.[467] They returned to Jewish towns and villages where they had killed all the men in July, to kill all the Jewish women and children in August.

At Bletchley Park in England, Enigma operators decoded the mounting death-toll in each region, as well as a single word, *Judenfrei*, where operations had ceased. The magnitude of the atrocity was soon apparent. "We are in the presence," Winston Churchill said, "of a crime without a name."[468]

As the invasion stalled, more than a million Jewish men, women and children were shot in Latvia, Lithuania, Ukraine and Belarus by the end of Christmas 1941.[469] Nearly 2 million more would be shot in

1942 and 1943. The perpetrators were Einsatzgruppen as well as Nazi-dominated Special Police units which were supposed to be thousands of miles east. Wehrmacht troops dug trenches and provided logistical support, and local collaborators pointed out where the Jews lived, and participated in their killing.

Many true believers, such as Bruno Muller, who told a two-year-old Jewish girl that she had to die so that the Aryan race could live, were lawyers.[470] So were many collaborators, like the policeman Victors Bernhard Arajs, who started a degree in Latvian law, studied Soviet law while working for the NKVD, and finished a degree in German law after the unit he led murdered 22,000 people, and helped to kill 28,000 more.[471]

The Holocaust was not a spontaneous manifestation of popular anti-Semitism. Unlike regular German forces, local police could be shot if they did not participate in the killings. Communists and Red Army veterans were told that they could wipe the slate clean by helping to kill a Jew.

To the chagrin of Himmler and Heydrich, less than 1 percent of the Jews who died in Lithuania in 1941 were killed in spontaneous pogroms, despite Nazi propaganda which blamed NKVD killings on the Jews.[472] No pogroms occurred in Lithuania where Germans were not present.[473]

Resistance to the genocide came from the most unlikely sources. The disillusioned German Nazi Party member and diplomat Georg Duckwitz warned the Social Democratic Party in Denmark about plans to deport Jews to concentration camps, enabling nearly the entire Jewish population – about eight thousand people – to be smuggled into Sweden.[474]

Zofia Kossak, a leader of the anti-Semitic Catholic Front for the Reborn Poland, made a public statement in August 1942 that "Whoever remains silent in the face of slaughter, becomes an enabler of the murderer". She founded the Zegota organisation a month later, smuggled thousands of children to safety, and refused to name her accomplices as her legs were broken at Auschwitz.[475]

At the same time, acts of kindness did not preclude participation in the massacres. The soldier who let a mother step out of line, so that she could hitch up her son's pants, was the same man who escorted them to the death-pits at Krupki, north-east of Minsk, on 18 September 1941.[476] The soldier who saved two-year-old Sara Sonja Griffin and her mother in the Netherlands, by shouting that there were no Jews in the attic before his comrades could find them, was the same man who led the other Jews hiding in the house to their doom.[477] The SS officer and chess-player Kurt Trimborn, who released his friend Eleazar Bernstein from custody after Kristallnacht, and drove his family from Zweibrucken to the French border, was the same man who organised the shooting of hundreds of Jews in the east, and shepherded children from an orphanage into a gas-van.[478] At his trial, he testified that he disliked orders to kill civilians, and occasionally let them escape if he could.

Since Germans could refuse to participate in the murder, they retained a level of agency which added to their sense of guilt.[479] The leader of Einsatzgruppe A, Franz Stahlecker, acknowledged that killing Jewish children was an "emotional strain", and that providing members of his unit with alcohol was not dulling moral angst. He pioneered the use of local proxies to "make it appear that the indigenous population had reacted naturally".[480]

The Higher SS and Police Leader in Ukraine, Friedrich Jeckeln, developed the use of the "sardine method" of execution. Under this method, the condemned were forced to stand over the dead before being shot themselves, speeding up the killing, and minimising sensory cognitive-dissonance from handling bodies.[481]

Walter Rauff, who introduced gas-vans with the Einsatzgruppen, said: "I cannot say whether I had misgivings about the use of gas-vans.

What was uppermost in my mind at the time was that the shootings were a great strain on the men involved, and that this strain would be removed by the use of gas-vans."[482] Perpetrators were spared sensory exposure to the deaths of their victims, but corpses still had to be manhandled before the vans could be used again, not to mention cleaning the residue of blood, shit, piss, flesh and vomit they left behind.

The deportation of Jews from around Europe for termination on Polish soil was rubber-stamped at the Wannsee Conference in January 1942.[483] The deployment of gas-chambers and crematoria facilities reflected the need to minimise sensory cognitive-dissonance in the murder of innocent men, women and children, as well as the acute labour-shortages facing the Reich.

Since the Eastern Front was consuming huge amounts of manpower, there were not enough Special Police officers to orchestrate mass-shootings. After starving to death 3 million Soviet prisoners-of-war, as well as a million civilians, in the Siege of Leningrad, the Reich started to feed Slavic POWs to plug labour deficits.[484]

Doubts about the ability of the *Herrenvolk* to win the struggle crept into Hitler's rhetoric a month after the Wannsee Conference, along with the consolation that at least the "Jewish question" would be resolved. "My prophecy will be fulfilled," Hitler said on the anniversary of the foundation of the Nazi Party, "that in this war not the Aryans will be exterminated but the Jew will be eradicated. Whatever the battle will bring, or how long it may last, this will be the ultimate legacy of this war."[485]

Some German administrators suggested that killing the residents of the ghettos was more humane than letting them slowly starve to death.[486] The Warsaw Ghetto would be liquidated in the gas-chambers of Treblinka, followed by the Jewish Police who corralled them onto transports, and then the prisoners of war who shovelled them into the crematorium.[487]

The facilities at Auschwitz alone claimed more than 1 million souls.[488] The vast majority of those who were scheduled to die at Auschwitz spent no more than a night there. The voices of these innocent victims were preserved by the survivors of the co-located labour camp.

As Nazi forces scoured occupied Europe, consent for persecution became a matter of life and death. Where local governments remained intact, a modicum of protection for Jewish citizens was still possible. Seventy-five percent of Jews in France survived. Seventy-five percent of Jews in the Netherlands died.[489]

At the end of the war, more than 5.7 million Jewish men, women and children would be dead, along with Roma, the handicapped and anyone else deemed unworthy of life.[490] Their lives, their stories, their hopes, fears and dreams can be reconstructed from the letters, diaries and mementoes they left behind, from messages of love and farewell thrown hastily out of trains, and from the remarkable archive of the Warsaw Ghetto.

They fought back where they could, melting into the forests near Minsk as partisans, or using arms from the Polish Home Army to stage an uprising in Warsaw. By 1945, the largest single group of Polish Jews left alive were the "class enemies" who had survived deportation to the Soviet Gulags.[491]

At the end of the war, minorities were ethnically cleansed across Central and Eastern Europe, in one of the largest population-movements in history. Hitler's body had been consigned to dust months before, along with the millions of victims of the Holocaust, who accounted for somewhere between 7 and 12 percent of the 50 million to 80 million people who perished in the Second World War as a result of the good strong lies the Nazis told themselves about their Social Darwinist utopia.[492] The war ended with mushroom-clouds over Hiroshima and Nagasaki, presaging an existential threat which hangs over us to this day.

III
The Pursuit of Kindness

Chapter Seven

From Patriarchy Back to Partnership

"It isn't enough to talk about peace. One must believe in it. And it isn't enough to believe in it. One must work at it."

ELEANOR ROOSEVELT

How do we move from cruelty back to collaboration again? How do we recognise our common humanity? How do we reconcile the competing aims and values which simmer within a deeply polarised society?

People have come up with various approaches to these problems. Joshua Greene suggests a "practical Utilitarianism" based on the greatest good for the greatest number. Michael McCullough champions a shared space for reasoned debate. Brian Hare and Vanessa Woods warn of our proclivity to dehumanise "them". Steven Pinker favours the promotion of Enlightenment values. The journalist Rutger Bregman highlights the detrimental effect of negative pereceptions – "nocebos" – and advises us to stop watching the news.

But none of these proposals address our cognitive biases, and the extent to which we skew our moral compass, as well as the evidence before us, in order to rationalise our passions. For thousands of years, violence and conflict have been part of the human narrative. Our ability to commit acts of unspeakable cruelty has been enabled by the lies we told ourselves to salve our conscience.

But when we say "we", we are talking mostly about men. Ever since criminologists have kept track of such statistics, men have perpetrated more than 90 percent of homicides and other serious crimes. The mere presence of women as partners leads to a pronounced fall in violence, as the story of the Wild West has shown.

The Impact of Women on Reducing Violence

During the Gold Rush of the late 1840s, the United States and Canada saw thousands of single young men go west to seek their fortune. Homicide rates in some towns in the Wild West were fifty to one hundred times higher than back east.[493]

In western Canada, where the Mounted Police maintained a semblance of order, the murder-rate was three times lower than in California, but the real game-changer was the arrival of single young women to marry the single young men.[494] With less competition over status, church attendance and other cultural norms of respectability increased, as young men married and settled down to raise a family.[495] As gender ratios re-balanced, the homicide rate in California fell ten-fold by 1910.

What is more remarkable than the declining homicide-rate in itself is the fact that after thousands of years of patriarchy, single young women could travel independently to the West to marry the single young men. With rising prosperity and education in the Industrial Revolution, women attained greater autonomy. With higher levels of gender equality, women could do more to advance the pursuit of kindness than swapping genes with rival bands. The journey from patriarchy back to partnership has been going on for generations.

As relations between nation-states came to be solemnised in legal treaties rather than dynastic hook-ups, and commercial success began to rely on contract law rather than kin-networks, arranged marriage fell out of fashion. We no longer relied on patriarchal marital alliances to deliver peace.

Women were seizing the opportunity to make an impact on the wider world. In 1792, Mary Wollstonecraft wrote *A Vindication of the Rights of Woman*.[496] In the 1850s, Harriet Beecher Stowe transformed attitudes to slavery in the northern United States.[497] In Germany, Rosa Luxemburg championed social democracy in the teeth of Freikorps paramilitary opposition both during and after the First World War, until she was killed in 1919.[498]

Weeks after Rosa Luxemburg was murdered in Berlin, and seven decades after the Seneca Falls Convention called for the right to vote – and following a litany of legal challenges, arrests and hunger-strikes – the National American Woman Suffrage Association under Carrie Chapman Catt secured the passage of the Nineteenth Amendment.[499] By 1927, similar campaigns led by Emmeline Pankhurst gained the vote for all women over the age of twenty-one in the United Kingdom.

Women acquired real political power for the first time. The question was what impact this would have on public policy, whether in attitudes to war, the spending priorities of government, or in relation to progress towards equality for all. Politicians can be held accountable at the ballot-box if they do not show that military action was necessary after peaceful means have been exhausted, but this is a comparatively new phenomenon in history. Equal rights to vote regardless of wealth, creed, colour or gender have existed for no more than a century in most western countries. Female political participation brought a fresh perspective.

Female Attitudes to War

Both men and women acquire high levels of emotional intelligence, but women typically develop empathetic skills earlier, and to a greater degree. Newborn girls look at other faces more than newborn boys, and are more likely to cry when they hear others crying – which is known as emotional contagion. Twelve-month-old girls comfort those in distress earlier than boys. Contagion carries into adulthood, with an Italian study showing that women are 33 percent more likely to yawn if someone else yawns.

The British psychologist Simon Baron-Cohen has found that three-year-old girls are better at understanding the emotions of others than boys of the same age, that girls play more generously and less roughly, and that women are typically better than men at reading emotions from people's facial expressions. Baron-Cohen also found that women are more likely to deploy snarky verbal put-downs rather than physical aggression.

Although females are less physically aggressive than males, emotional intelligence and empathy do not equate to pacifism. Men and women supported US forces in lockstep during the Second World War and the Cold War, as they do in other existential conflicts.

Some women have also joined terrorist groups. Female suicide-bombers are more lethal, and less likely to fail, than their male counterparts. Twenty percent of westerners who went to Syria to fight for ISIS were women. They have been patronised as "manipulated ingenues" or "jihadist cheerleaders", but they were more likely to initiate contact with a recruiter than vice versa. They were also more likely to be converts, to be married, and to have no criminal record.

But attitudes to war differ by gender. Support among women for the wars in Afghanistan and Iraq was consistently lower in Britain, France, Germany, Italy, Spain and the United States than among men. In survey after survey, women oppose unilateral wars of aggression.

A Chatham House YouGov poll in 2011 found that only one in ten British women would support war if the UK acted alone, compared to nearly three out of ten men. A multilateral conflict under a UN or NATO mandate commanded more support, but was still opposed by roughly six out of ten women, compared to four out of ten men.

The rising political, economic and social power of women in liberal democratic states over the past hundred years has been one of the strongest drivers of institutionalised kindness. Rosa Parks would galvanise the civil rights movement simply by refusing to go to the back of the bus in Montgomery, Alabama.[500] Malala Yousafzai, fifteen, was shot three times in the head, neck and shoulder, but survived, when she defied a Taliban ban on girls going to school in Pakistan. Sixteen-year-old Palestinian Ahed Tamimi served eight months in prison when she slapped an Israeli sergeant after her cousin Mohammed, fifteen, had been shot with a rubber bullet, and the boy had to have part of his skull removed to prevent brain-damage.

Female politicians are still underrepresented in legislatures around the world, but women have made an impact in terms of how our taxes are spent. As a percentage of GDP, spending on health, education and children has soared as democracies brought in welfare states, maternity leave and equal pay for equal work, as well as outlawing sexual discrimination.[501]

The Unfinished Struggle for Women's Rights

Despite these advances, inequality and abuse persist around the world. Only 1 percent of the titled land in the world is owned outright by women. One woman dies in childbirth every minute. In Ethiopia, one in seven die in childbirth, versus 1 in 19,000 in the UK. According to the United Nations, nearly 2.5 million women and children are victims of human trafficking each year. Eight out of ten victims of human trafficking are sexually abused.In some parts of the world, women are still treated as chattels. In Saudi Arabia, which issued driving licences to women for the first time in June 2018, unaccompanied women still need the written permission of a male guardian to travel, work or access healthcare.

Respect for traditional cultures and respect for individual human rights cannot always be easily reconciled. More than 200 million women have suffered genital mutilation at the hands of their mothers and grandmothers. In Chad, less than one in twenty girls go to school. Of the 1.2 billion people living in poverty, 70 percent are women or children, and nearly seven out of ten illiterate adults are women. Increases in female literacy have led to great improvements in prosperity, healthcare, birth-control and empowerment, but increasing levels of female literacy also correlate with higher levels of sex-selective abortion in China and northern India. In some areas, there are 120 boys under the age of six for every 100 girls. Writing in the *New York Review of Books* in 1990, the Nobel Prize-winning economist Amartya Sen estimated that at at least 100 million women had gone "missing" in the latter half of the twentieth century. Over the following thirty years, millions more sex-selective abortions have been performed, something *The Economist* magazine describes as "gendercide". In the West, discrimination and harassment are still significant problems. In Europe, fewer than one in twenty-five CEOS are women. In the United States, more than one in three lawyers are women, but just one in twenty partners in law firms are. In 2005, Donald Trump was able to make the lewd claim that "When you're a star . . . you can do anything. . . . Grab them by the pussy. You can do anything."

It took the downfall of the producer Harvey Weinstein to mobilise the #MeToo campaign, encouraging victims of endemic sexual harassment to speak out and demand an end to the abuse of power by men in the media industry and beyond.

The campaign for equal pay for equal work has seen the gap between male and female earnings in the same job narrow, but lower female participation in full-time, highly paid professions means that the overall gender pay-gap is still more than 20 percent in many western countries. The remaining pay-gap cannot be closed without addressing attitudes to childcare which focus on maternity leave rather than parental leave.

In countries which have mandated paternity leave, stay-at-home dads not only enable their partners to resume their careers sooner, they also report a sustained increase in the proportion of domestic chores which men perform long after they themselves return to full-time paid employment.[502] To close the gender pay-gap in industrialised societies requires a paradigm-shift in attitudes to parenting and remote working.

In the long term, Covid-19 may prove to be one of the greatest catalysts for change. The first lockdown hit women in the service sector particularly hard, in what has been described as a "she-cession", but it also saw men stepping up to provide more childcare. It proved that remote workers can juggle domestic obligations between Zoom calls and still be highly effective – a trend which is likely to be felt in much more flexible working practices and greater gender equality.[503]

Insidious cultural barriers to fulfilling potential remain. Twelve decades after the double Nobel laureate Marie Curie coined the term "radioactivity", and more than six decades after Rosalind Franklin's use of X-ray crystallography enabled the discovery of the double-helix structure of DNA, just one in four of the workforce in STEM (Science, Technology, Engineering, Math) industries are women.

The low participation of women in high-paying STEM jobs perpetuates gender pay-gaps, but the attitudes of parents, teachers and girls themselves reinforce the problem. A 2015 survey of four thousand females aged between eleven and twenty-three found that 60 percent of twelve-year-old girls thought that STEM subjects were too hard to learn, nearly half thought that STEM subjects were for boys, and one in three thought that these subjects better suited boys' brains, personalities and hobbies. Similar proportions of parents and teachers agreed.

A Female Candidate for President

If you want girls to believe in themselves, their dreams, and their ability to break the glass ceiling, it helps to have pioneering trail-blazers. The 2016 US presidential election was the first time that a leading party had a female nominee, former First Lady, Senator, and

Secretary of State Hillary Clinton, standing for the highest political office in the United States. It was also notable for being the first time that spending on digital advertising exceeded the spend on cable TV.

At $1.4 billion, political advertising on sites such as Facebook was more than five thousand times higher than when Barack Obama became President in 2008. [504] Donald Trump raised $280 million in campaign funds via Facebook; however, the ultimate source of funding for half of all digital political advertising in the election was unclear.

Facebook and Cambridge Analytica were caught in the crosshairs of Congressional hearings. According to Bloomberg Businessweek, Trump staffers paid Facebook for voter-suppression videos which discouraged idealistic white liberals, African-Americans and young women from voting for Hillary Clinton.[505]

One of the most disturbing features of the election was the involvement of a group of Russian hackers in St Petersburg known as the Internet Research Agency, who waged an information-war on social media to influence the outcome.

Details of their activities emerged after the election. Following the firing of James Comey, in May 2017 a former Director of the FBI, Robert Mueller, was appointed by Deputy Attorney General Rod Rosenstein as a Special Counsel to the US Department of Justice to investigate Russian interference.

US social-media companies, starting with Facebook, reported that they had identified Russian expenditures on their platforms to fund political and social advertisements. Facebook's initial disclosure stated that Facebook had "shared [its] findings with US authorities investigating these issues." Media reports said that Facebook was working with Robert Mueller and his investigators for the Special Counsel's Office of the US Department of Justice.

The Internet Research Agency started to destroy evidence. On 13

September 2017, Kaverzina (the alias of one of the hackers) emailed a family member: "We had a slight crisis here at work: the FBI busted our activity (not a joke). So, I got preoccupied with covering tracks together with the colleagues." Kaverzina wrote: "I created all these pictures and posts, and the Americans believed that it was written by their people." They were indicted by Robert Mueller, the Special Counsel, in February 2018.[506]

The indictment stated that by May 2014, the Internet Research Agency had decided to interfere with the 2016 US presidential election, with the stated goal of "spread[ing] distrust towards the candidates and the political system in general".[507] This included promoting allegations of voter fraud by the Democratic Party.[508]

The Internet Research Agency described its conduct as "information warfare against the United States of America".[509] By 2016, many of their social-media groups had hundreds of thousands of online followers.[510] Using the handle @TEN_GOP, the Twitter account "Tennessee GOP" claimed to be run by the Tennessee Republican Party. It eventually attracted more than a hundred thousand online followers.

The hackers posted derogatory information about a number of candidates, and by early to mid-2016, their operations included supporting the presidential campaign of Donald Trump and disparaging Hillary Clinton.[511] Some posed as US citizens to coordinate political activities with unwitting members of the Trump campaign.[512]

Former Trump staffers, including the campaign's chairman, Paul Manafort, and the campaign worker George Papadopoulos, pleaded guilty to making false statements to the FBI. In December 2017, the former National Security Advisor, Michael Flynn, pleaded guilty to "willfully and knowingly" [giving] "false, fictitious and fraudulent statements to the FBI".

In June 2016, the Internet Research Agency used their Facebook group "United Muslims of America" to promote a rally called

"Support Hillary. Save American Muslims" to be held on 9 July 2016 in the District of Columbia. They recruited a US person to hold a sign depicting Clinton and a quote attributed to her, stating: "I think Sharia Law will be a powerful new direction of freedom."

Three weeks later, they posted on the same Facebook page that Muslim voters were "between Hillary Clinton and a hard place". They used their false US personas to ask people to participate in the "Florida Goes Trump" rallies, paying one person to build a cage on a flatbed truck and another to pose as Hillary Clinton in a prison uniform.

In the aftermath of the election, the idea that Trump's connivance with Russia cost Hillary Clinton the presidency took on mythic proportions for Democrats, in a liberal version of the stabbed-in-the-back trope; the truth of the matter may have been that the Trump team was simply more effective online.

Trump's campaign budget was 30 percent lower than Hillary's, but they spent more heavily on Facebook. Trump paid Giles-Parscale Inc. $94 million – more than fifteen times what he gave to Cambridge Analytica – mainly for digital fund-raising, persuasion and get-out-the-vote campaigns. The Internet Research Agency bought 3500 Facebook ads between 2015 and 2017; the Trump campaign bought millions.[513]

Commentators have speculated that the Kremlin did not expect Donald Trump to win the 2016 US presidential election. The IRA aimed to "spread distrust towards the candidates and the political system in general". As with the hacking of Illinois voting-machines, a clumsy and easily detectable attempt to spread disinformation became a very cost-effective way to undermine faith in western democratic institutions.

In that, they succeeded. Prior to the election, 41 percent of Americans believed that if Donald Trump did not win, it would be because of vote-rigging by Democrats.

Female Leaders Stand Up to Populism

In 2016, the people of the United States were hoping for a strong leader. [514] They got President Trump. Within months, he would reject the terms of climate-change accords which had been signed by his predecessor, Barack Obama, and prompt German Chancellor Angela Merkel to say that the United States could no longer be relied upon to support NATO.

A country which had nothing to fear but fear itself under FDR, and fought the global threats of fascism, and then communism, for decades, came full circle. As Trump's "America first" policy became evident, the leaders of other Western democracies in Great Britain, France and Germany had to step up to the plate.

In the Cold War era, Golda Meier, Indira Gandhi and Margaret Thatcher had to be Iron Ladies to succeed, but a new generation of female leaders resisted populism without letting ego get in the way, from the calm political acumen of Chancellor Angela Merkel to the adroit crisis-management during the Covid-19 pandemic demonstrated by Jacinda Ardern of New Zealand, and the resilience of British Prime Minister Theresa May.

After the banking collapse of 2008, ancient fears about immigrants were renewed as Europe suffered under austerity measures. Pictures of Alan Kurdi, a three-year-old boy who drowned on the shores of Greece after fleeing the war in Syria, moved people to tears, but resistance to the influx from Syria and Libya remained.[515]

Chancellor Merkel's courageous determination to offer humanitarian assistance and shelter to Middle Eastern refugees in Germany exacerbated fears in the European Union about the free movement of people. This contributed to the Brexit vote in the United Kingdom to leave the European Union, even though the majority of Muslim immigrants to the UK came from the Commonwealth states of the former British Empire, rather than Europe.

Brexit became the catalyst for Theresa May to be elected as Prime Minister, and the leader of a profoundly divided Conservative Party, where she tried to wrest order from the chaos of irreconcilable factions. May stood up to President Trump when he re-tweeted images from the far-right Britain First group. After Brexit was approved in the referendum, police reported a 60 percent spike in hate-crimes towards minorities. Months after Brexit, hate-crimes remained 14 percent higher than they had been before the referendum vote.[516]

Britain's 3 million Muslims – including the Mayor of London, Sadiq Khan – made a huge contribution to the health and prosperity of the United Kingdom, but Islamists were committing atrocities across Europe in the hope that the active jihadist leanings of one in a thousand Muslims would lead to the persecution, and therefore the radicalisation, of the other nine hundred and ninety-nine.[517]

The terrorists have grounds for optimism. We still demonise "them" for not being "us".

Chapter Eight

It's the Illegal Immigrants, Stupid

"No one has ever made himself great by showing how small someone else is."

IRVIN HIMMEL

Three months after President Trump was elected, the author Elizabeth Kolbert wrote a pithy summary of confirmation-bias in the *New Yorker*. Citing the cognitive scientists Hugo Mercier and Dan Sperber, she argued that reason evolved to help us solve the problems of living in collaborative groups. "My-side bias" helped us to see the flaws in other people's views and to win arguments regardless of the evidence, she said – before likening the rise of Kellyanne Conway and "alternative facts" to a vast psychological experiment "being run either by no one or by Steve Bannon". Some on the Right clung on to Deep State conspiracy theories as tenaciously as some on the Left did to their view that Russian interference swung the election for Trump.

In truth, almost no one saw it coming. After two terms of President Barack Obama, America opted for a tax-avoiding billionaire maverick with no experience of political office, a series of failed marriages behind him, and a penchant for boasting about his virility while embroiled in allegations of affairs with porn stars.

Even more remarkable, a candidate who called Mexican illegal immigrants drug-dealers and rapists was able to poll more votes among

Hispanic Americans than his Republican predecessor, Mitt Romney, in the previous election. A man who bragged about "grabbing pussies" received 53 percent of the votes of white women.

The political scientist and best-selling author Amy Chua argued that his base loved him because The Donald was not afraid to use locker-room talk to call things as he saw them, to make mistakes while shooting from the hip, and to incur the wrath of the wealthy, entitled, liberal elite in 140 characters. Or less. He described himself as "the Ernest Hemingway of Twitter".[518]

It was an election characterised by what *The Late Show* presenter Stephen Colbert calls "truthiness": something that we feel is true regardless of evidence, logic or intellectual scrutiny.[519] An election where the facts didn't matter because there are always alternative facts. As America became even more polarised, it was more difficult to agree on anything.

Where many liberals saw bombast and bluster, *Dilbert* creator Scott Adams saw persuasive genius, calling the election for Trump after observing his intuitive grasp of confirmation-bias and cognitive-dissonance. Trump was popular among men who saw themselves as alphas, and women who liked alphas. The observation ended Adams' speaking career and reduced his income by about 40 percent.

Michael Moore also predicted that Trump would win: "I'm from the Rust Belt and know about that working-class male anger at being 'left behind'."

Trump was a master at fragmenting opposition, making listeners feel like "us" rather than "them" – but always with a scapegoat to hand. Isolation, marginalisation and exclusion were the leitmotifs. Like all bullies, he could pick on the weak kid in class and claim to be just having fun.

Senator John McCain, who was tortured as a POW for five and a half years in Vietnam, was, in Trump's eyes, not a war-hero because he got captured. The Donald denied saying that women who criticised him were fat pigs, dogs, slobs or disgusting animals – only Rosie O'Donnell. Jeb Bush liked "Mexican illegals because of his wife". Rick Perry "put on glasses so people will think he's smart, and it just doesn't work!"

He tapped into dog-whistle politics before he announced his candidacy, pandering to racists and Islamophobes when he challenged President Obama in 2011 to produce his birth-certificate. "He doesn't have a birth-certificate. He may have one, but there's something on that – maybe religion, maybe it says he is a Muslim. I don't know."

His previously positive Q Score TV approval ratings plummeted among African-American and Hispanic fans of *The Apprentice*. (Ironically, the show had been a beacon of diversity when it first aired in 2004, with female and minority candidates vying for the top prize in front of 20 million viewers each week.)

Not that Trump couldn't uncover plenty of legitimate grievances to talk about, including the corruption and affluence of Washington insiders. Median income in the DC Metro area of the Beltway was nearly 70 percent higher than the national average, outstripping Silicon Valley.

While Donald was stirring the birther pot, Peter Schweizer published *Throw Them All Out: How Politicians and Their Friends Get Rich Off of Insider Stock Tips, Land Deals, and Cronyism That Would Send the Rest of Us to Prison*, prompting Congress to pass the STOCK Act (Stop Trading On Congressional Knowledge).

Schweizer followed up with the *New York Times*-bestselling *Clinton Cash* in 2015, which showed how a donor to the Clinton Foundation won mining rights after flying Bill Clinton to Kazakhstan, and how the former President's speaking fees soared after Hillary Clinton became Secretary of State. The *Boston Globe* reported that a local branch of the Foundation had "uniformly bypassed" agreed rules for disclosure of Clinton Foundation donors to the White House while she was Secretary of State.

Trump claimed that people were getting screwed, and that only he could Make America Great Again. He was funding his own campaign – an outsider who could "drain the swamp" in Washington DC of politicians beholden to wealthy donors. Jeb Bush was ridiculed for having a Big Pharma heir as his finance chief when the refusal to negotiate Medicare drug prescriptions in bulk was costing America billions of dollars.

The Donald said he agreed with Bernie Sanders on two things: that "We're being ripped off", and that Hillary Clinton was "receiving a fortune from a lot of people". "Crooked Hillary" struggled to defend herself against the perception that she was the ultimate insider, saying that she accepted $675,000 from Goldman Sachs for a series of speeches because "that was what they offered". Donald Trump said: "Hillary Clinton only believes in government of, by and for the powerful."

She wasn't the first person to use a personal email account while Secretary of State, but Colin Powell never used it to discuss classified topics, according to FBI Director James Comey. According to Comey, email topics were classified by American Intelligence Agencies as either "Confidential", meaning that disclosure could cause "damage"; "Secret", which could cause "serious damage"; or "Top Secret", which could cause "exceptionally grave damage". Comey concluded that Hillary Clinton was "extremely careless" in participating in thirty-six email chains on "Secret" topics and eight chains on "Top Secret" topics, but he attributed it to her lack of tech-savvy about remote hacking, quoting her memoir *What Happened*, where she talked of the Secret Service agents guarding the server at her house. It didn't help her when the public discovered that roughly half of the emails on her personal server were deleted by her team before her correspondence was handed over to the FBI, or when more undisclosed emails were found on a computer belonging to the husband of her aide, Huma

Abedin, who was under investigation over allegations of sexting a minor. The FBI confirmed that the new emails did not change their findings, but days before the election, 60 percent of Americans thought Hillary was untrustworthy.

Donald Trump used the Republican Convention to stoke fears that this "was a moment of crisis in our nation . . . the attacks on our police, and the terrorism in our cities, threaten our very way of life . . . any politician who does not grasp this is not fit to lead our country". Almost no one expected him to win. Matt Taibbi of *Rolling Stone* magazine wrote in his book *Insane Clown President* that the media applied the "Seal of Death" to his campaign.

Then Trump pivoted. At the behest of Steve Bannon, Trump explicitly repudiated the Alt-Right in order to build a coalition among moderate Republicans and blue-collar Democrats. As he was moving to the centre, he looked to Taibbi "like Huck Finn taking a bath". His spokesperson Katrina Pierson explained: "He hasn't changed his position on immigration. He's changed the words that he is saying." Hate-crimes rose by 20 percent after his election.His base took Donald seriously rather than literally. He might never get Mexico to finance his wall, but he was speaking an emotional truth to people who were angry, and looking for a scapegoat. They wanted someone to fix the problems and punish the people who were taking them for a ride, not for sanctimonious virtue-signalling about tolerance and understanding.

Hyperbole around the threat Donald posed just made it easier for the base to dismiss liberals. He was capable of generating passionate loathing among opponents, but calling him out on facts didn't work when his base believed that America was in crisis. He may have inherited an economy with full employment, but it also contained a great deal of insecurity, inequality and hardship.

Mocking the ineptitude of the Trump administration gave liberals a moral high. They were trying to punish President Trump by gossiping about him, but despite his thin-skinned, narcissistic and compulsive tweets, he was far removed from the social censures which worked so effectively in hunter-gatherer societies thousands of years previously.

Like a good shock-jock, Trump understood that the only thing worse than being talked about was not being talked about. Bernie Sanders got nearly as many primary votes as Trump, but The Donald got twenty-three times as much television coverage. As the former President of CBS, Lee Moonves, said, in terms of ratings, Donald Trump was "good for business".

Taking President Trump Seriously

For many liberals, disbelief was replaced by a horrified sense that his elevation was a desecration of the office of President.[520] They found it hard to believe that decent human beings could see past the wild braggadocio and vote for a set of conservative social and economic policies which, they hoped, would Make America Great Again. The political columnist Salena Zito upbraided the media for taking Donald Trump literally but not seriously before the election. Following his inauguration, President Trump had an opportunity to Make America Great Again in practice, testing the boundaries of his authority and the separation of powers in the process.

It quickly became clear that he meant what he had said. He continued to scapegoat illegal immigrants and Muslim refugees, sought to tear up healthcare and climate -change accords, engaged in nuclear brinkmanship with North Korea, saw Hamas protestors shot in Gaza when the US Embassy moved to Jerusalem, demonstrated fitful support for NATO, placed protectionist tariffs on steel which could have sparked a trade war and another Great Depression, and announced that America would withdraw from the Iran nuclear deal. Donald Tusk, the President of the European Council, responded by saying: "With friends like that, who needs enemies?"

Within seven days of his inauguration, President Trump had signed a hastily drafted executive order entitled "Protecting the Nation from Foreign Terrorist Entry into the United States". The order placed an indefinite ban on Syrian refugees entering the United States, a 120-day ban on any other refugees, and a 90-day ban on people with visas from Iraq, Iran, Libya, Somalia, Sudan, Syria and Yemen.

Among the first to be detained were two Iraqi brothers who were granted visas after their service with the United States military. Federal judges injuncted multiple versions of the Executive Order, prompting the Supreme Court to allow those with "any bona fide relationship with a person or entity in the United States" to enter the country, but otherwise limiting travel from Iran, Libya, Somalia, Syria, Yemen and North Korea.

The restrictions imposed by the courts on President Trump were grist to the mill of right-wing conspiracy theorists who believed that Washington or the Deep State would try to stab Trump in the back. The mainstream media delivered Pulitzer Prize-winning investigative reportage as well as hard news about the administration based on daily tweets, announcements, actions, threats and proclamations, but viewers of Fox and MSNBC received vastly different assessments of the same behaviour.

Moderates who tried to work with the President were ostracised. Protestors chained themselves to the railings of Uber headquarters in San Francisco as President Trump was inaugurated, triggering the resignation of Uber CEO Travis Kalanick from the Strategic and Policy Forum, a business advisory council which had been set up by the President. At the same time, the President appeared "engaged", "interested" and "respectful" when talking to business leaders in the forum, listening to their ideas and asking relevant questions about how they could be developed.

Despite dire warnings from Democrat-leaning economists, including Nobel laureate Paul Krugman, the economy continued to prosper in President Trump's first term in office, and the stock market soared as the administration announced it was reducing uncompetitive corporate tax rates – which would, it was claimed, lead to the repatriation of billions of dollars held in overseas tax shelters. He was pilloried for his tepid response to Covid-19, but prompt bipartisan action mitigated the costs of the shutdown, tiding over people who had lost their jobs, and providing cheap finance for corporations. Within months, the S&P 500 would be trading at an all-time high again.

Tax cuts for the rich would lead to a yawning budget deficit, but the chickens would not come home to roost in President Trump's first term. Senator Charles Schumer confided to Steve Bannon that he feared that Donald Trump would announce a $1 trillion programme to address decades of underinvestment in infrastructure, which would lead a cohort of traditional blue-collar Democrats into the Republican camp for a generation.

For all the President's rhetoric on illegal immigrants, the *Washington Post* reported that the Trump Administration had deported nearly 33 percent fewer people in his first three years in office than his predecessor, President Obama. (Obama had been given the nickname "Deporter-in-Chief" by officials in Immigration and Customs Enforcement.)

The technocratic detail of healthcare reform was not Trump's strong suit, but having been heavily criticised by Paul Ryan during the Republican primaries, the President was willing to bury the hatchet and defer to him on replacing Obamacare with something even better. It soon became apparent that any alternative would not be palatable to all sections of the Republican Party, despite assurances from Ryan that it was "a done deal". Trump was heard to ask why they couldn't just extend Medicare to everyone.

A trade mission to Saudi Arabia netted a commitment to fight terrorist extremists, as well as the sale of $350 billion in American military hardware.[521] With the support of Egypt, Saudi Arabia and

Israel, Trump hoped that Palestinian leaders would come to the table – before the journalist Jamal Khashoggi was murdered in Turkey by "officials of the Saudi government acting outside their scope of authority".[522]

Many within Bannon's radical support-base favoured an isolationist approach in foreign policy, but President Trump dreamt of historic breakthroughs for peace, appointing his callow son-in-law Jared Kushner as an envoy to the Middle East. Having worked successfully behind the scenes with all parties to deliver NAFTA and criminal-justice reform, Kushner cut off aid to Palestinian refugees and moved the US Embassy to Jerusalem. Eventually, Israel agreed to suspend annexation in areas of the West Bank as part of a peace deal with the United Arab Emirates, but in alienating Palestinians, it was questionable whether Kushner had had any success in this position.[523]

On Afghanistan, Trump insisted on talking to enlisted soldiers about how the war was proceeding.[524] Afterwards, he told his generals that the soldiers on the ground could do a better job than them. "I don't know what the hell we're doing," he told an aide. "It's a disaster there. It's never going to be a functioning democracy. We ought to just exit completely."[525] He asked Rex Tillerson: "How many more deaths?"[526] No one could give him a straight answer as to how America was going to win.

The invasion of Iraq by the Bush Administration had led to Iran gaining influence among Shiite militias fighting ISIS in Iraq and Syria. While other powers were willing to give Iran latitude so long as they honoured the terms of the Nuclear Accord, Trump was determined to marginalise them. At the same time, Trump was criticised by one of his most hawkish advisors, John Bolton, for refusing to retaliate after a US drone was destroyed, because it would lead to "too many bodybags".

A warning of "fire and fury" to the "Rocket Man" of North Korea was followed by a tentative rapprochement, amidst hopes that the threat of nuclear war on the Korean peninsula could be averted.[527] US Intelligence officials testified that Kim Jong-un had continued to develop his nuclear arsenal in secret after their meeting in Singapore.

Trump railed against Chinese companies like Huawei, which had long been accused of stealing intellectual property from US businesses, and made public his determination to exclude them from vital US technology infrastructure in the future.

Not everyone agreed with President Trump that his aims were either right or realistic, but he had widespread support as he called on other world leaders to shoulder their fair share of the burden of maintaining peace. And then he fired James Comey.

"There Is No Chaos, Only Great Energy!"

Both Reince Priebus and Steve Bannon counselled against firing the Director of the FBI, who was then leading the investigation into Russian attempts to influence the election. It was clear that leading members of the Trump campaign, including his son Donald Junior, son-in-law Jared Kushner, and then campaign chief Paul Manafort, had met with a Russian lawyer, Natalia Veselnitskaya, and a lobbyist and former Soviet counter-intelligence officer, Rinat Akhmetshin. Donald Senior had even joked on national television about Russia hacking Hillary Clinton's missing emails.[528] On *The Late Show with Stephen Colbert*, he said: "Russia, if you're listening, I hope you're able to find the thirty thousand emails that are missing."

Trump frequently spoke impulsively, then forgot what he had said. Some who have worked with him said that it was like dealing with a spoilt child. In his book *Fire and Fury*, Michael Wolff wrote that Priebus and Bannon sought to postpone a decision on firing James Comey, since "delay worked advantageously with Trump's attention span".

Tony Schwartz, the ghostwriter of Trump's book, *The Art of the Deal*, said that he "has the attention span of a nine-year-old with ADHD". Matt Taibbi said that Trump "embraces and discards ideas at light speed". As President, he displayed an aversion to wonkish policy detail. He didn't read briefs. Officials thought he might be dyslexic – a common trait among people with Attention Deficit Hyperactivity Disorder, which is linked to dopamine deficiencies which impact the executive function of the brain.

One of the defining characteristics of people diagnosed with ADHD is that they live in the moment. Yesterday is ancient history. Tomorrow is too far away to worry about right now. People with ADHD tend to be drawn to creative pursuits rather than humdrum routine. At their best, they demonstrate tremendous energy and enthusiasm.

They often make terrific salesmen, even as their tendency to over-promise stretches the people around them to deliver. With brains revving at high speed, they rarely stay on message for long before something else occurs to them. It may be no coincidence that Candidate Trump demonstrated extraordinary energy, holding almost twice as many campaign rallies as Hillary Clinton.

But when your mind is working at high speed, it can be impossible to apply the brakes. ADHD is also associated with difficulty in regulating impulses. You say or tweet the first thing that's on your mind, without thinking about whether it's appropriate or true. It could be boasting about the allure of your star status, a journalist bleeding from "wherever", or that you saw thousands of people in Jersey City on 9/11 celebrating the fall of the Twin Towers.

Once you shoot your mouth off, you will bury yourself in absurd bluster and never admit to an embarrassing mistake, which could leave you even more humiliated. Like when a reporter you know on a first-name basis calls you out on the veracity of your statements, and you pretend you don't know what he looks like, even as you mimic his disability.

People with ADHD are often underestimated and misunderstood.

People mis-read their attention deficit as an *intelligence* deficit. According to Michael Wolff, President Trump was called "an idiot" by Secretary of the Treasury Steve Mnuchin and Chief of Staff Reince Priebus, "a dope" by National Security Advisor H. R. McMaster, "dumb as shit" by Chief Economic Advisor Gary Cohn, and "a fucking moron" by Secretary of State Rex Tillerson.[529] Former Deputy White House Chief of Staff Katie Walsh said that President Trump could be "demanding and petulant", and that getting a steer from him was "like trying to figure out what a child wants".

Despite issues with detail, people with ADHD can be principled, thoughtful and strategic, and they can often hyper-focus on topics they find fascinating. Their ability to follow through on their ideas with consistency can be missed in the radio chatter about outré comments.

Many disagreed with President Trump's protectionist instincts, but he had criticised the North American Free Trade Agreement for decades, publishing a book entitled *The America We Deserve* at the turn of the century. Since then, 5 million American manufacturing jobs have been lost, mostly to automation, and the number of illegal immigrants has risen to more than 11 million people.

Trump was championed by the Right, but part of his appeal was that he was a populist, not an ideologue. Following the murder of seventeen people in a mass shooting at a Florida High School, Trump suggested arming teachers who fire weapons "out of love", before making a 180-degree pivot in favour of gun control that the NRA called "bad policy".

Republican Senator Ben Sasse issued a statement: "We're not ditching any constitutional protections simply because the last person the President talked to today doesn't like them." Neither her enemies nor her allies knew what American policy would be from one day to the next.

Despite their confident demeanour, people with undiagnosed ADHD are often acutely sensitive about their shortcomings, and suffer from low self-esteem. They also find it hard not to take things personally.

Trump was vindictive towards those he deemed disloyal. Journalist Mika Brzezinski, a former Trump favourite, was once heard on audio asking if it would be OK to ask Trump a tough question on deportation. As she and her co-anchor on *The Morning Joe* show became more critical of the President, he tweeted that "low-IQ crazy Mika" had been "bleeding badly from a facelift" when he saw her on New Year's Eve.[530]

Having learnt from a TV news bulletin that he had been fired, as he visited a field office in Los Angeles, James Comey asked Andrew McCabe, the new acting Director of the FBI, if he could hitch a ride home to Washington DC. Trump chewed out McCabe, whose wife had just run for office as a Democrat, saying that McCabe should ask his wife "how it feels to be a loser". McCabe was subsequently fired.

The Trump Administration felt like a rerun of *The Apprentice*, with a new person being fired or resigning almost every week. In addition to the Director and Deputy Director of the FBI, in a little over a year in office President Trump lost four White House Communications Directors (including Sean Spicer and Anthony "The Mooch" Scaramucci), two National Security Advisors, a Homeland Security Advisor, a Chief of Staff, a Deputy Chief of Staff, a Secretary of State and a Chief Economic Advisor.

Following the resignation of Gary Cohn, the President tweeted: "The new Fake News narrative is that there is CHAOS in the White House. Wrong! People will always come & go, and I want strong dialogue before making a final decision. I still have some people that I want to change (always seeking perfection). There is no Chaos, only great Energy!"

His opponents doubled down on his unpresidential demeanor, calling him out for his bombastic and effusive praise of rogue dictator Kim Jong-un in the middle of negotiations to end Jong-un's nuclear-weapons programme, for planning to invite the Taliban to Camp David near the anniversary of 9/11, for cancelling a state visit to Denmark because they refused to sell Greenland to the United States, and for claiming, incorrectly, that Alabama was in the path of a hurricane. The general public was overwhelmed by the tsunami of criticism levelled at the President. It became hard for some to separate the wheat from the chaff.

CNN journalists had to resign after a story linking Anthony Scaramucci to the Russian Direct Investment Fund was found to be untrue. Trump lambasted the "fake-news" agenda of the media, but craved a legacy which would be admired by his critics.[531] "He just wants to be liked," according to Katie Walsh, the former White House Deputy Chief of Staff.[532]

When Trump was campaigning for the presidency, the columnist Salena Zito asked him if there was any question that he wished journalists would ask him. He laughed and said: "Honestly, at this stage, I think they've asked them all." He paused, then said quietly: "You know, I consider myself to be a nice person. And I am not sure they ever like to talk about that."

As the House of Representatives investigated whether military aid had been used to put pressure on the Ukrainian government to open an investigation into Joe Biden's son, they heard powerful testimony from the former US Ambassador to the Ukraine. Trump became the third President in history to face impeachment. Despite the moral courage of Mitt Romney, it was a foregone conclusion that the Republican-controlled Senate would not convict him. House Democrats argued that abuse of power by the Executive had to be brought to light regardless, but they were not addressing the fear and anxiety which had led to Trump's election in the first place.

The ability of a sitting President to act unilaterally is finite, corralled by the checks and balances of the US Constitution, but as polling day 2020 dawned, hyperbole crescendoed, with one journalist describing it as "arguably the most consequential election in the country's history" – leaving Washington, Jackson, FDR and Lincoln, whose victory in 1860 triggered secession, civil war and the end of slavery, to vie for second place.[533]

Those who saw the Trump era as an extended horror-show were in for one last jump-scare on election night, as it emerged that he had improved on his 2016 results across multiple demographics, including Latino voters in Miami. On Betfair, the UK betting exchange, nearly half a billion pounds was wagered on polling day as Trump's odds swung from 2-1 against to 5-1 on, before drifting out again as mail-in votes helped swing the election for Biden in one of the most tightly contested races in US history.

Those hoping for a peaceful and dignified transition of power were disappointed. President Trump declared victory while accusing Democrats of voter-fraud, and publicly attacking Republican officials in Georgia who could not give him the votes he needed. After being addressed by Trump at a rally, some of his supporters, along with a policeman, were killed while storming the Houses of Congress as they debated the ratification of the election results. President Trump was banned from Twitter, Facebook and Instagram. Former Republican President George W. Bush issued a statement that read: "This is how election results are disputed in a banana republic – not our democratic republic. I am appalled by the reckless behaviour of some political leaders since the election." White House officials resigned in protest amid talk of invoking the Twenty-fifth Amendment to declare President Trump unfit to discharge the powers and duties of his office. Trump would become the only person in history to be impeached twice.

Joe Biden would soon face the daunting task of bringing America together again, but the polarisation, deadlock and division that racked the country had preceded the election of his predecessor. Biden had always forged friendships across the political aisle in the Senate, but as he said: "Hate never goes away. It only hides."

Healing the divisions in the United States was never going to be a simple matter of impeaching Trump or electing Biden. As he scrambled to deal with Covid-19, The Donald's ratings might have sprung a leak, but the ship sailed on. Well into his term of office, nearly nine out of ten Republicans approved of him, but his political opponents still didn't *get* why they liked President Trump.

The barber in New York who used to cut his hair said that he talked to everyone, from billionaire to shoe-shine boy. He wasn't always successful – he went through bankruptcies – but he always had a charisma about him.

Michael Wolff told a story of Donald Trump trying to persuade an acquaintance and his girlfriend – a fashion model – to stop over at his casinos in Atlantic City. His friend demurred, saying that the place was full of white trash.

The model didn't understand what the phrase "white trash" meant. Donald answered: "They're people like me, only poorer."

Chapter Nine

The Lies We Tell Ourselves Today

"The good ended happily, and the bad unhappily. That is what Fiction means."

OSCAR WILDE

So maybe you were never the biggest fan of President Trump. At some point, you stopped arguing and started venting. Your mind was made up. Those who voted for him had to be either stupid or venal, or both. Why invest effort in understanding their point of view when snarkiness was keeping you sane?

For a species which invests a great deal of cognitive effort to persuade ourselves that we're great, we certainly have no shortage of moral outrage. It's just that our ire is generally, if not always, reserved for "them" rather than "us". Examining our own confirmation-bias is hard, but dissing the bad guys on social media offers a cheap moral high.

Where patriotism is concerned, having a nuanced mix of pride and regret in our past is harder than basking in the warm glow of half-remembered legends. In the UK, a rose-tinted view of the days when Britannia ruled the waves has persisted long after the heroic derring-do of the Royal Navy. Many think of Britain as a reluctant conqueror. "It is not in our custom," Queen Victoria wrote, "to annex countries, unless we are obliged and forced to do so."

There is much that is great in British history. The so-called Victorian age was an era of reform which saw the end of slavery, the expansion of democracy and the series of innovations which sparked the Industrial Revolution. The word for train station in Russian, *vokzal*, was coined after a Russian delegation inspected British railway ingenuity at Vauxhall in London.

But at its zenith, the British Empire fought two wars with China to force them to maintain the opium market, seizing Hong Kong as a bonus. A laissez-faire ideology saw the British imperialist elite preside over some of the worst famines in history, in India and Ireland. Politicians who funded the West Africa Squadron to end the slave trade also backed the slave-owning Confederacy which supplied the material for British cotton mills.

In 1865, the end of the American Civil War saw 10 percent of the African continent under European control. By 1910, this had risen to 90 percent, thanks to a combination of new anti-malaria drugs and the adoption of new industrial technologies.[534] Sir Roger Casement was knighted for bringing human rights abuses to light in the Belgian Congo, where up to half the population, or 8 million people, may have died, before being outed as gay and hanged for treason for his role in trying to secure Irish independence.[535]

The desire to impose straight imperial lines on crooked ethnic boundaries led Britain to project force around the globe, including the first use of chemical weapons in Iraq a century ago. Despite this legacy, in 2014 (prior to Brexit) a YouGov survey found that Britons who are proud of the Empire outnumber those who are ashamed of it by a ratio of three to one. Thirty-four percent of the people surveyed wished that the Empire still existed.

Fear of Foreigners

In the toxic miasma swirling around Brexit, it is easy to lose sight of the decent and honourable motivations on both sides. Passion blinds opponents to alternative points of view. Perspectives are dismissed because of the labels we attach to "them", rather than listening to what "they" have to say.

There are good reasons why people voted to "take back control" from the European Union, including the lack of direct democratic accountability within the Commission, the loss of national sovereignty to a nascent political super-state, the inability to exert complete control over immigration, and the bloated inefficiency of EU bureaucracy.

But Brexit also saw the rise of populist rhetoric about vassaldom and surrender, with a Government which abided by international law, except when they repudiated freshly signed treaties "in very specific and limited ways". A tabloid newspaper which had supported "taking back control" ran mugshots of British judges in a front-page rogues' gallery, under the headline "ENEMIES OF THE PEOPLE", because they had had the temerity to rule that the uncodified British constitution meant that Parliament was sovereign over the Executive in Brexit negotiations. This headline produced a chilling effect on the separation of powers that was more Orwell than Ibsen.

Fears of an influx of Muslim refugees influenced the outcome of the referendum. These fears had similar roots to the fears regarding the impact Polish migrants to Britain would have on the country after Poland joined the European Union in 2004. Decades before, immigrants were welcomed to British boarding-houses by classified ads that read "No Blacks, No Dogs, No Irish". Often, as in the New York Draft Riots, those fresh off the boat, or the plantation, are pilloried by other poor migrants who fear that "they" will undercut "us" for work. At one time or another in the English-speaking world, "they" included Muslims, Mexicans, Slavs, Africans, Chinese, Italians, Irish, Indians, Jews, Native Americans, Latvians, Lithuanians, Estonians, Romanians, Bulgarians, Germans and even Scots.

Fears of an "effluxion of people from the Northern parts" led the English Parliament to reject the unification of England and Scotland in 1604. Donald Trump's ancestors were among the Scottish migrants who were expected to swarm over the border.

"We shall be over-run with them," one English Parliamentarian said in 1606, "as cattle pent up by a slight hedge will over it into a better soil, and a tree taken from a barren place will thrive to excessive and exuberant branches in a better."[536] Although England and Scotland were both ruled by the same monarch after 1604, the Act of Union between them which formed the Kingdom of Great Britain would not take place for another hundred years.[537]

In recent times, it should not have come as a surprise that tensions over immigration rise during an era of austerity, especially as there have been profound demographic shifts over the last few decades. The proportion of foreign-born residents in the US more than trebled between 1970 and 2015, from one in twenty to one in six.[538]

America is tangibly more diverse than it was just a few decades ago. In 1970, six out of ten foreign-born residents were European, compared with just over one in ten today. The numbers of Asian-Americans grew from 1.3 million in 1965 to 18 million in 2015, and Hispanic-Americans grew from 8 million to nearly 57 million people in the same period.

The McKinsey Global Institute has shown that the economic impact of immigration has been positive, but people do not trust experts who bail out banks and ignore their hardship, so long as the S&P 500 rises.[539] In the UK and the US, reasonable concerns about sustainable levels of immigration, especially among the poorest members of society, were not adequately addressed.

Without income redistribution, what is good for the top 1 percent may not be so good for jobs, wage rates or affordable housing in lower percentiles. In the face of economic uncertainty, abstract intangibles like globalisation and automation are harder to pin down and scapegoat than "them next door".

At the same time as economic migrants from the southern states and abroad poured into the northern inner cities of the United States, effective law-enforcement declined. Homicide rates doubled from 1960 to 1980, triggering a change in attitudes to the right to bear arms. Science fiction painted a dystopian future where the legitimacy of the state monopoly on force was questioned, and no one knew who the good guys were. In the absence of objective policing, men took the law into their own hands.

But things are improving. From the nadir of the early 1980s, homicide rates in the United States halved in the 1990s and 2000s, as did the figures for rape, assault, robbery, abortion, teen pregnancy, divorce, sexually transmitted diseases and hate-crimes.[540]

From being a no-go area, New York is now one of the safest cities in America, with tourists and locals alike walking through Central Park at night safely. A more diverse America is also a more socially cohesive America in many ways.

Despite the reflexive frustration which led to Brexit and Trump, the prospects for peace and prosperity have never been better. As Steven Pinker wrote in *The Better Angels of Our Nature*, there has been a huge drop in international warfare from the latter half of the twentieth century, and annual deaths in battle have fallen by 90 percent.[541]

The risk of nuclear Armageddon has reduced the chances of all-out war between the Great Powers. The end of the Cold War paid a peace dividend, as superpowers curtailed the financing of proxy wars and sanctioned UN peacekeepers, reducing the recurrence of warfare by up to 80 percent, according to Virginia Page Fortna.[542]

Global interdependence has risen, along with a 140 percent uplift in trade as a proportion of GDP over the past fifty years.[543] The fall of the Berlin Wall coincided with the point where democratic states outnumbered autocracies for the first time. Now democracies outstrip autocracies by four to one.[544] The spread of democracy has defused political, economic and social crises through the peaceful transition of power.

An eleven-year-old ascending to the throne of Castile can no longer cause pogroms which force hundreds of thousands of Jews to convert to Christianity.[545] A ten-year-old head of state in France can no longer trigger a civil war between rival factions. Throwing a henchman out of a window, or assassinating an archduke, can no longer lead to millions of people being slaughtered in a conflict among major European powers.[546] The strategic benefits of coercing princesses into arranged marriages were lost in the ashes of ther First World War, when tens of millions died despite the fact that Queen Victoria's grandsons sat on the thrones of Germany, Russia and the United Kingdom.

Access to education and freedom of expression have allowed empirical insights to debunk myths which led to persecution. Even the Gestapo were embarrassed by having to investigate whether a Jewish farmer had poisoned a well, and they may have apologised to a Jewish suspect named Blumenthal in a blood-libel.[547]

The rule of law in liberal democracies protects human rights. So long as judges and juries are well fed, the monopoly of the State on justice reduces confirmation-bias, lowering the risk that people will take the law into their own hands or consent to the persecution of others by lynch-mobs.

Communism has not triumphed across the globe, and even notionally communist states like China and Vietnam have given way to private enterprise and a market economy. In western democracies, universal suffrage accelerated reforms.

Many of the demands made in *The Communist Manifesto*, such as investment in public education and the use of progressive income tax to provide a safety net, have become commonplace. At just under seventy-seven years, the life-expectancy for a child born in the poorest decile in the UK in 2013 is nearly double the average life-expectancy at the time *The Communist Manifesto* was written.[548]

As ideological barriers dissolved, more than a billion people have been lifted out of poverty. News outlets could have run the prosaically benign headline "137,000 Escape Poverty Today" every day for the past twenty years. It is no surprise that scandal-hungry media seek out dramatic copy about doom and gloom, but this creates a distorted picture of reality. If the truth doesn't bleed, the Fourth Estate has a tendency to bury the lead.

So if life is better than ever, why do people in the richest societies feel so pessimistic?

How the Absence of Hope Leads to Fear

Marx's insight into the cyclical nature of capitalist economies remains highly relevant following the global financial meltdown of 2008, as we over-invest in times of general confidence and over-correct when boom turns to bust.[549]

Intervention by the federal government may have prevented economic disaster on a scale similar to the Great Depression, but Thomas Piketty's *Capital in the Twenty-First Century* has shown that the American Dream is fraying at the seams.[550] Piketty's book charts the rising wealth of the top 1 percent in the United States in recent decades, and argues that without state action, inequality will continue to rise and growth will be depressed.

It has been estimated that 5 million US manufacturing jobs have been lost since the turn of the century. Parents working multiple shifts to make ends meet are struggling to build a better life for their kids. Poor education acts as a brake on social mobility.

Living standards for a large cohort in the United States have stagnated for decades. Mechanisation of traditional blue-collar jobs in the Rust Belt has meant a loss of income, status and self-esteem, and alienation from the affluent elites on the East and West Coasts.

The gap in life-expectancy between black and white America has narrowed, not so much because black America is living longer, but because white America is dying younger. Life expectancy has fallen among poor white high school drop-outs due to poor diet, as well as drug and alcohol abuse in the opioid epidemic.

There are no easy solutions. Piketty was criticised for focusing on wealth and incomes rather than living standards or social mobility. His theoretical remedies have also been disputed, with libertarians arguing that squeezing the rich – including a 2 percent wealth tax and an 80 percent income tax – is an apology for state coercion.

As white America slowly becomes a minority, two thirds of blue-collar white people believe "that discrimination against whites is as big a problem today as discrimination against blacks and other minorities". Twenty-nine percent of black Americans agree with them.[551]

White America may stay relatively affluent, but psychology experiments show that we fear losses more than we value gains. Losing ten dollars reduces happiness by twice as much as a ten-dollar windfall increases it.[552]

In surveys, less than one in four white Americans believe that their children will be better off than they were, compared to nearly half of African-Americans and more than six out of ten Latinos. When wages are flat and your kids face a harder life than you did, your well-being is compromised. Relative prosperity means little without faith in the future, but in the absence of faith, people will respond to fear.

A Polarised America

Commentators argue that the polarisation of America between affluent coastal "blue" states and stagnant heartland "red" states is a gross over-simplification, with urban and suburban divisions being more significant, but if white America had opted for Hillary Clinton in the same proportions as Black, Hispanic, Asian or LGBTQ America did, she would have won with more than 70 percent of the vote.

Electoral-college winner-takes-all arithmetic encourages pundits to see life through a red or blue lens, but the most worrying trend is the physical and virtual isolation of "red" and "blue" America. In 1976, just over one in four people lived in counties where either the Republican or Democratic nominee for President had a majority of 20 percent or more. Forty years later, more than six out of ten people live in "landslide counties". Gerrymandering has reduced the number of competitive electoral districts.

Americans receive more election news from social media (27 percent) than cable television (23 percent), local papers (21 percent) or national papers (11 to 17 percent), with the under-fifties twice as likely to read a national paper in print or online for election news as the over-fifties. With social media curating news-feeds to pander to our prejudices, more and more people are living in an echo-chamber, partly of their own making, where dissenting voices are not heard.

In a 2017 survey by Pew Research, 55 percent of Republicans said that they had few or no close friends who were Democrats. Among Democrats, 65 percent said that they had few or no close friends who were Republicans.

The alienation of working-class white America was already well under way prior to the banking crisis. The success of Trumpism was foreshadowed in the derailing of John Kerry's bid for the presidency twelve years before. When Kerry's wife and prospective First Lady, the heiress Teresa Heinz, was traduced for being "kinda French-looking", her withering response was to question whether her critics could even speak French. It's fair to say that her blow fell short, and a populist perception of an out-of-touch elite resonated.

Intriguingly, that out-of-touch elite includes left-leaning liberals as much as it did the right-wing bankers and speculators who were blamed for the crash. As a study carried out by the City University of New York has shown, the Occupy Wall Street movement was not their first rodeo for many activists. At one demo, one in four protestors were undergraduates, while most of the remaining protesters held more than one college degree. They were far more likely to have an income in excess of $75,000 than the general public, and nearly half of them had already participated in more than thirty other protests before the Occupy campaign. The irony of the top 1 percent chanting about kicking the ass out of the ruling class without any obvious sense of privilege was not lost on those they claimed to represent.

The working poor pull down too many jobs to join clubs or political demonstrations. They are more likely to serve their country in the police or armed forces, and they are used to seeing their honour-codes, like God, corps and country, mocked by those whose lives they are pledged to protect with their own.

The hauteur of the elite enables cosmopolitans to excoriate "them" for not being "us" as they fly over Middle America. In her book *Political Tribes*, Amy Chua quotes a scathing *National Review* op-ed from March 2016. Kevin Williamson lambasted the nascar-loving white working class for "drug and alcohol addiction . . . the whelping of human children with all the respect and wisdom of a stray dog . . . the incomprehensible malice . . . of poor white America . . . . The truth about these dysfunctional, downscale communities is that they deserve to die."

The mainstream "legacy" newspapers split 57-to-2 in their endorsements of Hillary over Donald, but in a campaign where over 60 percent of her advertising was negative, antipathy to Hillary Clinton was growing.

During the election, Hillary Clinton described Trump supporters as coming from a "basket of deplorables . . . racist, sexist, homophobic, xenophobic, Islamophobic". A study of television advertising found that Hillary spent twice as much as Trump overall, and was far more negative and personal.[553]

The antagonism was mutual. Fifty-three percent of Trump voters opted negatively for him because of their dislike for Hillary, with only 44 percent voting positively because they liked Trump. Based on exit polls, negative voting was three times higher among Republicans and twice as high among Democrats, compared to earlier elections.

Speaking in Mumbai long after her defeat, Hillary characterised her support-base as "optimistic, diverse, dynamic, moving forward . . . his whole campaign was looking backward". Married white women voted for Trump due to "ongoing pressure to vote the way that your husband, your boss, your son, whoever, believes you should". Her rationale for losing the votes of white women was tenuous, given the existence of the secret ballot.

*

The bipartisan spirit that sustained America throughout the Cold War seems a distant memory. According to the 2017 Pew Research survey, 45 percent of Republicans and 44 percent of Democrats hold very unfavourable opinions about the other party, compared to 17 percent and 16 percent respectively in 1994.

A deadlocked Congress cannot agree on how to change for the better. The Culture Wars apparently divide Americans on everything from the effectiveness of initiatives to tackle climate-change to the right to bear arms and the right to choose when it comes to abortion.

In an era of profound distrust, politicians are accused of using coded language and euphemisms, ostensibly framing dilemmas in moderate terms for a wider audience, when, rather like a dog-whistle, their words contain a higher-pitched message for the ears of their base.

The Obama campaign ran an ad in Ohio stating that Mitt Romney, who is a Mormon, was not "one of us". Politicians who, playing on racial prejudice, might once have spoken of "states' right", might speak of food-stamps and "welfare queens" today. We all interpret evidence selectively in a way which reinforces our beliefs and values, but the hard-fought battle for civil rights has been followed by a gradual acceptance of African-American rights, as well as women's rights, gay rights and children's rights. In the 2017 Pew Research survey, most Republicans agreed that homosexuality should be accepted in society, that religion should be kept separate from government policies, and that affirmative-action programs designed to increase the number of black and minority students on campus are a good thing.

After President Obama was elected, the number of Republicans who identified discrimination as the main reason why black people cannot get ahead collapsed, but even this indicator rallied by 40 percent between 2014 and 2017. Forty-two percent of Republicans said that immigrants strengthen the country because of their hard work and talents, up from 29 percent in 2010. Pro-immigrant sentiment among Republicans in 2017 was more than 30 percent stronger than it had been among Democrats in 1994.

What is clear is that the sharp increase in isolation and antipathy between Republicans and Democrats lends air-cover to obnoxious policies, like separating migrant children from their parents, that do not reflect the views of the silent majority. Conservatives are more tolerant of difference today than liberals were just a few decades ago.

Perhaps the biggest lie of all is that the so-called Culture Wars, on climate-change, gun-control and abortion rights, have left America irretrievably divided. We used to believe that differences of opinion in an open society should be respected, even cherished. So how do we break out of the cycle of dog-whistle politics?

Acknowledging Our Biases

The ability to manipulate evidence effectively to support confirmation-bias is strongly linked to higher intelligence. In experiments run by Dan Kahan of Yale Law School, highly educated subjects who displayed the greatest competence in analysing data on neutral topics were more likely to skew data in line with their existing beliefs on issues like climate-change and gun-control.

The smarter, or at least the more educated, we are, the more adept we are at using data to justify foregone conclusions. Smart people come up with smarter excuses.[554] We dismiss evidence to the contrary rather than considering alternatives fairly and objectively. Passionate idealism is blind to facts which conflict with our values.

Terrorists muster confirmation-bias to commit horrific atrocities in response to what they see as legitimate grievances. Khalid Shaikh Mohammad wrote to President Obama from Guantánamo Bay, saying that the razing of the Twin Towers was a "natural reaction" to US foreign policy.[555] Amedy Coulibaly, who killed four Jewish customers at a kosher supermarket in Paris, told his hostages that he was defending Muslims (especially Palestinians) and avenging Syrian attacks on ISIS and Western military operations in Mali, Iraq and Afghanistan.[556]

The selective use of evidence to reinforce our own beliefs and values is not limited to terrorists. Psychologists have shown that identical policies are viewed very differently if the subject believes them to be Republican or Democratic recommendations, and to approve or disapprove based on their own pre-existing partisan affiliation.[557]

Once we tell ourselves a good, strong lie, it is hard to acknowledge the inconvenient truth. In an experiment run by Thomas Asch in 1951, participants had to judge which lines on a card were the same length. On average, three out of four subjects gave a blatantly wrong answer if six actors in the room had repeated the same thing.[558] How can we trust our judgement when when we are bedevilled by cognitive-biases which rely on proximity, peer pressure, and sensory cues?

Ninety-two percent of Democrats believe that there is solid evidence that the average temperature on Earth has been getting warmer. This compares to the 52 percent of Republicans who are more likely to say that not enough is known about whether warming is a result of human activity.

No one has a monopoly on truth or wisdom. Many of us scorn those who express skepticism about the impact of humans on global warming, or our ability to reverse the process, without looking at the detailed scientific evidence for ourselves.

As early as 1983, the Environmental Protection Agency stated that global warming was a "threat whose effects will be felt within a few years", possibly with "catastrophic" results. Reputable estimates by the Intergovernmental Panel on Climate Change show a range of possible increases in global surface temperatures, from 0.3 degrees Celsius to 4.8 degrees Celsius over the next eighty years, depending, among other things, on the level of future global CO_2 emissions.

The Paris Climate Change Accord aims to keep global warming below 2 degrees Celsius, and preferably below 1.5 degrees Celsius, by the end of the century. It has no policing mechanism and no binding targets. No major industrialised nation has met its objectives to reduce CO_2 emissions, and Developing Nations have been allowed to increase CO_2 emissions as they play catch-up with the West.

Research suggests that even if all current proposals are implemented, this will not stop global warming. By 2050, temperatures are likely to rise by more than 3 degrees Celsius. It is reasonable to ask why coal-miners in the Rust Belt should be laid off in order for the United States to meet its objectives, while other nations continue to pollute, under a programme that will not achieve the required outcome anyway.[559]

We might like to think that we are open to being open-minded, but none of us wants to challenge our deeply cherished beliefs and values. The number of Republicans who believe that stricter environmental laws are worth the cost entailed, has fallen from 58 percent in 2010 to 36 percent in 2017, compared to 77 percent of Democrats.

If we are asking people to take painful cuts to their livelihoods, at the very least they should feel confident that their sacrifice will make a difference, and that other nations are doing their fair share. The combination of political will and scientific insight can make a real difference. After a global ban on CfCs in aerosols and refrigerators in the 1990s, the depletion of atmospheric ozone was rapidly repaired.

Letting the Truth Get in the Way of a Good Story

Better gun-control is not a Red-versus-Blue issue. According to a survey from the Pew Research Center, banning the mentally ill and those on no-fly lists from owning guns has bi-partisan support from more than eight out of ten citizens. Republicans as well as Democrats favour stronger background checks, and Democrats as well as Republicans support the right to bear arms.

No one knows how many guns are legally held by Americans, but it is more than in any other country. Estimates range from 265 million to over 400 million weapons – nearly twice as many per head as Yemen, in second place, and more than three times as many per head as Iraq, according to a 2011 small-arms survey. Roughly half of that total are possessed by just 3 percent of adults, who own seventeen weapons each on average.

The proliferation of weapons has led to profound differences with other Developed countries. Nearly two-thirds of all homicides in the United States in 2016 were gun-related, compared to less than one in twenty in England and Wales. These homicides are heavily concentrated in poorer areas, with 25 percent occurring in neighborhoods which contain just 1.5 percent of the population. Americans are twenty-five times more likely to be killed in a gun homicide than citizens of other Developed countries, but residents in high-risk neighbourhoods are four hundred times more likely to be killed, mostly by handguns.

America has always been an outlier when it comes to gun-ownership, with the right to bear arms as part of a well-regulated citizen militia guaranteed by the Bill of Rights. Commentators talk of a frontier spirit which saw vigilante justice meted out in the Wild West, but until the 1960s most Americans were in favour of banning handguns, according to Gallup.[560]

In 1967, the numbers opposed to banning handguns exceeded those in favour of a ban for the first time. The following year, the moderate leadership of the National Rifle Association was ousted after their endorsement of the 1968 Gun Control Act. The NRA morphed from an association for training hunters into a powerful lobby-group.

It is no coincidence that this change in attitudes tracked the spiralling homicide rate, which doubled between 1960 and 1980. The NRA lobbied for gun rights under the banner of self-defence. Advertisements in the 1970s depicted home-intruders being confronted by gun-owners.

This fear of violent crime continues, despite the fact that homicide rates have halved, approaching levels not seen since the 1950s. The Centers for Disease Control estimates that there were 33,594 gun-deaths in 2014. Of these, 21,386 were suicides. Homicides accounted for less than one-third of the total. Americans are nearly twice as likely to kill themselves with their own guns than to be a victim of gun homicide.

Despite this, roughly three million Americans carry concealed weapons in self-defence on a daily basis, and nine million carry concealed weapons every month. Following the mass shootings at Sandy Hook Elementary School in Connecticut and Parkland High in Florida, two-thirds of Republicans supported teachers and officials being permitted to carry guns in schools, versus one in four Democrats.

Paradoxically, for many people the best way to combat mass shootings is to put more guns in the right hands. Support for gun-rights among young adults doubled between 2000 and 2016, briefly exceeding half of eighteen- to twenty-nine-year-olds, before the Orlando attack on a gay nightclub, which saw a dramatic and sustained decline in support for gun-ownership.

The hundreds of millions of guns held by ordinary Americans will not be mothballed any time soon. Two-thirds of people live in gun-free households, but few of them want to remove weapons from the cold, dead hands of hunting enthusiasts. Apocalyptic hype has to be challenged. Background checks are not a slippery slope to the destruction of the Second Amendment.

What Unites as Well as Divides

People fundamentally disagree on how the right to choose should be weighed against the right to life of the foetus. In Gallup surveys, roughly one in four are pro-choice in almost all circumstances, and a little over one in five are pro-life except where the life of the mother is in danger.[561]

A foetus is not a blank slate. Her unique DNA, inherited at conception, influences adult height, weight, musculature, colouring, gender and physiognomy, as well as intellectual potential, personality, and predisposition to certain diseases. The instinct to walk and talk is hard-wired by nature, as is a rudimentary moral sense.[562] In healthy pregnancies, the difference between "them" and "us" is simply a matter of time.

Ethicists do not agree on a stage of foetal development where the right to life of unique human beings outweighs the right to choose, whether after identical twins separate in the blastocyst stage, or after the first heartbeat at four weeks, the first brainwaves at eight weeks, the development of the brain and central nervous system at twelve weeks, the development of hearing at eighteen weeks, or the stirrings of consciousness at week twenty-six, when neurons reverberate between the thalamus and cerebral cortex – a few weeks after foetal humans can start to become independently viable.[563]

Pro-life groups have tried to engage our sensory moral mode to increase our empathy for pre-natal human beings, hoping that being able to see and hear the unborn during ultra-sound scans will light up the ventromedial prefrontal cortex. Kellyanne Conway, the spokesperson and pollster for Donald Trump's presidential campaign, told the 2017 March for Life that science had led "Americans to rethink just how fragile and how triumphant human life truly is . . . . Look at a sonogram".[564]

Philosophers have tried to abstract the ethics from the emotions by framing them in other ways, most famously Judith Jarvis Thomson.[565] Thomson imagines a woman being kidnapped while unconscious by a fanatical group of music-lovers, who wakes up to discover that her kidneys are being used to keep a famous violinist alive. In surveys, the public agree that offering life-support for nine months would be praiseworthy, but not obligatory.

Critics have argued that the scenario is analogous to rape rather than consensual sex. Changing the story so that the woman consents to life-support and changes her mind, prompted a majority in one online survey to agree that she is obliged to continue.[566]

Abortion on request is available to the end of week twelve across much of the European Union, including France and Germany. In Italy, the limit is ninety days. In Finland and the United Kingdom, the limit is twenty-four weeks. In the United States, it is limited by the viability of the foetus outside the womb.[567] Over nine out of ten terminations occur in the first trimester.[568]

This lack of consistency in legal codes is reflected in surveys which suggest that Americans favour a right to choose in some, but not all, circumstances, and they distinguish moral disapproval from legal prohibition. Most support the right to choose in cases of rape, incest and foetal abnormality, or if the life or health of the mother is at risk, but only 35 percent approve of termination on economic grounds, and a similar proportion supports the right to a termination after the first trimester.[569] [570]

There may always be disagreement, but we need to recognise what unites as well as divides. Feminists of all shades agree that more should be done to support women in crisis-pregnancies. A right to choose is spurious when single-parenthood condemns families to the poorest decile of society. A right to life in poverty, without affordable education and childcare, is a meagre aspiration for generations as yet unborn.[571]

We also need to look at those in the middle. In a recent survey, 39 percent said that they were neither pro-life nor pro-choice, or both. Many who are pro-life accept that the harm from forcing a woman to continue with a pregnancy can exceed the harm from termination in cases of rape, incest or fatal foetal abnormality. Many who champion the right to choose acknowledge that a pre-natal human being is more than just a cluster of cells, and should be treated with dignity and compassion.

Addressing the challenges of the Culture Wars requires leadership and solidarity from across the political spectrum. Prior to Covid-19, President Obama's administration had staved off the greatest economic crisis since the Great Depression, as well as introducing substantial healthcare reform, but the headwinds his administration faced never allowed it to live up to the potential of his rhetoric.

To bury the dog-whistle, we need the audacity of hope. As Obama said in his speech to the Democratic National Convention in 2004:

> There is not a liberal America and a conservative America: there is the United States of America. There is not a black America

and a white America and Latino America and Asian America: there's the United States of America.

The pundits like to slice-and-dice our country into Red States and Blue States . . . But I've got news for them, too: we worship an awesome God in the Blue States, and we don't like federal agents poking around in our libraries in the Red States. We coach Little League in the Blue States, and, yes, we've got some gay friends in the Red States.

Hope! Hope in the face of difficulty! Hope in the face of uncertainty! The audacity of hope! In the end, that is God's greatest gift to us, the bedrock of this nation. A belief in things not seen. A belief that there are better days ahead.

Yes we can.

Chapter Ten

Profiles in Kindness

"Without stories we would go mad. Life would lose its moorings or orientation. . . . Stories can conquer fear, you know. They can make the heart larger."

BEN OKRI

There is an old story: two men are being chased by a hungry lion. One says to the other: "Why are we trying to outrun him? He's faster than either of us." The other one pants: "I'm not trying to outrun him, I'm trying to outrun you!"

They say that the needs of the many outweigh the needs of the few, or the one, but if our hunter-gatherer ancestors had thrown each other to the lions, we would not have survived. Without the passion to stand and fight together, we would have died alone.

When I get into an argument, I have to remind myself that the more passionate I am, the more selectively I skew evidence in my favour. We all suffer from cognitive biases of which we are only dimly aware, but who wants a world without passion?[572]

Passion is what drives us to exceed expectations. Passion breaks the chains of human bondage, and tears down the walls of totalitarian states. Passion is our innate moral compass pointing us towards a better place. Passion is what compels us to speak up for others. It is crucial in making any sort of judgement at all.[573]

Less than one in three of us will spontaneously step up to help a person in distress if anyone else can rush in instead, but almost all of us are wired to be nice. We have the faculties we need to do good, and the potential to use our heads as well as our hearts in the pursuit of kindness. All it takes is a spark to light the flame.

Offering Practical Compassion

Médecins Sans Frontières, or Doctors Without Borders, was set up in 1971 to deliver emergency medical aid to those affected by conflict, epidemics, disasters, or exclusion from health care.[574]

In 1999, Médecins Sans Frontières won the Nobel Peace Prize in recognition of "the organisation's pioneering humanitarian work on several continents". By then, Doctors Without Borders had treated tens of millions of patients in more than eighty countries around the world.

Accepting the award, the President of the International Council of MSF, Doctor James Orbinski, used the occasion to condemn Russian violence under President Boris Yeltsin against civilians in Chechnya. Orbinski said this:

> Silence has long been confused with neutrality, and has been presented as a necessary condition for humanitarian action. From its beginning, MSF was created in opposition to this assumption . . . . We are not sure that words can always save lives, but we know that silence can certainly kill.[575]

Shining a Light in the Darkness

After George Zimmerman was acquitted in the shooting of seventeen-year-old unarmed Trayvon Martin in 2013, a community organiser named Alicia Garza wrote a Facebook post called "A Love Note to Black People". Her friend Patrisse Cullors responded: #BlackLivesMatter. With Opal Tometi, they ran an online campaign against police and vigilante assaults, as well as a series of demonstrations.

Within two years, "#BlackLivesMatter" had been tweeted over 30 million times. The supporters of the movement speak out in protest against police killings of black people, and broader issues such as racial profiling, police brutality, and racial inequality in the US criminal-justice system.

From the outset, #BlackLivesMatter was a movement rather than an organisation. It embraced those who were marginalised for reasons other than race, and many others all over the country.[576]

Anyone with mobile-phone footage of police brutality was a potential member, as Feidin Santana had of a white North Charleston police officer, Michael Slager, shooting an unarmed black man, Walter Scott, in the back. Scott had run away after a traffic-stop for a non-functioning brake-light led to him being tasered. Eight times. Will Smith later said: "Racism is not getting worse. It's getting filmed." #BlackLivesMatter stimulated a debate within the African-American community over attitudes to law enforcement, as well as the need to reduce intra-racial homicide.[577] It helped to empower seventeen-year-old Darnella Frazier to record the last moments of George Floyd.

By shining a spotlight on vigilante and police violence against African-Americans, #BlackLivesMatter has highlighted the work that still needs to be done. President Obama said: "there is a specific problem that is happening in the African-American community that's not happening in other communities . . . that is a legitimate issue that we have to address".

Letting Go of Fear

When she was eleven years old, Malala Yousafzai started a blog for the BBC Urdu website about what life was like in the Swat Valley in Pakistan, and her fear of going to school after the Taliban had destroyed dozens of schools and issued an edict banning all girls from attending school. Excerpts from her blog were published in local newspapers. A month later, boys' schools were re-opened, and the Taliban allowed girls to attend primary school. Malala criticised the Taliban on a national radio show, *Capital Talk*. Three days later, the local Taliban leader lifted the ban on girl's education, provided they wore burqas. Refugees fled the region as the Pakistani army moved in to eject the Taliban.

Malala continued to fight for women's education, lobbying US Ambassador Richard Holbrooke for help days after her twelfth birthday.[578] When she was fourteen, she was awarded Pakistan's National Peace Award for Youth, but the Taliban issued a death-threat against her. "Even if they come to kill me," she said, "I will tell them what they are trying to do is wrong, that education is our basic right."

Months later, a twenty-three-year-old graduate student boarded a school bus and shot Malala through the head, neck and shoulder; he also shot two of her friends. She was rushed to hospital and survived. Part of her skull had to be removed to allow for swelling, before being re-built with a cochlear ear implant, to allow her to hear again. She was fifteen years old.[579]

The Taliban claimed that they had to shoot her because she had been brainwashed by her father to use "dirty language" against them. Fifty Islamic scholars issued a fatwa against the Taliban, and the Sunni Ittehad Council denounced their justification of her attempted murder.

On her sixteenth birthday, Malala spoke at the United Nations General Assembly: "The terrorists thought they would change my aims and stop my ambitions, but nothing changed in my life except this: weakness, fear and hopelessness died. Strength, power and courage was born."

She met President Barack Obama later that year, and took the opportunity to warn him that innocent people were being killed in drone-strikes, leading to resentment among the Pakistani people. She urged him to refocus efforts on education.

At the age of seventeen, she became the youngest person ever to win the Nobel Prize for Peace. She continued her education at Lady Margaret Hall in Oxford, England.

Showing Solidarity

As allegations of a litany of sexual assaults circulated around Harvey Weinstein, the actress Alyssa Milano responded with #MeToo, saying: "if all the women who have been sexually harassed or assaulted wrote 'Me Too' as a status, we might give people a sense of the magnitude of the problem." As a result, over 4 million users of Facebook posted #MeToo more than 12 million times in the first twenty-four hours after Milano's initial post.[580]

More than half of American women have suffered from "unwanted and inappropriate sexual advances". Many have been sexually harassed at work, but few incidents are reported, for fear of reprisal. Outside the workplace, assaults are often perpetrated by friends and family members who are in positions of authority.

A movement which began in order to empower women through empathy has now become a campaign to address the legal, cultural and economic barriers to reducing sexual assault and harassment in eighty-five countries around the world, to educate men and women, and to end the decades of silence by those who have suffered abuse.

Bearing Witness

A Red Cross worker knew who to call after rumours filtered through of a mass-grave of Taliban fighters, who had been killed in Northern Afghanistan after a failed prison revolt.

Physicians for Human Rights was established in 1986 to use medicine and forensic science to document and fight against mass atrocities and human-rights violations around the world. Since its inception in 1986, they have examined mass-graves in Rwanda and Bosnia, highlighted the use of chemical weapons in Iraq, and provided evidence of torture and extra-judicial killings in Colombia, Honduras, Libya, Mexico, Peru and Sierra Leone.

The organisation's founder, a Boston doctor named Jonathan Fine, had secured the release of three prominent physicians from prison in dictator General Augusto Pincohet's Chile in 1981. Inspired by this, he founded Physicians for Human Rights with four other American doctors in 1986.

They have established international standards for evaluating and documenting torture and unlawful death. In 1997, they shared the Nobel Peace Prize for their work on the clearing and banning of land-mines around the world, after research in Cambodia on the health-impact of anti-personnel mines.

They are not always successful, however. In northern Afghanistan, they had to flee the site of the Taliban graves, which were in a region controlled by an Uzbek warlord friendly to coalition forces. The bodies were subsequently moved before they could be examined. But their meticulous tenacity assisted in the conviction for genocide of the Bosnian Serb leader Radovan Karadzic at the International Criminal Tribunal in 2016.[581]

Standing Up against Violence

After Israel captured the West Bank in the Six Days War in 1967, more than three out of four Israelis supported full or partial withdrawal as part of a peace-settlement with a new Palestinian state.

Today, most West Bank citizens are governed by the Palestinian Authority, but more than 80 percent of the territory is under Israeli military occupation. Nearly 400,000 Israelis live in West Bank settlements, as well as 200,000 in East Jerusalem.

The Way to the Spring by Ben Ehrenreich, published in 2016, chronicles the lives of Palestinians in the West Bank under Israeli occupation. The book describes the displacement of families who lived there for centuries, the corruption of the Palestinian elite, and the quotidian humiliations of life under military rule.

Ehrenreich writes about weekly protests that occurred in the village of Nabi Saleh against arrests, detentions and the way in which village farms have been cut off from a nearby spring. Days after President Donald Trump announced that the US Embassy was moving to Jerusalem, the Israeli Army quelled stone-throwing in Nabi Saleh. Fifteen-year-old Mohammed Tamimi had to have part of his skull removed after being hit in the head by a rubber bullet.

His sixteen-year-old cousin Ahed Tamimi was filmed while slapping an Israeli Captain and Sergeant, demanding that they leave. They did not retaliate. After the film went viral, Ahed was arrested and threatened with a fourteen-year jail-term.

Ahed was awarded the Hanzala Prize for Courage by Turkey when she was thirteen years old, and she has been nominated for other international awards for her protest against the Israeli occupation. She has also been described as a serial provocateur who uses social media to antagonise and provoke Israeli soldiers.

She agreed to serve eight months in prison for slapping the soldiers – a month less than an Israeli border guard who had shot dead an unarmed demonstrator. The sentence was heavily criticised by the UK Foreign Office as well as many other institutions and organisations.

Few commented on the common humanity of an outraged sixteen-year-old girl and the two young soldiers who stoically took her blows, or asked why things had to be this way. In a region where conflict and cynicism has corroded empathy, it takes courage to make room for the middle ground.

Defending the Rights of Those Who Oppose You

When the American Civil Liberties Union agreed to defend the First Amendment rights of Nazis to free speech by challenging a legal ban on their march through the predominantly Jewish neighbourhood of Skokie, Illinois, in 1978, the Guild of American Lawyers accused them of a "poisonous evenhandedness".[582]

Hundreds of residents of Skokie were survivors of the Holocaust. One resident asked how the ACLU would feel if the Nazis were marching through their neighbourhood. The ACLU lawyer David Goldberger said that defending them already felt that way. Despite this, Goldberger argued that banning their march for fear of a breach of the peace amounted to a "heckler's veto" which could just as easily have been applied to Martin Luther King's march through Cicero, Illinois, ten years earlier.

The decision to take the Skokie case exacerbated a crisis in funding and membership which had begun several years before, but the reforms it forced on the ACLU ultimately made the organisation stronger. In the face of condemnation from the American Jewish Congress, the ACLU "kept faith with our principles", as its President, Norman Dorsen, said. In the opinion of Professor Lee Bollinger, the "capacity for toleration" shown by the ACLU indicated a deeper confidence in the enduring strength of democracy.

The ACLU continues to defend the rights of individuals in hundreds of lawsuits across the United States. In 2018, it filed a federal lawsuit to stop President Trump's policy of family separation of illegal immigrants, and to demand that these children be reunited with their parents.

Stepping Outside the Echo-chamber

The Foundation for Individual Rights in Education (thefire.org) was founded in 2009 to defend the rights of students and faculty at America's colleges and universities, including the rights to freedom of speech, freedom of association, due process, legal equality, religious liberty, and sanctity of conscience. FIRE argues that the best way to advance the frontiers of human knowledge and to challenge distasteful beliefs is to scrutinise them in the "marketplace of ideas".[583]

FIRE has raised concerns that anonymous submissions to the Bias Incident Report Team at the University of Kentucky restrict free speech by policing incidents of "intentional or unintentional" bias, including "any activity that intimidates, demeans, mocks, degrades, marginalises, or threatens individuals or groups".[584]

At a time when campuses across America are working to create a safe space to learn, free from harassment and intimidation, FIRE seeks to ensure that intellectual vitality is not compromised by censorship, when students or faculty fear being punished for expressing unpopular points of view, or prevented from forming like-minded groups.

Encouraging a safe, plural academic environment should not mean that the Christian Legal Society cannot select leaders based on their religious beliefs, or insist that they lead "Bible Study, prayer and worship". Nor should the Campus Bible Fellowship be prevented from asking members to accept Jesus Christ as their personal Saviour. Nor should Students For Life have to enrol members who do not believe in the sanctity of human life.

FIRE filed an amicus brief in support of a political-science professor who lost tenure over a blog which championed the right to speak out against same-sex marriage, even if it offended others. They support fair and transparent disciplinary procedures which follow the principle of due process.

Chapter Eleven

Learning from Our Mistakes

"Difference is the essence of humanity."

JOHN HUME

Maintaining the pursuit of kindness in civil society takes substantial cognitive effort in order to check our own biases. Passion for our values, whether liberal or conservative, still leads us to dismiss opponents or policies because of the labels we attach to them, making it harder to consider dissenting voices.

In an era of populism and polarisation, we harden our hearts and demonise our opponents. More than half of Republicans have few or no close friends who are Democrats, and even fewer Democrats have Republican buddies. Science seeks genetic explanations for our liberal or conservative bias.[585] How else could a right-thinking person hold a different point of view?

The banality of evil is that no matter how smart we think we are, we are blinded by our partisan biases, and convince ourselves that we are always the good guys.[586]

But hope remains. We have the ability and self-awareness to learn from our mistakes, and to acknowledge our biases. Republicans hold more liberal views on immigration, gay rights and minorities than Democrats did twenty-five years ago.

Amos Tversky once said: "All too often, we feel like kicking ourselves for failing to foresee that which later appears inevitable. . . . The handwriting might have been on the wall all along. The question is: was the ink visible?"[587] Or as John Connor says in *The Terminator*, the future is not set.[588]

We know that the United States will support energy autarky through fracking over the next few decades, but we have no idea whether America will become more isolationist if it does not need stable foreign governments to deliver oil or gas. We also know that Caucasians may be one of many minorities in the United States by 2050, and that with declining birth-rates, the population of Germany will fall by 25 percent without an influx of economic migrants from Muslim nations like Turkey. Immigrants from poorer regions will have a further impact in reducing global poverty, by sending money home to their families. What we do not know is how Western society will respond to these changes, and to what extent it will adapt.The West will become more diverse, and that is a wonderful thing. Minorities matter: they see past the biases of the herd. A subtly different perspective can put them at the vanguard of social change, nudging us all in a better direction.[589]

There is still no room for complacency. We have to avoid ghettoisation and alienation, which can subvert plural democracy. The Founding Fathers framed the American War of Independence as a way to build a society free from tyranny, including the tyranny of the majority against a minority. They prioritised a Bill of Rights over universal suffrage.

Not that a plural society is a one-way street. There is no inevitable destination. We struggle to understand how our ancestors resisted female suffrage, or the abolition of slavery. Our descendants may question our skepticism on climate-change, our ability to eat sentient animals, or how at least half a billion abortions around the world over the last fifty years, with 100 million because of gender, met the aspiration of: "safe, legal and rare".

Hope for the Future

In his book *Homo Deus*, Yuval Noah Harari pictures a brighter future where "War is obsolete, famine is disappearing" and death is "just a technical problem".[590] Steven Pinker argues that collective rationality should "whittle away at the short-sighted and hot-blooded impulses towards violence". He believes that we are a more enlightened species in comparison to our "morally retarded" forebears.[591]

Of course, not all conflicts are short-sighted and hot-blooded. The strategic use of violence, and the threat of violence, yields dividends. In the absence of deterrence by the international community, wars of aggression by the strong against the weak can achieve their aims with minimal costs to the aggressor.

The morality of the Golden Rule – that we should treat others as we ourselves would like to be treated – is predicated on our ability to share and develop our resources. "Might is right" is a rational alternative, if not a moral one, when there are not enough resources to go around.

The overwhelming evidence from history is that progress is not inevitable, and that short-term crisis measures adopted with the best of intentions can erode pluralism and civil rights for decades, if not centuries. Innocent Japanese-Americans were imprisoned by FDR during the Second World War, and the federal government was running a Cold War witch-hunt long before Joseph McCarthy presided over the Senate Committee on Government Operations. CIA-backed coups against governments in Guatemala, Iran and Chile which strayed too close to the Soviet Union led to appalling human-rights abuses. The invasion of Iraq after 9/11 ultimately led to ISIS, and regime-change in Libya left it a "failed state".

In the midst of crisis, neither the survival nor the destruction of democratic states is guaranteed. The ancient Athenians fell into tyranny when the *demos* lost a war. Rome became a dictatorship by winning one, when Caesar was emboldened by the conquest of Gaul to cross the Rubicon. The rights enshrined in the US Constitution have been a bulwark against overweening power for centuries, yet the Union was plunged into a civil war merely by electing a President who favoured placing slavery in the course of ultimate extinction. There is a clear and present danger that a mis-step could lead to a nuclear war, that disengagement from the international community will lead to further genocide, ethnic cleansing and refugee crises, or that further polarisation will leave America even more profoundly fractured.

We have a growing appreciation of how precious and unusual our world is.[592] There may well be intelligent life "out there" in the universe, but our moral duty to look after our own planet, and all the people on it, has never been clearer.

We forget how close we have come to annihilation. If Khrushchev had called President Kennedy's bluff during the Cuban Missile Crisis, or Mao had launched a pre-emptive missile-strike against the Soviet Union, or Gorbachev had sent tanks into East Germany and Poland, we might have been wiped out in a nuclear conflagration.

The potential lurks around the corner for the cyber-manipulation of news-feeds to escalate into a full-scale attack on democracy, for a rogue state or a terrorist group to detonate a nuclear weapon, for the rise of artificial intelligence to lead to massive blue-collar job losses, for a black-swan event like Covid-19 to lead to economic collapse, or for a global famine to occur due to climate change.[593]

In such circumstances, our moral instinct is to find and punish those who are deemed culpable – which facilitates the persecution of ethnic, religious and political minorities. Rather than learning from our mistakes, our faculties provide the cognitive bias which justifies scapegoating "them" for what has happened to "us".

This Stupid Kindness

We cannot rely on the "right" type of heavyweight philosopher to take us up the escalator of reason. The more passionate we are, the harder it becomes to listen to dissenting voices. Something more is needed. We need the audacity of hope. We need to have faith in what we hope for, and to recognise what we have in common.

People all over the world showed solidarity with the most vulnerable in the face of Covid-19. They chose to hail the heroes of the lockdown, not harass minorities over a "foreign" virus.

Vasily Grossman, the war correspondent who witnessed both Soviet anti-Semitism and Nazi extermination camps at first hand, and wrote about the dehumanisation at the heart of both regimes, finally concluded that "kindness, this stupid kindness, is what is most truly human in a human being".[594]

In his 2015 book *Sapiens,* Yuval Noah Harari frames some of the most influential ideas of abstract reasoning, including religion, money and the nation-state, as "useful fictions". Making light work of reciprocal altruism, he argues that "there are no such things as rights in biology". Human rights are a myth we tell ourselves. Far from being created equal, we "evolved differently", with "mutable characteristics" such as "life and the pursuit of pleasure".[595] I disagree.

The ideals behind the American Declaration of Independence are consistent with the insights of evolutionary biology. We hold these truths to be self-evident: that we are a profoundly collaborative species, whose survival depends on treating others as we would like to be treated. We hold that laws, to be just, must involve a reciprocation of right, and that among these rights are life, liberty and the pursuit of happiness.

In the midst of a pandemic, viewers across the world were revulsed by the sight of a Minnesota police officer with his hand in his pocket as an African-American called George Floyd choked to death under his knee. Police brutality sparked moral outrage and protests. Righteous anger erupted into violence. But in Flint, Michigan, the local sheriff put down his riot-gear and told the crowd that "these cops love you". In cities across the United States, police marched and knelt with civilians.

In Kenosha, Wisconsin, a twenty-nine-year-old African-American called Jacob Blake was shot seven times in the back by police. The incident was captured on video by bystanders. As her son lay grievously wounded in hospital, his mother Julia Jackson, in a public appeal for calm, said that she was praying for police officers and their families, as well as her black and brown sisters and brothers. "Let's begin to pray for healing for our nation. . . . Let's use our hearts, our love and our intelligence to work together, to show the rest of the world how humans are supposed to treat each other."

We have a choice. We can reach beyond our biases. If we are to rekindle the pursuit of kindness, the time to act is now. Walk with us.[*]

---

[*] "Walk with us" was the chant made by protestors when Sheriff Christopher Swanson removed his riot-gear.

Acknowledgements

They say it takes a village to raise a child. Thanks to Seán O'Keeffe and everyone at Liberties Press for persisting with this book, instead of handing it back to me every time I had a meltdown.

To Alan Rinzler, who believed enough in the premise to take on a "repetitious boring list of facts without advocacy or a strong narrative voice" and help to restructure it beyond recognition. If there is any coherence to the flow it's down to you.

To the many academics who took time out from a busy schedule to respond to an unsolicited email from an unknown author, including Daniel Kahneman, Joshua Greene, Elizabeth Anderson and Steven Pinker – I'll keep sending you verbs from Dublin Zoo. Thank you Paul Bloom for saying the book "sounds fascinating" – I nearly put that on the cover, absent the "sounds". To Professor Michael McCullough, author of *The Kindness of Strangers*, who was thoughtful enough to respond to my rambling queries, and to both Professor Francis Pryor, author of *Britain BC*, and Professor Fergus Shanahan, author of *The Language of Illness,* who endorsed the finished manuscript.

To the literary agent Jane Dystel, who believed enough in the book to overcome any reticence about representing an unknown author, and to the many New York editors who almost said yes, as well as the one who said he had had enough of consultants with world-changing visions.

To Laura Duffy, for a wonderful front cover, and for being flexible, supportive and phenomenally great to work with.

To my many friends and family members who offered advice, encouragement and pre-orders. Thanks to Richard Murphy and David Young for your suggestions to improve the book. Yes, the chapters could do with better introductions, no, I don't want to live in a world without passion, and maybe the opening passages are better now. Michael O'Donovan, I never forgot.

They also say all it takes is a spark to light the flame. To my primary school teacher in Larkhill, Geraldine Quinn, my history teacher at St Aidan's CBS in Whitehall, Tom Ward, and my tutor at St Hugh's College, John Robertson, who let me into Oxford despite the fact that "once started, I was not easily stopped" at interview. Thanks also to Edward and Virginia Lawlor, whose generosity helped me to study there.

To my late sister Marie, who walked with me to Ballymun Library when I should have been out playing football, my brother and sister Fergal and Caroline, and to my late parents Danny and Margaret, who taught me so much about the pursuit of kindness. I think of you all the time.

To my wife Jennifer, who read an early draft and observed, "You can tell this was written by a man", sending me back to the drawing board and changing the book for the better. I love you. I couldn't have done this without you.

To our brilliant son Dylan, who has taught us so much about love, laughter and kindness – as well as music, memes and Five Nights at Freddy's. Thanks for all your enthusiasm and inspiration. We are so proud of you every single day.

Notes

1   See (Mandela 1994)

2   According to the Pew Research Center Religious Landscape Survey, roughly 34 percent of Americans reject the theory of evolution, believing that humans and all other living creatures, including plants and vegetables, have existed in their present form since the beginning of time.

3   For a more nuanced view of how collaborative behaviour increases the fitness of organisms in the "snuggle for survival" see https://getpocket.com/explore/item/survival-of-the-friendliest, an article by Kelly Clancy which first appeared in *Nautilus* (23 March 2017)

4   The familiarity with their mother's voice has been used to aid the development of premature babies. See https://www.cbsnews.com/news/special-pacifiers-equipped-with-moms-voice-can-aid-premature-babies-development/

5   For evidence of pre-sapiens hominin activity in Britain, see (Pryor 2004), pp6-45

6   Systematic butchering of large game animals during the lower Paleolithic in Qesem Cave, Israel. Avi Gopher, Ran Barkai (Tel Aviv University) and Mary Stiner (University of Arizona) 2009. For potential effects on egalitarian social selection, see (Boehm 2012), pp 159-63

7   Recent research by Holly M. Dunsworth suggests that the primary constraint on extended pregnancy in humans may be the burden placed on the mother's metabolic rate, rather than pelvis size. See https://blogs.scientificamerican.com/observations/why-humans-give-birth-to-helpless-babies/

8   See (Hare and Woods 2020), pp73-4

9   Mama's Boys of Nature, see (Bloom, Just Babies: The Origins of Good and Evil 2013)

10   For a summary of the work of Robert Trivers et al on kin and reciprocal altruism, see (Trivers March, 1971) and (Dawkins 1989)

11   Investment in childcare by male sapiens, see (Diamond 1999). Earlier hominins such as Australopithicus may have been polygynous. Some scientists have speculated that changes to foraging practices, rather than male investment in child rearing, may have encouraged the shift to monogamy. See (Christakis 2019)

12   For sexual dimorphism, see (Diamond 1999)

13   For evolutionary pros and cons of monogamy, see (Wright, The Moral Animal 1995), pp89-102

14   Boston study of recidivism quoted by (Pinker, The Better Angels of our Nature 2011), p106

15   About 90 percent of bird species and 9 percent of mammal species are monogamous. In most mammal species, it seems that pair-bonding between solitary animals evolved first, followed by increased paternal investment in childcare. This does not explain the rise of monogamy among humans. Twenty-nine percent of primate species are monogamous, but primates tend to be social rather than solitary. Some scientists speculate that pair-bonding was a pre-adaptation that helped ease the parenting burden on our ancestors as our brain-size grew. See (Christakis 2019)

16   Some date the rise of sapiens to 300,000 years ago. See (Christakis 2019), p132

17   For the rise of intelligent Homo sapiens, see (Sykes 2006), p127

18   Origins of life on earth. Evidence for life on earth appears in the fossil record around three and a half to four billion years ago, but the speciation of Homo sapiens occurred around three hundred thousand years ago, and only two hundred thousand years separate mitochondrial Eve from Neil Armstrong's giant leap for mankind. If the entire history of life on earth is represented by one twenty-four-hour day, hominins would be around for roughly two minutes, and Homo sapiens for around six seconds. We started to live in large-scale settlements when we invented agriculture, with about a quarter of a second, or 12,000 years, left on the clock. See (Peter D. Ward 2004), p 57

19   For data on the likely size of the human population 75,000 years ago, see (Zhivotovsky, Rosenberg and Feldman May, 2003)

20   For home-range of 32 square miles see (Hamilton, Milne and Brown 2007), as well as Tim De Chant's guest blog in *Scientific American* (16 August 2011)

21   Uganda, Somalia, Eritrea, Rwanda, Burundi, Djibouti, Mozambique, Malawi, Zimbabwe and Zambia
22   For the benefits of reciprocal altruism, see (Trivers March, 1971)
23   For the benefits of living in bands of around a hundred people, see (Hamilton, Milne and Brown 2007)
24   Something that Nicholas Christakis, the head of the Human Nature Lab at Yale, says is "exceedingly rare in the animal kingdom". He lists eight features in our "social suite": the capability to recognise individual identity, love for our partners and children, friendship, social networks, cooperation, in-group bias, higher status for those who can teach us or introduce us to others, and social learning. See (Christakis 2019), p13
25   For evidence of hard-wired language ability see (Pinker, The Blank Slate 2002) as well as his earlier book *The Language Instinct,* and the work of Noam Chomsky
26   See (Haidt 2012), p207
27   One of the leading exponents for the argument that war was widespread among "primitive" societies, Lawrence H. Keeley, concedes that when a hunter-gatherer band can easily avoid conflict by moving to another fertile area, the most that they risk is their "composure". See (Keeley 1996)
28   Studies of the Hadza and other non-segmented hunter-gatherer bands show that nuclear families move freely between them: humans lived in bands where most of their neighbours were not close kin. See (Christakis 2019)
29   For arrival in Australia, see (Clarkson, et al. 2017). For arrival in Siberia, see (Pitulko, et al. 2004). For arrival in the Americas, see (Bonatto and Salzano 1997)
30   For arrival in Europe, and the impact of subsequent migrations, see (Gibbons 2014)
31   For evidence of early migration to the Near East, see (Armitage, et al. 2011) and (Balter 2011). For evidence of sapiens in China, see (Xing, et al. 2015)
32   See 2014 report by Professor Thomas Higham of Oxford University in *Nature* or https://www.ox.ac.uk/news/2014-08-20-neanderthals-overlapped-modern-humans-5400-years
33   For the inheritance of Neanderthal dna by sapiens, see the work of Erik Trinkaus (Washington University, St Louis), David Reich (Harvard Medical School) and Svante Paabo (Max Plaank Institute for Evolutionary Anthropology, Leipzig). See also (Mooallem 2017) and https://www.irishtimes.com/news/science/the-cavemen-within-did-love-not-war-bring-an-end-to-neanderthals-1.4170477
34   For evidence of rudimentary morality, see (Bloom, Just Babies: The Origins of Good and Evil 2013)
35   Evolutionary biologists define altruism as reducing your own reproductive fitness to help another organism. Helping another organism in a way which does not reduce your reproductive fitness is not deemed altruistic, although, confusingly, biologists use the terms "kin altruism" and "reciprocal altruism" where collaboration with family or other organisms *increases the reproductive fitness of our genes.*
36   There is a temptation to ascribe goal-seeking behaviour to genes which have the self-awareness of a photocopier, or a "blind replicator". Instead of anthropomorphising genes, we can define genetic "success" as the ability to make copies, whether through collaborative, predatory or parasitic strategies. See (Dawkins 1989)
37   See (Rosa Parks 1996)
38   For pushing off a footbridge or flicking a switch in the Trolley Problem, see (Greene 2013) pp113-116
39   Recent research has suggested that the number of people willing to push someone onto the track has risen among younger age-cohorts, especially millennials in the West: on average, roughly 1 in 2 people would push the stranger onto the track. In China, it is closer to one in three. See https://www.ncbi.nlm.nih.gov/pubmed/28963983, and (Edmond Awad 2020) https://www.pnas.org/content/117/5/2332
40   For the Doctrine of Double Effect, see (Greene 2013), p218
41   For modular myopia, see (Greene 2013), p224
42   For aversion to prototypical violence, see (Greene 2013), pp247-8
43   Analysis of the Ju/'hoansi bushmen of Botswana by Polly Weissner indicates that 98 percent of disputes were resolved without any form of violence, let alone homicide. See (Hauser 2006), pp101-3
44   For the Ultimatum Game, see: (Greene 2013), pp70-1 and (Hauser 2006), pp77-9
45   Critics of this experiment have stressed that environmental influences are a key factor, and that offering beer-money to psychology undergraduates in weird societies (Western, Educated, Industrialised, Rich, Democratic) is hardly conducive to getting an unbiased sample. Studies by Joseph Henrich and others have proven that cultural norms are of great importance. For a synopsis of Joseph Henrich's findings on cultural differences in the Ultimatum Game, see (Hauser 2006), pp83-5
46   In a series of experiments on collaboration between groups, the psychologists Ernst Fehr and Simon Gachter found that the ability to pay to punish others who had not shared fairly, resulted in cooperation soaring. See (Haidt 2012), pp207-9

47   The desire to punish stinginess perplexed socially impaired participants with autistic-spectrum disorders, who were more likely to accept low offers and did not understand why their low-ball offers were not accepted. They certainly were not suffering from a logical impairment. Within the rules of the Ultimatum Game, punishing a stranger by refusing an offer in a one-off experiment is cutting off your nose to spite your face. The Ultimatum Game is not the only example where someone with an autistic-spectrum "disorder" behaves more rationally than socially unimpaired humans. See (Sally and Hill 2006)

48   See studies of the !Kung people cited by (Bregman 2020), p230, among many others

49   For evidence of ridicule and social censure as a form of relatively cost-free moral suasion among the Mbuti and !Kung, see (Boehm 2012), pp38-47

50   For a great summary of the work of Richard Alexander on indirect reciprocity, see (McCullough 2020), pp107-8. With the advent of modern communications amd transportation, McCullough believes that our reciprocal altruism, need for a positive reputation (indirect reciprocity) and ability to reason were the primary psychological traits behind the expansion of the moral circle and kindness towards strangers

51   We are also twice as likely to litter in a cycle-park which is covered in graffiti. Graffiti study (Keizer, Lindenberg and Steg 2008), reported by (Bryner 2008)

52   We have dedicated neurons in the superior temporal sulcus which fire only when we see eyes – especially human eyes with white sclerae surrounding the pupil. See (Hare and Woods 2020), pp75-6

53   See (McCullough 2020)

54   See (Bloom 2016)

55   For the alleged quote on the Ukrainian famine, see Leonard Lyons (*Washington Post, 1947*)

56   For a discussion of Paleolithic art and warfare, and the work of Fred Wendorf at Jebel Sahaba, see (Kelly 2003), pp148-61. Death by warfare and raiding can be inferred from the injuries received. The death of children indicates a level of feuding or raiding where individual culpability had become less important than collective responsibility. For Kelly, warfare implies a level of social substitution.

57   Some scientists argue that, as humans became increasingly collaborative, their social intelligence soared. For further insight on the self-domestication theory, see (Hare and Woods 2020).

58   Three-quarters of Upper Paleolithic hand-stencils in caves in France and Spain may have been made by women, according to a 2013 *National Geographic* paper published by Dean Snow of Pennsylvania State University in the journal *American Antiquity*

59   See (Fry 2013), Chapter 10, by Jonathan Haas and Matthew Piscitelli

60   For egalitarianism among hunter-gatherers, and the use of punitive homicide as a form of social control which may have had an impact on genetic selection, see (Boehm 2012)

61   For a table summarising the causes of capital punishment in fifty Late Pleistocene Appropriate (lpa) foraging societies, see (Boehm 2012), pp84-7

62   For a discussion of homicide rates in allegedly peaceful societies, see (Kelly 2003). New York City had 339 murders in 2014, in a population of 8.55 million people – a homicide rate close to 1 in 25,000.

63   In recorded history, population peaks have been followed by warfare peaks in the Roman Empire, Han and Tang China and early Modern England, as modelled by Turchin and Korotayev. See also (Turchin 2015)

64   See the essay by Jonathan Haas and Matthew Piscitelli entitled "The Prehistory of Warfare, Misled by Ethnography", where they quote Kelly (2000): "Warfare is not an endemic condition of human existence but an episodic feature of human history" (Fry 2013), Chapter 10, pp168-90

65   The cultural anthropologist Robert L. Carneiro has argued that states were formed as a result of circumscribed resources and rising population densities.

66   Recent work using the History Database of the Global Environment, or HYDE 3.1, suggests a population of two million people 12,000 years ago (Goldewijk, Beusen and Janssen June, 2010). Earlier, Thomlinson suggested a range between 1 million and 10 million (Thomlinson 1975), and McEvedy and Jones estimated a global population of 4 million (McEvedy and Jones 1978).

67   For the natural advantages of the Fertile Crescent, see (Diamond 1999)

68   The HYDE database suggests a global population 2,000 years ago of 188 million people. See (Goldewijk, Beusen and Janssen June, 2010); (Durand 1974) suggests 270 to 330 million

69   For a detailed treatment of Neolithic farming in Britain, see (Pryor 2004), pp107-33

70   For more on the hunter-gatherer ancestry of modern Britons, see (Sykes 2006), pp26-7. That Neolithic farmers were at least as adept at making love, not war, see the influence of Y-chromosome DNA from Anatolia across Europe in (Balaresque, et al. 2010)

71   See (Pryor 2004) on the spread of agriculture, pp107-33

72   See (McCullough 2020), pp116-9. Ninety-five percent of farms in the United States and Europe continue to be owned by single families.

73   Fred Wendorf's conclusion was that population pressures and a deteriorating climate led to the warfare at Jebel Sahaba. See (Wendorf 1968) and (Kelly 2003), p150

74   For a discussion of the impact of drainage and irrigation in Sumeria, see (Cowen 2011), Chapter 18, on ancient irrigation

75   Data has emerged which correlates warfare with increasing village-size and localised population bottlenecks. This led Robert Carneiro to develop Circumscription Theory, which suggests that the creation of large-scale states was a means to reduce conflict. See (Carneiro 1970)

76   A three-fold drop in mortality compares the average among "pre-State" societies with the estimate for the pre-Colombian Mexican state (Pinker, The Better Angels of our Nature 2011): the Pacification Process. None of the pre-State data is more than 16,000 years old – by which time population densities were far higher than they had been for the previous 150,000 years. That some pre-State societies are violent is irrefutable, but Pinker had to use the available data without knowing how representative it was.

77   See *sumerianshakespeare.com*, as well as the work of Helmut Uhlig (1992) and (McCullough 2020), p123, on the Reforms of Uruinimgina, the Code of Ur-Nammu and the Code of Hammurabi

78   For the importance of material capital over social or embodied capital, see (McCullough 2020), pp119-20

79   For the Sumerian description of slaves as mountain people, see *fsmitha.com*

80   See (McCullough 2020), p123

81   For the impact of exogamy, see (Kelly 2003), p73. He concludes that low levels of exogamy, high levels of food storage and high levels of population density are all linked to increased warfare. In the Paleolithic, with more freedom to roam, membership of nomadic bands was probably more fluid, with nuclear families moving between groups, and women marrying as they pleased – similar to non-segmented hunter-gatherer societies today. Non-segmented hunter-gatherer cultures impose far fewer restrictions on women. With less freedom to migrate from established territories, membership of what anthropologists call segmented hunter-gatherer bands is relatively fixed, often with a strong sense of group identity in an extended family, and formal marriage-contracts between bands. High levels of exogamy, or inter-band marriage, are strongly linked to lower rates of warfare. Rival groups diffuse tension by swapping genes, whereas warring bands are much less likely to permit marriage between them – like Romeo and Juliet. Rather than being free to choose her own partner, or practise serial monogamy, the chastity of a young girl becomes a strategic consideration.

82   He also believed that Egyptian women peed standing up, and Egyptian men squatting.

83   For simple fornication, see (Kamen 2014), p286

84   "I take on a passenger only when the ship's hold is full." Macrobius, *Saturnalia, Book II, 5:9*

85   In the grasslands north of the Black Sea, archaeologists discovered that one in five of the Scythian and Sarmatian warriors buried with bows and armour were female, prompting speculation that their prowess was the inspiration for the Amazonian stories. Irish myths tell of Queen Maeve of Connacht, who led her armies in battle – and, incidentally, needed seven men to satisfy her when her husband wasn't around. Scholars suggest she was a sovereignty goddess, whose favour had to be secured before rulers could be anointed. In recorded history, Queen Boudica, the widow of King Prasutagas, led the Iceni in rebellion against the Roman occupation of what would become England, after her daughters had been raped and her lands seized in the year 60. She sacked St Alban's, Colchester and London, killing 80,000 Roman citizens before she was defeated.

86   Helena exerted a powerful influence over Constantine, but women were also able to demonstrate authority as religious leaders in their own right. The early Christian writer Paul advised women to cover their heads as a sign of respectability in pagan societies, but he had no qualms about working with Priscilla and her husband Aquila, who led the Christian church in Corinth before becoming missionaries with Paul.

87   Estimates of third-century Christian numbers are necessarily hazy. See (Freeman 2002), p 152

88   The persecution of Christians by Nero in the year 64 is mentioned by Tacitus in the year 116 in his *Annals of Imperial Rome. Nero sought to divert suspicion that he had started the Great Fire of Rome by "fastening the guilt . . . on a class hated for their abominations . . . called Christians by the pop-ulace".* Tacitus says a "most mischievous superstition" broke out in Judea and then Rome after Pontius Pilate had ordered the execution of Jesus. See (Ehrman 2012), pp54-6. The expulsion by Claudius, within twenty years of the crucifixion, of followers of "Chrestus" is cited by Suetonius

in his *Lives of the Caesars, written in the year 121.* See (Ehrman 2012), pp 53-4. Pliny the Younger discussing illegal assemblies of Christians in the year 112 in his tenth letter to the Emperor Trajan. See (Ehrman 2012), pp51-2

89   As a new religious group, Christians did not have to pay the special tax which exempted Jewish believers from sacrificing to the gods. The Fiscus Judaicus tax was imposed by Vespasian after the destruction of the Second Temple in the year 70, and was used to finance the Temple of Jupiter Optimus Maximus in Rome.

90   For the origin of the pejorative "*traditores*", see (Lindberg 2009), p45

91   For "By this sign, conquer" ("*in hoc signo vinces*"), see (Lactantius 315) and (Eusebius 339)

92   For Constantine's devotion to Sol Invictus, see (Freeman 2002), p 160

93   From that moment, Christianity was expected to bless the arms of the state. Constantine's biographer, Bishop Eusebius, would describe him as God's commander-in-chief. See (Eusebius and Williamson, The History of the Church from Christ to Constantine 1965). Decades later, Saint Ambrose, a Roman Prefect hastily baptised after his acclamation as Archbishop of Milan, would state in his book *De Fide that the Roman Army was led by the name and worship of Jesus.* See (Freeman 2002), pp 176-7

94   For Christian tax exemptions, see (Freeman 2002), p 161

95   For Libianus commenting on the need for intercession among peasants, see (Freeman 2002), p267. For Bishop Paulinus creating saintly cults, see (Freeman 2002), p264. For the Virgin Mary displacing female pagan deities, see (Freeman 2002), pp241-3

96   Christology had been overwhelmed by the austere and awesome nature of the immutable Platonic Supreme Being. Eusebius said that if Jesus were fully divine, his physical presence on earth would have been as devastating as a collision with the sun. See (Freeman 2002), p145. Despite his role as Constantine's biographer, Eusebius' skepticism about the subordination of Jesus led him to be accused of heresy by Alexander of Alexandria. See www.britannica.com.

97   For the Arian controversy, see (Freeman 2002), pp163-71. Squabbles among Christians were not a new phenomenon. Despite the teachings of Jesus to "love one another", the New Testament records multiple instances of paranoia, jealousy and infighting, especially in the letters of Paul and the Acts of the Apostles. See Paul's Letter to the Galatians for his argument with Peter over eating with Gentiles in Antioch, and the Acts of the Apostles for his quarrel with Barnabas over John Mark. But after the Battle of Milvian Bridge, the political context had changed. A question-mark over the moral legitimacy of clerical authority would quickly come to hover over imperial authority as well.

98   For the rebuke to Arius and Alexander, see (Freeman 2002), p166

99   Constantine's fear of schism undermining him is cited by (Freeman 2002), p162

100   For bishops spreading discord, see (Freeman 2002), p163

101   For the execution of wife and son, see (Freeman 2002), p172

102   Thereafter, the toxic struggle over power, orthodoxy and lucrative tax-exemptions intensified among different factions of the clergy. Bishop Theodosius of Phrygia was on his way to the emperor to complain about the heretics in his diocese, when one of their leaders, Agapetus, recanted and deposed him. See (Freeman 2002), p 215. More than a hundred people were killed during the election of a new bishop of Rome when the ultimate winner, Damasus, called on the *fossores, or catacomb diggers, to support him.* See (Freeman 2002), p204. Saint Ambrose was acclaimed as Archbishop of Milan, even though he was an unbaptised Roman Prefect, after an eloquent speech appealing for peace between Homoousians and Arians. See (Freeman 2002), pp217-20

103   When the Christian heretic Priscillian was executed by the Emperor Maximus in 385 – technically for sorcery – both Ambrose and Siricius, the bishop of Rome, denounced and excommunicated his accusers. See (Hughes 1947). The Theodosian Code imposed some restrictions on Jewish participation in public life, but also said: "We especially command those persons who are truly Christians that they shall not abuse the authority of religion and dare to lay violent hands on Jews and pagans, who are living quietly and attempting nothing disorderly or contrary to the law. For if such Christians should be violent against people living in security or should plunder their goods, they shall be compelled to restore triple or quadruple that amount which they robbed." See *Codex Theodosianus* (439).

104   For persecution by Theodosius, see (Freeman 2002), pp192-4

105   Using the logic of divine retribution, familiar to agricultural societies for millennia, this calamity was attributed to the punishment of God for the heretical faith of Emperor Valens, a Homoean Christian, and his insistence that the Goths, who defeated him, should also adhere to Homoean

Christianity. See (Freeman 2002), pp185-6

106 For the defacing of pagan temples, see (Freeman 2002), pp266-7

107 The redirection of funds to the Nicene church echoed the redirection of funds from the Fiscus Judaicus towards the Temple of Jupiter Optimus Maximus. See (Freeman 2002), p267

108 For the suppression of cult worship, see (Freeman 2002), p225

109 Prior to his conversion to Christianity, Augustine had enjoyed a hedonistic life. In his autobiography, *Confessions,* he admits to praying: "Grant me chastity and continence, but not yet." As a young man in North Africa, he fathered a child, Adeodatus, before moving to Italy with his partner and son to embark on a stellar academic career as the Professor of Rhetoric for the Emperor in Milan. When he was around thirty, he dumped the mother of his son to marry a ten-year-old heiress, in a match arranged by his Christian mother, Monica. "My mistress being torn from my side as an impediment to my marriage, my heart, which clave to her, was racked, and wounded, and bleeding." His misery did not stop him from finding another mistress while waiting for his bride to come of age, but before his fiancee turned twelve, he became a Christian and took up a life of celibacy. He returned to North Africa, where his brilliant son died young. For explanations of the Sack of Rome based on divine wrath, see (Freeman 2002), p267

110 *The City of God, or De ciuitate Dei contra paganos, Book XIII,* outlines the concept of Original Sin. To explain how a Platonic God could nevertheless deign to take on human form, Augustine seized on a quote from the Gospel of Matthew, who drew on the Greek Septuagint translation of the Hebrew Bible (Isaiah 7) to claim that the Messiah would be born to a virgin – although the original Hebrew word, *almah,* is more conventionally rendered as "a young girl". Jesus escapes the taint of Original Sin by being born to the Virgin Mary, who herself was declared free from Original Sin through her Immaculate Conception by Pope Pius IX in 1854 in his bull *Ineffabilis Deus.*

111 Four years after writing *The City of God,* Augustine died, on 28 August 430, at the age of seventy-five, with Vandals besieging the gates of Hippo. Jovinian was branded a heretic, especially by St Jerome, and condemned by Councils in Rome and Milan. For the denunciation of Jovinian by Jerome, see (Freeman 2002), pp243-4

112 Hypatia's contemporary, Socrates Scholasticus, wrote: "On account of the self-possession and ease of manner which she had acquired in consequence of the cultivation of her mind, she not infrequently appeared in public in the presence of the magistrates. Neither did she feel abashed in going to an assembly of men. For all men on account of her extraordinary dignity and virtue admired her the more."

113 Socrates Scholasticus wrote: "She fell a victim to the political jealousy which at that time prevailed. For as she had frequent interviews with Orestes, it was calumniously reported among the Christian populace that it was she who prevented Orestes from being reconciled to the bishop." Cyril of Alexandria later spent 78,000 gold pieces bribing the imperial court to have Nestorius, the bishop of Constantinople, denounced as a heretic. This was enough to feed and clothe 19,000 people for a year. Such behaviour was not ubiquitous. For every Cyril of Alexandria there was a Cyril of Jerusalem, selling off the wealth of the church to feed the poor. The conflict made a mockery of claims about Christians loving one another. See (Freeman 2002), p215. As Socrates Scholasticus commented: "Surely nothing can be farther from the spirit of Christianity than the allowance of massacres, fights and transactions of that sort." The second-century Carthaginian theologian Tertullian imagined pagans saying: "Look at these Christians! See how they love one another." For an account of the murder of Hypatia, see (Scholasticus 439)

114 She became an inspiration for a Catholic saint as well as anti-Catholic polemics by atheists like Gibbon, for whom Christianity caused the decline and fall of the Roman Empire, as well as Deist philosophers such as Voltaire, who said: "When one strips beautiful women naked, it is not to massacre them." Hypatia was used as a metaphor for the end of Greek philosophy, even though Plato's Academy thrived for a hundred more years, until the Emperor Justinian shut it down after nine hundred years of operation. Justinian was determined to restore control over the Western Empire, but first of all he dealt with catechumens who clung on to traditional pagan festivals. "All those who have not yet been baptised must come forward, whether they reside in the capital or in the provinces, and go to the very holy churches with their wives, their children and their households, to be instructed in the true faith of Christianity. And once thus instructed and having sincerely renounced their former error, let them be judged worthy of redemptive baptism. Should they disobey, let them know that they will be excluded from the state and will no longer have any rights of possession, neither goods nor property; stripped of everything, they will be reduced to penury, without prejudice to the appropriate punishments that will be imposed upon them." Practitioners

in pagan cults faced the death-penalty. Jewish worship in Hebrew was forbidden, the Shema Yisrael prayer was proscribed, Jews were not allowed to testify against Christians, and their citizenship was rescinded. See Codex Justinianius (529). In 526, the last Temple of Isis was closed, and Plato's Academy was shut down in 529 by the new Emperor Justinian (527-65), after nine hundred years of continuous operation. See (Freeman 2002), p269

115   Charlemagne convened the Council of Frankfurt in 794, which called belief in witchcraft "superstitious" and imposed the death-penalty on witch-hunters. Councils in Paderborn in 785 and Ireland in 800 echoed this stance, as did the Canon Episcopi in 900. King Coloman of Hungary banned witch-hunting in 1100 because "witches do not exist". Pope Gregory VII forbade the execution of Danish witches for causing storms or crop-failures in 1080, and in Russia, Serapion of Vladimir rejected the superstitious belief that witches caused crop-failures in 1274.

116   Legal-codes of Babylon (Code of Hammurabi, 3770 bp), Egypt and Rome (Twelve Tables of Roman Law, 2468 bp) prohibited sorcery. For capital punishment in hunter-gatherer societies, see (Boehm 2012), pp 84-7

117   Catholic teaching was influenced by Augustine's view of divine omnipotence (*City of God*, Book 9, 420).

118   The Synod of Elvira in Spain (306) prescribes excommunication for those who have killed others by sorcery or magic (Canon 6); the Synod of Ankyra in Turkey (314) prescribes five years of penance for those Christians who have practised divination or sorcery (Canon 24).

119   The Lombard Code (643) bans witch-hunts, stating: "Let nobody presume to kill a foreign serving maid or female servant as a witch, for it is not possible, nor ought to be believed by Christian minds." For more, see (Hutton 1993)

120   Persecution and inquisition for heresy, as opposed to sorcery, ramped up after the First Crusade in 1095. When the nineteen-year-old Joan of Arc was captured by the Burgundian allies of England during the Hundred Years War between England and France, they needed a reason to kill her which would tarnish her visionary reputation. She had led an army armed only with her banner, lifting a key English siege at Orléans to restore the occupied territory to France. She was burnt at the stake in 1431 on a trumped-up charge of heresy, using her proclivity for cross-dressing (as a soldier) to light the pyre.

121   The Papal bull *Super illius specula* (1326), where John XXII authorised the Papal Inquisition to investigate sorcery as a form of heresy

122   *Summis desiderantes affectibus (1484)*. Papal Bull by Innocent VIII against devil worshippers

123   *Malleus Maleficarum*. A number of editions, 1487 to 1520; 1574 to 1669. See (J. B. Russell 1984)

124   For the exchange of information on witches across denominations, see (Scarre and Callow 2001)

125   The death-toll from witchcraft persecution has been estimated variously at 40,000 (Scarre and Callow 2001) and 60,000 (Behringer 2004).

126   Voigt estimated that 133 local people had been killed out of a population of eleven thousand in the previous century, during the most intense phase of the persecution. He assumed that the same death-toll had occurred across all of Europe for the previous eleven hundred years. For the story of Gottfried Christian Voigt's massive over-estimate of witchcraft fatalities, see (Behringer 2004)

127   For Salazar and witchcraft during the Spanish Inquisition, see (Kamen 2014) pp291-9

128   In times of crisis, these minorities could quickly become scapegoats. The Sephardic Jewish population was persecuted by the Muslim Almohads, forcing Maimonides to leave Spain, and Jews were targeted during a civil war among Christian rulers in 1366. Minority groups, whose allegiance was suspect after hundreds of years of Muslim rule, were vulnerable during periods of political instability. The ascension of an eleven-year-old to the throne of Castile in 1391, and the concomitant power-vacuum, led to riots which killed thousands of Sephardic Jews, and forced tens of thousands more Sephardi to convert to Christianity, despite the prohibition on forced conversions under Canon Law. For the anti-Semitic riots of 1391 (Kamen 2014), see pp15-16

129   For 1474 Jewish and *converso population*, see (Kamen 2014), pp27-8

130   For the refusal to acknowledge forced conversions outside Aragon, see (Kamen 2014), p16

131   As Ferdinand wrote to the Pope: "many who seemed to be Christians were found to be living not simply not as Christians but even as godless persons". See (Kamen 2014), p53. The Pope approved the Spanish Inquisition with reluctance, mindful that Rome could not defend itself against the Muslim Ottoman Empire, which had captured Istanbul twenty-five years before.

132   For the Alhambra decree expulsion, see (Kamen 2014), p 25

133   For the Jewish death-toll from the Spanish Inquisition, 1480 to 1530, see (Kamen 2014), pp253-4

134   For criticism of the Inquisition, see (Kamen 2014), pp74-91

135 For Juan Mariana's justification of persecution based on the needs of the times, see (Kamen 2014), p76

136 On welcoming Jews in 1492, Rodrigo Borgia said they were to be "permitted to lead their life, free from interference from Christians, to continue in their own rites, to gain wealth, and to enjoy many other privileges".

137 For propaganda against the Spanish Inquisition in northern Europe, see (Kamen 2014), pp374-93

138 A few Protestant sailors were hauled before the Inquisitors, but the execution-rate was lower than for many secular courts in Spain or elsewhere in Europe. For the death-toll between 1540 and 1700, see (Kamen 2014), pp253-4

139 An Inquisitor at an auto-da-fé in 1719 wrote of a Jewish man who converted on the stake: "This caused great pleasure and joy among all. . . . And desirous that the soul which had given so many signs of conversion should not be lost, I went round casually behind the stake to where the executioner was, and gave him the order to strangle him immediately. . . . This he did with great expedition." (Kamen 2014), p 260

140 For committing blasphemy to come under jurisdiction of Inquisition, see (Madden 2004)

141 For Grosse Aktion Treblinka, see (Snyder, Black Earth: The Holocaust as History and Warning 2015), p202. The Spanish Inquisition killed a total of between three thousand and five thousand people over four centuries.

142 It took more than a hundred years from the fall of Granada before the Moriscos were expelled from Spain, in 1609. Church leaders had been reluctant to persecute Muslims who had not been thoroughly catechised. Noblemen were reluctant to lose a lucrative labour-supply – at least until they were compensated by receiving the land of the 300,000 expelled Moriscos, who made up more than 90 percent of the Muslim population. For the expulsion of Moriscos, see (Kamen 2014), pp160-75. Although the Inquisition was not responsible for their expulsion, their zeal in hunting out recusant Muslims, who accounted for between 80 and 90 percent of Inquisition defendants in the late sixteenth century, contributed to the fear and paranoia which led to their ethnic cleansing, ending centuries of coexistence. Muslim targets of the Inquisition were described as an "enemy race" by Florencio Janer. See (Kamen 2014), p 174. The Chief Minister of Louis XIII of France, Cardinal Richelieu, described it as "the most barbarous act in human annals". For Richelieu's description of the expulsion of Moriscos as a "barbarous act", see (Kamen 2014), p173. Thereafter, persecution declined – but not before coarsening cultural norms. Under *limpieza de sangre*, or "pure-blood rules", the descendants of *conversos could not join the most prestigious faculties, military orders and monasteries in Spain. Juan Martinez* Siliceo, a populist Archbishop of Toledo, was proud of his humble origin and Old Christian peasant roots. Invoking the psychology of disgust, he was scathing of the noble families of Toledo, who were "contaminated" with *converso* blood. For Juan Martinez Siliceo and the contamination of *conversos*, see (Kamen 2014), pp301-27. Institutions which resisted *limpieza de sangre were accused of being a party of Jews. Many who joined the Jesuits after its foundation in 1540 came from converso families, including the second Father General, Diego* Lainez, but by 1593 anyone with Jewish or Muslim lineage was forbidden from becoming a Jesuit. This met with substantial resistance within the order, and in 1608 this rule was amended so that anyone whose Jewish or Islamic heritage was five generations distant could join – effectively almost the entire *converso* population. For more information on the 1608 Decree preventing *conversos* from becoming Jesuits, see (Kamen 2014), p318-20

143 An excellent account of the habituation of the German people to anti-Semitic persecution within the Nazi state can be found in (Confino 2014)

144 For more on the Saint Bartholomew's Day Massacre, especially the tensions in provincial towns with significant Huguenot minorities, see (Holt 2005)

145 For the death-toll from the French Wars of Religion, see (Holt 2005)

146 Edward refused to recognise the claims of either of his sisters, nominating Lady Jane Grey to succeed him. Her reign lasted for nine days before she was deposed and beheaded.

147 Mary's courtiers crushed a rebellion of Protestant nobles led by Thomas Wyatt. Elizabeth was suspected of conspiring with them.

148 Mary acknowledged that her sister would succeed her if she remained childless, despite the fact that the Catholic Church regarded Henry's marriage to Ann Boleyn as illegitimate.

149 She was crowned by a Catholic bishop, but retained her Protestant faith. Since Henry's marriage to her mother, Ann Boleyn was not recognised by the Catholic Church, and could only claim to be a legitimate heir to the throne as a Protestant. After the first stirrings of sedition, she insisted that her English subjects swear loyalty to the Crown and the reformed church in an Act of Uniformity

in 1562, but she tried to restore religious balance, allowing priests to wear vestments and frowning on the lengthy sermons beloved by evangelical Protestants.

150   Earl Grey summarised the strategy as "burning their corn, spoiling their harvest and killing or driving their cattle". One English soldier, Pelham, said that the poor "offer themselves [and] their wives and children to be slain by the army [rather] than to suffer the famine". See (Dorney 2012)

151   For anatomies of death, see (Spenser 1596)

152   For Lord Deputy Mountjoy's grief in a letter to Carew, 2 July 1602, see (Bardon 2012), p41

153   For corpse-eating, reported by Sir Arthur Chichester and Sir Richard Moryson to Fynes Moryson, Secretary to Lord Mountjoy, see (Bardon 2012), p42

154   For old women murdering and eating children, reported by Captain Trevor to Fynes Moryson, Secretary to Lord Mountjoy, see (Bardon 2012), p42

155   For the Treaty of Mellifont, see (Bardon 2012), pp 43-8

156   Undertakers were enthusiastic in selling the benefits of Plantation to prospective colonists, who were led to believe that the land was "utterly depopulated" before moving there. Thomas Blennerhasset issued a pamphlet that said: "Fayre, England, she hath more people than she can well sustaine: goodly Ulster for want of people unmanured, her pleasant fields and rich groundes, they remaine if not desolate, worse. Art thou a tradesman? . . . go thither, thou shalt be in estimation, and quickely inriched. Art thou an husbandman, whose worth is not past ten or twenty poundes? . . . go thither . . . thou shalt whistle sweetely, and feed thy whole family." So long as you were not a "poor, indigent fellow . . . get thee to Ulster". The Scottish allocation of land was heavily oversubscribed. Calvinists from south-west Scotland formed the backbone of Dissenting, Presbyterian settlers. "Naughty" Border Reivers from the English and Scottish Marches were transported to County Fermanagh, where they became farmers and enthusiastic adherents of the Anglican Church of Ireland, 180 years before the foundation of a penal colony in Australia. To further entrench their rights, pocket boroughs were gerrymandered in 1613, so that the Anglican New English would form a majority in the Irish Parliament.

157   Francis Bacon feared that overpopulation in Great Britain "doth turn external peace into internal troubles and seditions . . . what an excellent diversion of this inconvenience is ministered . . . in this plantation of Ireland – wherein so many families may receive sustentations and fortunes, and the discharge of them out of England and Scotland may prevent many seeds of future perturbations." See (Bardon 2012), pp135-6. Ethnic cleansing was contemplated. Although the "deserving Irish" who had fought for Elizabeth were allowed substantial estates where locals could settle, English and Scottish Undertakers were forbidden to have any native tenants on their lands. James, whose Catholic mother, Mary Queen of Scots, had been executed by Elizabeth for treason, was advised that Ulster could be re-stocked by loyal Anglican subjects "to establish the true religion of Christ among men . . . almost lost in superstition". For the motivation for Ulster Plantation, see (Bardon 2012), pp111-41. There had been mass expulsions before, notably following the Alhambra Decree in 1492, and 300,000 Moriscos were expelled from Spain months after the Orders and Conditions for the Ulster Plantation were published in London, but the removal of an indigenous people to create living-space for Planters was without parallel in Renaissance Europe. Courtiers drew precedents from the Roman Empire, the Spanish conquest of the New World, and the defeat of Canaan in the Hebrew Bible. The famine caused by Mountjoy's scorched-earth tactics was also cited as a rationale: "these estates are so depopulated, as there is not a sufficient number of natives to inhabit and manure the third part thereof". For the justification of plantation on the basis that the land was underpopulated, see (Bardon 2012), p129

158   For the plantation of Laois and Offaly, see (Bardon 2012), p6

159   For more information on the benefits expected from the colonization of Ulster see (Bardon 2012), p119, 133

160   For the advantages of Plantation, see (Bardon 2012), pp 135-41

161   For Plato's advice that kings should lie for the benefit of the state, see (Popper 2011), p131

162   For Plato and the Myth of the Metals, see (Popper 2011), p132

163   For Hegel's Great Man despising public opinion, see (Popper 2011), p283

164   See (Popper 2011), p279

165   For a critique of Hegel's belief that reason sets the passions to work for itself, see (Popper 2011), p283

166   For more on self-serving biases, see (Babcock and Loewenstein 1997)

167   For the results of their experiments on self-serving biases, see (Babcock and Loewenstein 1997)

168   For more on the Peterborough study, see (Wikstrom 2012)

169   For the Constantine Sedekides prisoner study, see (Sedekides, Meek and Alicke 2013)
170   For more on our cognitive biases, see (Kahneman 2011)
171   We need to call out cheats. A major reason for capital punishment among hunter-gatherers is bully-ing. For a table summarising the causes of capital punishment in fifty Late Pleistocene Appropriate (lpa) foraging societies, see (Boehm 2012), pp 84-7
172   Ninety percent of homicides are morally punitive. See (Pinker, The Better Angels of our Nature 2011), p 83
173   Homicide by men study quoted by (Pinker, The Better Angels of our Nature 2011), p63
174   In a Dutch study of collaborative games, men who were sprayed with oxytocin became more self-less towards their group, and follow-up studies found that participants became clannish, favoring Dutch names and focusing life-saving efforts on Dutch people. This in-group bias did not lead to to increased hostility towards out-groups: being pro-Dutch did not increase resentment, e.g. of Mus-lims. Jonathan Haidt describes this response as "parochial altruism". See (Haidt 2012), pp 271-2
175   Later studies were unable to replicate the same effects, amid controversy over how much direction was given to prisoners and guards in the original experiement. See (Bregman 2020)
176   For more on Ned Kelly's theories that kings were sacrificed to appease the gods after bad har-vests, see the BBC television documentary "Four-thousand-year-old Cold Case: The body in the bog (O'Halloran 2013)
177   Blood-letting was used to ensure the fertility of the harvest in Mesoamerica, starting with the Ol-mec civilisation approximately 3,500 years ago. See (Joyce, et al. 1986)
178   For accounts of Mayan child-sacrifice, see the writings of the notorious iconoclast Friar Diego de Landa in (Landa and Gates 2012)
179   See Voltaire's "Poem on the Lisbon disaster" (1756), as well as his wonderful satire Candide (1759)
180   For the crucial role of plate-tectonics in regulating the biosphere, see (Peter D. Ward 2004)
181   See Kathy Sheridan in the Irish Times: https://www.irishtimes.com/opinion/kathy-sheridan-we-need-to-start-acting-like-grown-ups-over-covid-19-1.4191669
182   On governors seeking cordons sanitaires to prevent an Ebola outbreak in the United States, see (Crow and Harding 2014)
183   For the ebola outbreak, see https://www.huffpost.com/entry/white-house-ebola-quarantine_n_6050448
184   See (Marshall 1947). For a challenge to S. L. A, Marshall's claims, see (Engen Autumn, 2011)
185   For further information on killology, see (Grossman 1996)
186   For more on Audie Murphy, see (Smith 2015)
187   For more on cognitive dissonance, see (Festinger 1962)
188   See the recent translation of the Epic of Gilgamesh, (George 2003)
189   See (Hare and Woods 2020), Chapter Six, especially pp112-14 and their citation of the experiments of Albert Bandura, pp134-6
190   For Facebook response to Myanmar, see (Osnos 2018)
191   Exaggerating the 1641 death-toll to 150,000 Protestants, twelve to thirty times the true figure (Bar-don 2012), p277, was used to justify Cromwell's atrocities in the seventeenth century (Bardon 2012), p285, and by nationalist historians in the twentieth century to exculpate the killing of 11 to 27 per-cent of the colonists.
192   For the Cromwellian death-toll, famine, and so on, see (Bardon 2012), p 286
193   See (Bregman 2020), p 218
194   Bruno Muller, quoted in (Snyder, Black Earth: The Holocaust as History and Warning 2015), p145
195   Letter home, written on 5 October 1941. See (Confino 2014), p 186
196   For more on China under Mao and Deng Xiaoping, see (Salisbury 1992)
197   For death-toll estimates for the Great Leap Forward, see (Dikötter 2010)
198   From 1968 to 1979, 17 million city dwellers were sent to work on farms as part of the Down to the Countryside Movement. See (Ebrey 2005)
199   For the purification of the populace, see (Hannum 1989)
200   For the death-toll in Cambodia, see (Power 2007), p143
201   For Boat People, see (Butterfield 1979)
202   For a summary of George Kennan's doctrine of containment, see (Kissinger 1994), pp 446-72
203   The build-up of defence spending in the Cold War led President Eisenhower to give a remarkable warning, in his farewell address in 1961, against the influence of the "military-industrial complex" on foreign policy. As the arms industry grew, the United States was criticised in 1971 for allowing hundreds of thousands of civilians to die in the war between their client state, Pakistan, and the

seceding state of Bangladesh. A detailed treatment of us involvement in Pakistan and Bangladesh can be found in (Bass 2013). In 1973, a cia-backed coup in Chile enabled the Pinochet dictatorship to kill thousands of opponents when it deposed the democratically elected Allende government. See *cia.gov for an overview of covert actions in Chile in the 1960s and 1970s*. In the 1980s, the United States supported right-wing movements in Nicaragua and El Salvador which were accused of human-rights violations, as well as Saddam Hussein during the Iran-Iraq War. Support included satellite imagery, technology and training. See (Friedman 1993).

Insofar as the public were aware of what was happening, support by the American government for authoritarian proxies which had a dismal record on human rights, or the subversion of democratic regimes which leant too close to the ussr, engendered massive cognitive dissonance. As the presence of investigative journalists and television crews brought the horrors of war into the living room, enabling the folks back home to form a closer sensory connection to the suffering on their screens, Vietnam became the defining engagement of the Cold War. Ho Chi Minh fought the Japanese with American support during the Second World War, before stopping French colonial forces in 1954, when the country was split into North and South Vietnam. A picture of Ho Chi Minh alongside oss operatives is in the Vietnamese Museum of the War. He spent the next twenty years fighting to unify the country under a Communist regime. Fifty thousand people may have been executed in land reforms in the Red River Delta (Turner, Robert F., 1975. Vietnamese Communism: Its Origins and Development. Stanford: Hoover Institution Publications). The North Vietnamese rigged elections and plebiscites without scruple, but then, so did their opposite numbers in the South, who once secured more than 130 percent of the popular vote in Saigon. For a history of American involvement in Vietnam, see (Halberstam 1992) Halberstam, David. 1992. The Best and the Brightest. New York: Ballantine.and (Sheehan 1988) Sheehan, Neil. 1988. *A Bright Shining Lie*. London: Pimlic).

American policymakers framed Communism in monolithic terms which barely registered the hostility between China and the Soviet Union until the election of President Nixon. Having seen North Korea and China fall like dominos into the Communist fold, and a Communist insurgency in Malaya which was suppressed with the help of Britain's sas, they wanted to create a firewall in Vietnam which would prevent the spread of Communism to Laos, Burma, Thailand and India. Nearly ten thousand aerial sorties would be conducted on nva lines in neighbouring Cambodia.

204   "'It became necessary to destroy the town to save it,' a United States major said today. He was talking about the decision by allied commanders to bomb and shell the town regardless of civilian casualties, to rout the Vietcong." (Arnett 1968)

205   The journalist Seymour Hersh publicised his report on the My Lai/Son My massacre, 12 November 1969

206   For a Vietnamese death-toll exceeding one million in the Second Indo-China War see (Lewy 1978) and the Armed Conflict Database

207   For American post-war hostility to colonialism, see (Kissinger 1994), pp522-49. Kissinger attributed us antagonism to an idealistic American desire to oppose colonialism after the Second World War, yet in 1953, the cia mounted a coup to overthrow the democratically elected Prime Minister of Iran, who wanted to nationalise the Anglo-Iranian Oil Company. A year later, the cia had helped depose the democratically elected President of Guatemala, at the behest of the United Fruit Company, after he had seized and redistributed their lands to the peasantry. America demonstrated an extraordinary degree of resilience in the Cold War, and a willingness to sacrifice blood and treasure. Billions of dollars were spent under the Marshall Plan in Europe to rebuild the shattered economies of wartime enemies. American logistical might have prevented Stalin from seizing Berlin, and the North Atlantic Treaty Organisation prevented Warsaw Pact forces from contemplating the invasion of Western Europe. Tens of thousands laid down their lives in Korea, when the United States helped repel an invasion by North Korea under a United Nations mandate. President Kennedy faced down a potentially lethal expansion of short-range nuclear weaponry in the Cuban Missile Crisis, and idealistic Americans tried to help less developed nations under the auspices of the Peace Corps. American political and economic freedoms allowed the West to out-spend the Soviet Union until its collapse at the end of the Cold War, when the truth about life and persecution behind the Iron Curtain could be heard. Tiananmen Square was a reminder that the authoritarian suppression of human rights had not gone away, but even Red China recognised that it would have to adapt and reform, if it was to compete with the American innovation and prowess exhibited in the first Gulf war.

208   Yes, you read that right. Now *that's* an interesting story. See Chapter Seven

209   For the death-toll of the Thirty Years War, see (Wilson 2011)

210   For Swedish troops destroying one third of German towns, see (Trueman 2015)

211   For the death-toll in wars of religion, see (Phillips and Axelrod 2004)

212   For the religious impulse behind totalitarianism, see (Hitchens 2009)

213   Experiments which encouraged categorisation into in-groups and out-groups, see (Bazalgette 2017)

214   For a detailed exposition of the case for the existence of Jesus by an agnostic, see (Ehrman 2012)

215   For more on Gibbon's view of Christianity, see (Gibbon 1776-1789), especially Volume I

216   For a summary of the ethical teachings of Jesus, see (Aslan 2013)

217   For Dawkins' view of Jesus, see (Dawkins, The God Delusion 2008)

218   In the Sermon on the Mount, Jesus was clear about who would be blessed by God: the gentle, the pure in heart, the poor in spirit, and those who were persecuted in the cause of uprightness. Those who hungered and thirsted for uprightness would have their fill; those who mourned would be comforted; peacemakers would be called children of God; and the merciful would have mercy shown to them (Matthew 5). For Gandhi's views on Jesus, see (Gandhi 2009)

219   For the Letters of Paul written roughly two decades after Jesus' crucifixion, see (Ehrman 2012), pp117-32. For the Gospels and Acts written between thirty-five and sixty-five years after the crucifixion, see (Ehrman 2012), pp69-93 and pp106-13. The earliest authenticated papyrus fragment from the Gospels dates to around 125, and the oldest complete copy of the New Testament, in the Codex Sinaiticus, has been dated to between 325 and 360. See (Milne and Skeat 1981). Although reliant on overlapping sources, the four canonical Gospels contain discrepancies which suggest they were in relatively wide circulation before anyone could substantially doctor them. Matthew has an angel appearing to Joseph and urging him to marry Mary (Matthew 1:20). Luke has an angel appearing to Mary to tell her she will conceive by the Holy Spirit (Luke 1:26-28). Matthew says the child Jesus was rushed out of Bethlehem to exile in Egypt (Matthew 2:13-16). Luke has the Holy Family return to Nazareth after presenting Jesus at the Temple in Jerusalem (Luke 2:22-23 and 2:39-40). Mark ignores the birth of Jesus completely, while John starts his Gospel with a new creation story which affirms Jesus as God: "In the beginning there was the Word: the Word was with God, and the Word was God." John 1:1. Christology, the study of Jesus, remains a highly tendentious field, but it is clear that a large collection of the sayings of Jesus and the reflections of his followers were in circulation at an early stage, and form the basis of Christian moral teaching.

220   The first letter of John states: "God is love." (John 1:4). The Gospels are full of teachings about love, forgiveness and compassion. Jesus told his followers to love one another (John 13) and to follow the Golden Rule: "Treat others as you would like people to treat you" (Luke 6).

221   For a definition of faith, see (Hebrews 11)

222   God is love (1 John 4)

223   In A History of Western Philosophy, Bertrand Russell lamented the lack of philosophical and intellectual rigour among early Christians. See (Russell 1945). The theologian Tertullian argued that blending Greek philosophical conceits with Christianity was pointless: "What has Athens to do with Jerusalem?" See (Tertullian, On the Prescription of Heretics 208 or earlier), Chapter 7. Paul debated with Greek philosophers, but claimed a higher wisdom, through the revelation of God, which superseded their sophistry (Acts 17). For a history of philosophical development in the early church, see (Freeman 2002). Eventually, Christian doctrine co-opted aspects of Greek cosmology and philosophy, especially neo-Platonism; however, this worldview was endowed with the full force of moral zeal, rather than being seen as one hypothesis among many. Intellectuals such as Celsus and Galen scorned the Christian reliance on revelation rather than reason. See (Freeman 2002), pp141-4. However, Jesus was admired as a wise man and teacher by a variety of religious groups, including Gnostics, Ebionites and followers of Theos Hypsistos.

224   "You must therefore set no bounds to your love, just as your heavenly Father sets none to his" (Matthew 5).

225   "I came to call not the upright, but sinners" (Mark 2).

226   "How can you say to your brother, 'Let me take the speck out of your eye', while there is still a beam in your own eye? You hypocrite! First take the beam out of your own eye, and then you will see clearly to remove the speck from your brother's eye" (Matthew 7).
      "Be compassionate just as your Father is compassionate. Do not judge, and you will not be judged; do not condemn, and you will not be condemned; forgive, and you will be forgiven." (Luke 6).
      "Let he who is without sin cast the first stone." (John 8).

227   Doing the will of God was more important than working miracles (Matthew 7). Good deeds were more important than Sabbath proscriptions; mercy was pleasing to God, not ritual sacrifices (Matthew 12).

228   Jesus scorned people who fasted, prayed and gave alms ostentatiously (Matthew 6); who devoured the property of widows while offering long prayers (Mark 12); who sought the place of honour at banquets and the front seats in the synagogues; who did not practice what they preached; who gave tithes fastidiously while neglecting "the weightier matters of the Law: justice, mercy, good faith!"; who strained gnats and swallowed camels; and who cleaned the outside of the cup while the inside was full of extortion and intemperance – like whitewashed tombs, which were handsome on the outside but inside were full of corruption. "From the outside you look upright, but inside you are full of hypocrisy and lawlessness." Jesus publicly excoriated them: "You serpents, brood of vipers, how can you escape being condemned to hell?" (Matthew 23). It was easier for a camel to pass through the eye of a needle than for a rich person to enter the Kingdom of God (Mark 10).

229   For the full context for Jesus saying he had come not to bring peace, but a sword, see Matthew 10: "For I have come to turn 'A man against his father, a daughter against her mother, a daughter-in-law against her mother-in-law. A man's enemies will be the members of his own household.'"

230   When he is asked to clarify who should be loved as a neighbour, Jesus tells the story of a Good Samaritan, moved to care for a stranger who had been beaten, robbed and left for dead. He bandages his wounds, carries him to an inn and pays for his care. His choice of neighbour is freighted with meaning (Luke 10).
Samaritans were seen as heretics and foreigners, rejecting worship at the Temple in Jerusalem, but Jesus shows that the compassionate behaviour of the Good Samaritan is morally superior to that of a Priest and Levite, two pillars of society, who pass the injured man without helping him. The parable of the Good Samaritan provides a clue as to how Jesus, a Jewish teacher who told his Jewish followers to obey the commandments of Jewish law (Matthew 5), wound up nailed to a Roman cross for sedition; with the title "King of the Jews" over his head.

231   His followers were described by the chief priests as the rabble from Galilee (John 7). Jesus likened the authorities to guests who made excuses not to attend a banquet, leading the host to invite "the poor, the crippled, the blind and the lame" (Luke 14). He told a rich young man to sell everything he owned and give the money to the poor, and he told his disciples that no one could serve two masters, both God and money (Luke 16).

232   For the assassination of Ananus, see (Aslan 2013), pp197-212, quoting (Josephus 93)

233   For the destruction of the Second Temple in Jerusalem, see (Aslan 2013), pp 67-8

234   For the historical evidence for Pontius Pilate, see (Ehrman 2012), pp 44-5, and for more on Jesus' ministry near the Roman garrison in Capernaum, see (Aslan 2013), pp95-100

235   For academic techniques to assess Biblical authenticity, see (Ehrman 2012), pp 288-93. Scholars try to discern whether passages are original or a later addition by a copyist, known as a linear interpolation. Certainly, the reference to Jesus made by the Jewish historian Flavius Josephus in Book 18, Chapter 3 of his *Antiquities of the Jews, written around* 94, has been touched up by a later hand: "At this time there appeared Jesus, a wise man, if indeed one should call him a man. For he was a doer of startling deeds, a teacher of people who receive the truth with pleasure. And he gained a following both among many Jews and among many of Greek origin. He was the messiah. And when Pilate, because of an accusation made by the leading men among us, condemned him to the cross, those who had loved him previously did not cease to do so. For he appeared to them on the third day, living again, just as the divine prophets had spoken of these and countless other wondrous things about him. And up until this very day, the tribe of Christians, named after him, has not died out." See the *Testimonium Flavianum in Antiquities of the Jews* (93) 18.3.3) in (Ehrman 2012), pp57-66. The idea that Flavius Josephus, a former Jewish aristocrat writing for the Emperor Vespasian, would acknowledge Jesus as the Messiah, is absurd. Origen, writing of *Antiquities in the third century, explicitly says that Josephus did not recognise Jesus as the Christ in his writings.* For Origen, Commentary on Matthew (10.17) and Contra Celsum (1.47), see (Grabbe 2014) and also (Mizugaki 1987). Bart Ehrman refers to a multiplicity of techniques used by biblical scholars to assess the authenticity of Christian traditions, including contextual credibility, multiple attestation, and the criterion of dissimilarity. Contextual credibility rejects phrases which could not have been said by a first-century speaker of Aramaic. Passages written in or obviously translated from Aramaic into Greek are more likely to be original, such as the exhortation given for a little girl to rise "*Talitha kum*" in the *Gospel of Mark. Similarly, the words of Jesus on the cross* – "*Eloi, Eloi, lama sabachtani*" – are quoted in Aramaic and then translated by Mark as "My God, my God, why have you forsaken me?" Multiple attestation occurs when a variety of sources refer to the same event, particularly if they use

different language or exhibit slight discrepancies in their interpretation of events. The execution of John the Baptist by Herod Antipas is attributed in the Synoptic Gospels to Herod's lust for Salomé. Flavius Josephus reports that Herod, fearful of John's influence and virtue, killed him to prevent revolt – an unjust act which, for the local Jewish population, led to Herod's subsequent defeat in battle. More controversially, the criterion of dissimilarity suggests that any New Testament story that clashed with or caused difficulties for early Christian doctrine is more likely to be reliable. The crucifixion itself was problematic for early Christians, since no Jewish tradition anticipated a crucified Messiah, and with multiple independent attestations it is considered to be authentic.

236 Faith without actions is dead (James 2)

237 Efforts to proselytise Gentiles were boosted when Peter, James and the church elders in Jerusalem agreed that they did not have to be circumcised in order to become Christians (Acts 15). The second-century Carthaginian theologian Tertullian imagined pagans saying: "Look at these Christians! See how they love one another."

238 Gentiles who followed their conscience were a "law unto themselves", with the commandments of God engraved in their hearts (Romans 2). People who fed the hungry, welcomed strangers, clothed the naked and visited the sick or those who were in prison would sit at the right hand of God on the Day of Judgement (Matthew 25). Showing love to others was the way to love God.

239 Within a few years of the crucifixion, a young Jew called Stephen, from the Greek diaspora, was stoned to death for his belief in the divinity of Jesus (see Acts 7:54-8:2); at the behest of Gamaliel, the Sanhedrin soon decided to leave the Christian community alone (Acts 5).

240 According to the Jewish historian Flavius Josephus, the death of James outraged the most observant Jews in the city, who told Albinus what had happened. Ananus was deposed a year later. The Christian historian Hegesippus, writing in the second century, has the authorities asking James to dissuade people from calling Jesus the Messiah. See (Aslan 2013), pp197-200. For the Roman Governor Lucceius Albinus deposing the High Priest Ananus ben Ananus following his execution of James, the brother of Jesus, see (Josephus 93) 20.9.1

241 A detailed account of the Bar Kokhba revolt was written by Cassius Dio in his *Roman History*

242 All the canonical Gospels identify the Temple authorities as the primary culprits, but Matthew goes further. After Pilate, implausibly, washes his hands of the matter, the mob shouts: "His blood be upon us, and on our children" (Matthew 27).

Since Matthew was writing for a Jewish community for whom Jesus fulfilled the Law of Moses (Matthew 5), it is unlikely that he believed that all Jewish people throughout history had assumed collective responsibility for the crucifixion.

243 Apart from the events of the Hebrew Bible, there were many instances of killings and expulsions in antiquity, and some Egyptian, Greek and Roman pagans who mocked Jewish beliefs.

Whether the blood-libel in Matthew 27 was a later interpolation is academic. For Melito of Sardis, himself of Jewish origin, the elimination of Jesus to prevent sedition had become an act of deicide. By 167, the Jewish Jesus of Nazareth had been lost in a Platonic concept of the Son of God. For more on Melito of Sardis and his Peri Pascha sermon, see (Bibliowicz 2013), pp180-18

Ambrose of Milan opposed compensation for Jews whose synagogue had been destroyed by Christians in Callinicum, arguing that Christians could not be responsible for re-building a house where "Christ was denied". In 415, Severus of Minorca boasted of burning out a synagogue with the help of Christians from the surrounding countryside. Jerome argued that "the ceremonies of the Jews are harmful and deadly to Christians".

John Chrysostom denounced Christians who visited synagogues or participated in Jewish festivals, saying that synagogues were "worse than brothels", "the source of vice and heresy" and the "refuge of the debauched". Jewish people "continued to rejoice in the death of Jesus"; "demons dwelt in their souls"; "they were growing fit for slaughter"; they should be shunned "as if they were a plague". The fact that John Chrysostom railed against Christians, particularly women, who celebrated Rosh Hashanah and applauded rabbinical preaching, indicates that relations between Jews and Christians in Antioch were far too convivial for his liking. See (Chrysostom 387) and (Michael 2008)

244 For a first-century rebuttal of pagan Greek blood-libels of Jews, see (Josephus, Against Apion 100?)

245 Justinian reconquered the Western Empire before his death, but after the extreme global cooling of 536, the advent of plague in 541, which continued sporadically through to 750, led to the deaths of millions of people, including up to a quarter of the population of the eastern Mediterranean. The ability of the Emperors of Byzantium to project power in the Western Empire collapsed after

the Lombard invasion of northern Italy in 568, and their sphere of influence shrank. See (Freeman 2002), pp302-3

246   Coercing conformity to Nicene Christianity invited unwelcome analogies with the persecution of Christian martyrs by Diocletian. Resolving the cognitive dissonance required an intellectual rationale, which was provided by Saint Augustine. He drew inspiration from the piety and orthodoxy exhibited by former Donatists after their movement had been suppressed in northern Africa. He believed that many had been led astray by the Donatist clerical elite. Having been initially hostile to interference with freedom of conscience, Augustine came to see a utilitarian benefit in the imposition of orthodoxy as a way of ensuring the salvation of more souls. The end justified the means. Suppression of heresy therefore became a moral obligation, even if collateral damage among the heretical elite was required so that their followers could see the light. "What then does brotherly love do? Does it, because it fears the short-lived fires of the furnace for the few, abandon all to the eternal fires of hell?" Augustine never endorsed the execution of heretics, but he rationalised the abrogation of an individual right to liberty of conscience. It would be deployed to lethal effect in the centuries to come.

Some measure of respite was offered by the reiteration of tolerance in 438 as a cornerstone of Roman law. The Theodosian Code imposed some restrictions on Jewish participation in public life, but also said: "We especially command those persons who are truly Christians that they shall not abuse the authority of religion and dare to lay violent hands on Jews and pagans, who are living quietly and attempting nothing disorderly or contrary to the law. For if such Christians should be violent against people living in security or should plunder their goods, they shall be compelled to restore triple or quadruple that amount which they robbed." The ability to enforce this law in the Western Empire was heavily constrained by continued incursions, which forced the Latin Church to operate independently of the Emperor. Within seventeen years of its promulgation, the bishop of Rome, Leo the Great (440-61), had to ask Attila the Hun to leave northern Italy, and negotiated terms with Gaiseric the Vandal when he plundered Rome in 455. Doctrinally, Leo was one of the most influential bishops of Rome in centuries. His predecessor, Sylvester I, had not even attended the synod which approved the Nicene Creed in 325, although he subsequently ratified it.

The Emperor Justinian was determined to restore control over the Western Empire, but first of all he dealt with catechumens who clung on to traditional pagan festivals. "All those who have not yet been baptised must come forward, whether they reside in the capital or in the provinces, and go to the very holy churches with their wives, their children and their households, to be instructed in the true faith of Christianity. And once thus instructed and having sincerely renounced their former error, let them be judged worthy of redemptive baptism. Should they disobey, let them know that they will be excluded from the state and will no longer have any rights of possession, neither goods nor property; stripped of everything, they will be reduced to penury, without prejudice to the appropriate punishments that will be imposed upon them." Practitioners in pagan cults faced the death-penalty. Jewish worship in Hebrew was forbidden, the Shema Yisrael prayer was proscribed, Jews were not allowed to testify against Christians, and their citizenship was rescinded.

Justinian reconquered the Western Empire before his death, but after the extreme global cooling of 536, the advent of plague in 541 (which continued sporadically through to 750), led to the deaths of millions of people, including up to a quarter of the population of the eastern Mediterranean. The ability of the Emperors of Byzantium to project power in the Western theatre collapsed after the Lombard invasion of northern Italy in 568, and their sphere of influence shrank. Into the vacuum stepped Pope Gregory the Great (590-604), who asserted the primacy of the bishop of Rome over all other episcopal sees.

Gregory had been a wealthy Prefect of Rome before selling all his possessions to give the money to the poor. He instituted a sophisticated system of famine relief, and re-connected Rome with bishoprics in Spain, France and Italy, lobbying local rulers to suppress paganism and prevent the sale of church offices, or simony. Ignoring the doctrinal disputes which had preceded the adoption of Nicene Christianity, he was hostile to the forced conversion of Jews and heretics, arguing that compassion and good example were the way to win hearts and minds. His mission to the pagan Angles in Britain was sensitive to their traditions, and became a tremendous success.

While evangelisation flourished in Europe, philosophical inquiry declined, and Western civilisation lost contact with Greek and Arab thought. Despite being a papal legate to Constantinople earlier in his career, Gregory himself spoke no Greek. In his *History of Western Philosophy*, Bertrand Russell highlights only one figure of real substance, Johannes Scottus Eriugena (815-77), in the six centuries between Gregory's death and the birth of Thomas Aquinas. In his own time, Johannes

Scottus, or John the Irishman, was more remarkable for his fluency in Greek than his original thinking. Literary output was focused on biblical commentaries, many of them crafted in peripheral regions unaffected by the depredations of Goths, Visigoths, Huns, Vandals and Lombards. Approximately half of all known biblical commentaries written in Western Europe between 650 and 850 were composed by Irish monks, who founded monasteries across Britain, France, Germany, Switzerland, Austria, Hungary and northern Italy.

247 Before the First Crusade, Augustine had stressed the moral obligation to fight just wars when peaceful means were not available, to thwart great wrongdoing. Whether Jesus would have agreed with this concept is moot. After the adoption of the stirrup allowed Islamic heavy cavalry to sweep though Visigothic Spain in seven years, Charles Martel was celebrated for halting them at the Battle of Tours in France. His grandson Charlemagne used Christianity to justify his conquest of pagan Saxons; yet his massacre of 4,500 rebellious captives at Verden in 782 was a risky move, given the clerical desire to evangelise rather than eviscerate. Charlemagne was an enthusiastic participant in mass-baptisms of Saxons, and instituted the death-penalty for recalcitrant pagans. For more on Charlemagne, see (Barbero 2004). When his Carolingian Empire collapsed, the Church established rules against harming unarmed civilians, especially women and children, and safe havens where feuding was forbidden under the Peace and Truce of God. Until the Crusades, the church was reluctant to sanctify acts of violence. Afterwards, a necessary evil had been re-branded as a positive good. See (Asbridge 2005), pp24-5

248 For more on Visio Tnugdali, see (Easting 1997)

249 The Domesday Book (1086) quantifies church land ownership (see *nationalarchives.gov.uk*)

250 Urban's predecessor, Gregory VII, managed to rustle up a few hundred knights under Robert of Flanders to defend Constantinople, but decades after the Eastern Orthodox and Roman Catholic churches separated in the Great Schism, Norman knights in the south of Italy preferred to steal from the Byzantines rather than fight the Seljuks, who went on to take Jerusalem from the Shiite Fatimids of Egypt.

251 Urban had learnt from the mistakes of his predecessors. Leo IX had triggered the Great Schism with the Orthodox Church forty years previously, by asserting his authority over Patriarch Michael of Constantinople. The document he relied on, the Donation of Constantine, ostensibly written after Constantine was cured of leprosy by Pope Sylvester, was later shown to be an eighth-century fraud. Urban's mentor, Gregory VII, had excommunicated the Holy Roman Emperor, Henry IV, twenty years previously, following a campaign to stop local rulers from selling church offices to the highest bidder. Gregory's papacy was derailed when Henry marched on Rome, appointing his own rival candidate, Clement III, as anti-pope. Urban had been Gregory's papal legate to Germany as relations with Henry declined, and he used diplomacy and moral suasion where confrontation with secular rulers had failed. The astute use of bribes allowed him to regain the Lateran Palace in 1094, and he instituted a permanent Roman Curia to advise him. Before launching the First Crusade, he preached throughout France, and convened Ecclesiastical Councils in Piacenza and Clermont which brought lay and spiritual leaders together. His politicking worked. Adhémar, bishop of Le Puy, volunteered to act as the Pope's emissary as soon as Urban finished speaking. Adhémar's ally, Count Raymond of Toulouse, pledged his military support the following day. See (Asbridge 2005)

252 "A race absolutely alien to God has invaded the land of Christians, has reduced the people with sword, rapine and flame. These men have destroyed the altars polluted by their foul practices. They have circumcised the Christians, either spreading the blood from the circumcisions on the altars or pouring it into the baptismal fonts. And they cut open the navels of those whom they choose to torment with loathsome death, tear out their most vital organs and tie them to a stake, drag them around and flog them, before killing them as they lie prone on the ground with all their entrails out. What shall I say of the appalling violation of women, of which it is more evil to speak than to keep silent?"

"On whom, therefore, does the task lie of avenging this, of redeeming this situation, if not on you, upon whom above all nations God has bestowed outstanding glory in arms, magnitude of heart, litheness of body and strength to humble anyone who resists you?"

For Robert the Monk's transcript of Urban II's speech, see (Asbridge 2005), p1

253 Tancred's biographer was Ralph of Caen, who wrote *Gesta Tancredi after Tancred died in 1112*.

254 Many of the First Crusaders were wealthy, and not close to the Pope. See (Asbridge 2005)

255 For the *Diary of Anna Comnena, Alexius I's* daughter, see (Asbridge 2005), p104

256 For Peter the Hermit, encouraging untrained civilians to join the First Crusade, see (Asbridge 2005)

257 The Caliphate benefited from the special taxes levied on Jews and Christians under the *dhimmi sys-*

tem, and had been ambivalent about converting them. In 649, a Nestorian Patriarch wrote that "These Arabs fight not against our Christian religion; nay, rather they defend our faith, they revere our priests and saints, and they make gifts to our churches and monasteries." See (Freeman 2002), p324

258   For more on the expulsion of French Jews in Limoges, see (Bokenkotter 1979)

259   In Speyer, the local bishop prevented a massacre by sheltering the Jewish community. In Regensburg, the entire Jewish population was forced into the Danube to be baptised. By the time Emicho reached Worms, he had hit upon a different tactic to incite the crowd. According to an anonymous Jewish chronicler from Mainz:

"They took a 'trampled corpse' of theirs, which had been buried thirty days previously, and carried it through the city, saying, 'Behold what the Jews have done to our comrade. They took a gentile and boiled him in water. Then they poured the water into our wells in order to kill us.'" Isaac of Worms was dragged through the streets with a rope around his neck, then decapitated when he refused to convert to Christianity. Crusaders breached the episcopal palace. Jewish families sheltering there were "killed like oxen and dragged through the market places and streets like sheep to the slaughter".

In Mainz, a few days later, the bishop accepted "an incredible amount of money" to protect the Jewish population, and some local burghers tried to shelter their Jewish colleagues, but according to Albert of Aix they were soon overwhelmed: "Breaking the bolts and doors, they killed the Jews, about 700 in number, who in vain resisted the force and attack of so many thousands. They killed the women, also, and with their swords pierced tender children of whatever age and sex. . . . Horrible to say, mothers cut the throats of nursing children and stabbed others, preferring them to perish thus by their hands." For the massacre at Worms, see (Asbridge 2005), pp87-8

260   There were plenty of precedents for the Rhineland Massacre. Persecution of minorities to appease the gods pre-dated Christian hegemony; Jews had had to defend themselves against false accusations, whether poisoning wells or sacrificing Greeks in temple rituals, since Josephus wrote the rebuttal Against Apion in the first century. The Byzantine Emperor Heraclius forcibly baptised Jews after the massacre of Jerusalem in 629, and the Twelfth Council of Toledo initiated twenty-eight laws against Jews, as well as preventing *conversos from returning to Judaism in 681*, eight hundred years before the foundation of the Spanish Inquisition. See (Asbridge 2005), pp84-8. With the sanctification of violence through Crusade, ancient fears about religious minorities were given full rein. For centuries, Canon Law had been a counterweight against lynch-mobs, forbidding persecution and forced conversion of the vulnerable in times of famine or sickness to appease the gods. These prejudices festered until the Crusades opened the floodgates. For Canon Law (Codex Episcopi) against forced conversions, see (Kamen 2014), p16

261   Rivalries between Muslim rulers were exploited by Crusaders who knew that the best way to defeat a large force was to fracture it into rival groups. They negotiated astute alliances with Muslims, accepting food, tribute and intelligence about the road ahead. Christian and Muslim alike were fearful of traitors in their midst, and with good reason: the Crusaders had captured Antioch, after an eight-month siege, by bribing a guard called Firuz to let them in. See (Asbridge 2005), pp200-11. The Fatimids expelled Christians from Jerusalem in order to avoid similar treachery. In the eyes of the Crusaders, this gave them licence to be less discriminating in the subsequent conquest.

262   Albert of Aix wrote: "After a very great and cruel slaughter of Saracens, of whom 10,000 fell in that same place, they put to the sword great numbers of gentiles who were running about the quarters of the city, fleeing in all directions. . . . They were stabbing women who had fled into palaces . . . seizing infants by the soles of their feet . . . and dashing them against the walls." For the death-toll in the capture of Jerusalem, see (Asbridge 2005), p376, note 35

The only person to honour the terms of quarter made when the garrison surrendered was Raymond of Toulouse, who allowed the Fatimid commander, Iftikhar al-Daulah, and his cavalry, to leave unharmed. For an account of the massacre of Jerusalem, see (Asbridge 2005), pp316-19

263   For the massacre of the Latins in 1182, see (Fossier 1986), pp506-8

264   Pope Innocent III wrote a jeremiad, asking how the Eastern Orthodox Church could recognise the Holy See "when she has seen in the Latins only an example of perdition and the works of darkness" so that "with reason [she] detests the Latins more than dogs?" Innocent lamented that the swords of the Crusaders, "which they were supposed to use against the pagans, drip with Christian blood". He recognised Baldwin of Flanders as the new Emperor nonetheless, and received treasures stolen from the churches of the city. For more on the Sack of Constantinople, see (Hughes 1947)

265   The Cathars of Southern France believed that the evils of the world were attributable to a demiurge, the *rex mundi, and that all things of the flesh were to be repudiated. They did not think that Jesus*

had taken on human form, and their most devoted adherents, the Perfecti who had undergone the spiritual rite of Consolamentum swore vows of celibacy. Local clerics had preached against the heresy for decades, but the Cathars were protected by Raymond VI, a descendant of the First Crusader, Raymond of Toulouse. The trigger for the Albigensian Crusade was the crisis caused by the murder of the papal legate, Pierre de Castelnau, following the excommunication of Raymond VI. For more on the Albigensian heresy and Cathar beliefs, see (Lambert 1998)

266   Arnaud-Amaury reported what happened next: "While discussions were still going on with the barons about the release of those in the city who were deemed to be Catholics, the servants and other persons of low rank attacked the city without waiting for orders from their leaders. To our amazement, crying 'To arms, to arms!' within the space of two or three hours they crossed the ditches and walls, and Beziers was taken. Our men spared no one, irrespective of rank, sex or age, and put to the sword almost twenty thousand people. After this great slaughter, the whole city was despoiled and burnt." Letter from Arnaud-Amaury to Pope Innocent III, August 1209. The rumour that Arnaud-Amaury told the soldiers to kill them all was circulated twenty years later by Caesarius of Heisterbach.

267   Popes continued to preach old-school Crusades against pagans in the Baltic in the thirteenth century where the Teutonic Knights founded the monastic state of Prussia.

268   Innocent IV sanctioning the use of torture in the Inquisition in *Ad extirpanda, 1252*

269   Of 5,400 people interrogated between 1245 and 1246 in Toulouse, 184 were ordered to wear a yellow cross, twenty-three were imprisoned for life, and none were executed. For more on the Inquisition in Toulouse in 1245 and 1246, see (Pegg 2001)

270   Bernard Gui of Carcassone had forty-two people killed out of nine hundred he found guilty in a fifteen-year span, the equivalent of less than three people per annum. For more on Bernard Gui, see (Sullivan 2011)

271   For Gregory VII's excommunication of Cambrai in 1077, see (Borst 1974)

272   For Montsegur's burning of two hundred Cathars in 1244, see (Sumption 2000)

273   The Holy Roman Emperor Frederick I (Barbarossa) warned priests not to preach against Jews before departing on the King's Crusade, but within twenty-five years *Judensau, anti-Semitic images, would start to be carved in churches across Germanic principalities. The oldest Judensau known today was carved in 1210 underneath a seat in Cologne Cathedral. The Fourth Lateran Council under Pope Innocent III would mandate special clothing for Jews and Muslims, ostensibly to avoid intermarriage with Christians.* See the edict by the Fourth Lateran Council (1215) on special clothing for Jews and Muslims (Canon 68). See also Canons 67 (ban on Jews charging interest), 69 (ban on Jews holding public office) and 70 (against Judaising)

274   Alleged victims included William of Norwich (1144), Hugh of Lincoln (1255), Werner of Oberwesel (1287), Andreas of Rinn (1462), Simon of Trent (1475) and Christopher of Toledo (1491). In 1235, five children from the same family were murdered on Christmas Day in the Prussian town of Fulda. Thirty-four Jews were killed by passing Crusaders before the Holy Roman Emperor, Frederick II, exonerated the Jewish population. He meticulously demolished the blood-libel, summoning temporal authorities and Christian converts from Judaism to give testimony. Frederick concluded: "There is no evidence to be found either in the Old or the New Testament that the Jews are desirous of human blood. On the contrary, they avoid contamination with any type of blood. . . . Those to whom even the blood of permitted animals is forbidden cannot have a hankering after human blood."

275   Repudiation of blood-libel [insert: by] Gregory X in 1272: "And most falsely do these Christians claim that the Jews have secretly and furtively carried away these children and killed them, and that the Jews offer sacrifice from the heart and blood of these children, since their law in this matter precisely and expressly forbids Jews to sacrifice, eat, or drink the blood, or to eat the flesh of animals having claws." Letter quoted by Brian Tierney in *The Middles Ages (1998)*

276   Jews in Norwich and York were massacred in 1190, forty-six years after the death of William of Norwich, when Richard the Lionheart joined the King's Crusade.

277   Five thousand Jews were identified as victims of the Rintfleisch Massacres in the German Civil War (1298), according to the Nuremberg Chronicle. See (Green 2014)

278   The Jews of Strasbourg were burnt to death on St Valentine's Day, 14 February, 1349.

279   Despite pressure from some nobles, Casimir IV of Poland continued to offer protection and religious freedom because of "the principle of tolerance, which, in conformity with God's laws, obliged him to protect them". For the quotation on tolerance by Casimir IV of Poland, see (Weinryb 1973), p50. Poland had been a refuge for Jewish refugees since the Statute of Kalisz (1264) issued by Boleslaw the Pious.

280   Martin Luther had called for a reformation within the church following the sale of indulgences to rebuild St Peter's in Rome, but the last "good" Pope he recognised was Gregory the Great, nine hundred years earlier. He railed against the "Babylonian Captivity" of the Papacy as clients of the King of France, which began after the last Crusader colonies fell in 1291, when the Papal Inquisition was turned against an order whose raison d'être was the defence of the Holy Land.

Since 1139, the Knights Templar had been answerable only to the Pope, who gave them the right to move crusading armies across borders. Due to tax-exemptions, they were also extremely wealthy, bankrolling the French King Philip IV in his war with Edward Longshanks of England.

By 1307, Philip was desperate to reduce his liabilities. He had already followed Edward I's lead by expelling his Jewish and Lombard bankers and seizing their assets, and he sought shelter with the Templars during a riot in Paris over his debasement of the currency. With the election of a French Pope, Clement V, the Papacy moved from Rome to Avignon, and King Philip accused the Templars of heresy, corruption, sodomy and blasphemy.

At dawn on Friday 13 October 1307, Philip struck. Dozens of Knights Templar were arrested simultaneously across France. Many confessed under torture by the Inquisition, and although Clement absolved them of heresy in the Chinon Parchment of 1308, Philip used their earlier confessions to have them burnt at the stake. Clement dissolved the order, and Philip seized the bank.

The Chinon Parchment of Clement V was discovered in the Vatican in 2001 by Barbara Frale.

As famine and the Black Death cut down tens of millions of people across Europe, French Popes stayed in Avignon for sixty-seven years, living in great wealth from payments made by candidates to secure clerical office.

After Gregory XI died in Rome in 1378, two rival Popes were elected by the College of Cardinals in the same year. Neither would make way for the other. Embroiled in the Hundred Years War, France and England took opposing sides in the controversy, and other states followed suit. It took forty years to sort out the Western Schism at the Council of Constance – by which time there were three legitimately elected rival Popes, making a mockery of the concept of Apostolic Succession.

281   For more on Protestant works in circulation, see (Edwards 2004)

282   For Martin Luther's views on the expulsion of the Jews by the Elector of Saxony, John Frederick, in 1536, see (Brecht 1999)

283   For the "Argument between monks" attributed to Charles V at the Diet of Worms (1521), including the phrase "German money for a German church", see (Bainton 1978), p76

284   In *Against the Murdering, Thieving Hordes of Peasants, Luther* wrote: "Therefore let everyone who can, smite, slay, and stab, secretly or openly, remembering that nothing can be more poisonous, hurtful, or devilish than a rebel." For the death-toll of the Peasants' Revolt of 1524, estimated at 100,000, see (Blickle 1981), p165

285   For Martin Luther's advice to the bigamous Landgrave Philip I of Hesse on his second marriage, see (Brecht 1999), pp205-15

286   The Tridentine Index under Pius IV (1564) replaced a withdrawn Roman Index from 1557.

287   The use of the leap-year in the Gregorian calendar was proposed by Petrus Pitatus of Verona in 1560, who noted that it conformed with the mean tropical year in Copernicus' *De revolutionibus.*

288   For the Tycho Brahe stellar parallax objection, see (Graney and Danielson Jan, 2014)

289   For the existence of galaxies beyond the Milky Way, see (Hubble 1924)

290   For more on Galileo's persecution, see (Sobel 2000)

291   For more on the use of the Bodleian Library as a Protestant redoubt, see (Nelles 2007)

292   Alexander Leighton, sentenced by Archbishop William Laud's High Commission Court in 1630

293   For John Toland's comments on his persecution by Parliament, see (Gilbert 1861) vol. 3, p66

294   Martin Luther's *Invocavit Sermons, Lent 1522*

295   See the study by Phillip Goff cited in (Hare and Woods 2020), p136

296   John Wesley, the founder of Methodism, had written *Thoughts Upon Slavery in 1774. He said*: "Liberty is the right of every human creature, as soon as he breathes the vital air; and no human law can deprive him of that right which he derives from the law of nature." Despite this, the Georgia Methodist Conference applauded bishops who suppressed "excitement . . . on the subject of abolitionism", resolving that "we view slavery as a civil and domestic institution, and one with which, as ministers of Christ, we have nothing to do, further than to ameliorate the condition of the slave, by endeavoring to impart to him and his master the benign influences of the religion of Christ, and aiding both on their way to heaven".

297   The Moral Circle was a concept invented by the nineteenth-century Irish historian William Lecky.

For a discussion of the Moral Circle, see (Wright, The Moral Animal 1995), pp371-5

298   For further information on the 81.2 percent turnout among the white, male, voting-age population in the 1860 presidential election, see (Ragsdale 1998)

299   The first slaves in the Thirteen Colonies were Native American prisoners of war. Planters in South Carolina profited from laws which allowed them to enslave captive Tuscarora and Yamasee. Slavery was not the exclusive preserve of the New World at this time. Crimean Tatars and Barbary Pirates enslaved millions of white Europeans between the sixteenth and eighteenth centuries, and in some African states a third of the people were enslaved. For more on the East African slave trade, see (Campbell 2003)

300   Thirty years earlier, Johnson was one of only five men out of fifty-seven on the Plantation where he was a servant to survive the Indian Massacre of 1622, when the Powhatan killed a quarter of the Virginia colony. We know he was well respected because he and his wife Mary were given tax relief after an accidental fire on their farm, three years before the Casor ruling.

301   For an account of Antonio Johnson enforcing his right to own a slave, see (Berlin 2003), pp30-1

302   The Dominican Friar Bartolomé de las Casas wrote *A Short Account of the Destruction of the Indies, a scathing attack on the exploitation of native Americans, prompting Charles V to provide them with notional protection under his New Laws of 1542. The morality of the entire colonial project was publicly called into question in the famous Valladolid Debate of 1550. De las Casas argued that the native Americans were fully human, and therefore entitled to human rights, making their "civili*sation" by Spanish *encomanderos unjustifiable.* See (De Las Casas 1550). Sadly, de Las Casas' initial enthusiasm for the replacement of native Americans with Africans had more impact than his later condemnation of all forms of slavery.

303   For the number of slaves imported by century, see *Voyages: The Trans-Atlantic Slave Trade Database*

304   The state of Georgia banned slavery in 1735.

305   Less than one in fourteen of those transported from Africa would travel directly to the colonies of North America. For the proportion of slaves sent directly to North America, see (Behrendt 2005)

306   For the death-toll of slaves trafficked on the Middle Passage, see (Manning 1992)

307   For the quote "stark mad after negroes", see (Berlin 2003), p144

308   Conflict between native Americans and frontier colonists, who coveted their lands, led to the revolt. When Nathaniel Bacon rebelled against Governor Berkeley's forces, his Choice and Standing Army was made up of black and white indentured servants in equal measure.

309   An Act Concerning Servants and Slaves, Virginia, 1705

310   For utopian exhortations in *Common Sense*, see (Paine 1987), p93 and p109

311   For more on the purpose of government [insert: being] to protect property, see (Paine 1987), p67. For the circulation of *Common Sense in Revolutionary America*, see (Loughran 2007) and (Raphael 2013)

312   "There are thousands and tens of thousands, who would think it glorious to expel from the continent, that barbarous and hellish power, which hath stirred up the Indians and Negroes to destroy us." For Thomas Paine's reference to slaves and Indians, see (Paine 1987), p93

313   For the proportion of slaves in the population of the United States, see (Berlin 2003), pp369-71

314   For a list of slaves owned by us presidents prior to Lincoln, see (Center 2012)

315   For "Yelps for liberty among drivers of negroes", see (S. Johnson 1775)

316   "He has waged cruel war against human nature itself, violating its most sacred rights of life and liberty in the persons of a distant people who never offended him; captivating and carrying them into slavery in another hemisphere, or to incur miserable death in their transportation thither. This piratical warfare, the opprobrium of Infidel Powers, is the warfare of the Christian King of Great Britain. Determined to keep open a market where men should be bought and sold, he has prostituted his negative for suppressing every legislative attempt to prohibit or restrain this execrable commerce." Congress's Draft of the *Declaration of Independence, 1776*

317   Reflecting on the talks, General Charles Cotesworth Pinckney, a delegate for South Carolina at the Constitutional Convention, said: "In short, considering all circumstances, we have made the best terms for the security of this species of property it was in our power to make. We would have made better if we could; but on the whole, I do not think them bad." General Charles Cotesworth Pinckney, speaking in South Carolina House, 1788

318   Notes on Debates in Congress, Jefferson 2-4 July [1776]

319   "The Migration or Importation of such Persons as any of the States now existing shall think proper to admit shall not be prohibited by the Congress prior to the Year one thousand eight hundred and eight." Article V of the Constitution (1787)

320 "Representatives and direct Taxes shall be apportioned among the several States which may be included within this Union, according to their respective Numbers, which shall be determined by adding to the whole Number of free Persons, including those bound to Service for a Term of Years, and excluding Indians not taxed, three fifths of all other Persons." Three Fifths Compromise, Article I, Section 2, Clause 3 of the Constitution (1787)

321 James Madison, a slave-owner and architect of the Constitution, said: "We have seen the mere distinction of color made, in the most enlightened period of time, a ground of the most oppressive dominion ever exercised by man over man ... where slavery exists, the republican theory becomes still more fallacious." See (Madison 1787)

322 Jefferson had this to say about slavery: "The whole commerce between master and slave is a perpetual exercise of the most boisterous passions – the most unremitting despotism on the one part, and degrading submissions on the other. Our children see this, and learn to imitate it ... the parent storms, the child looks on, catches the lineaments of wrath, puts on the same airs in the circle of similar slaves, gives a loose rein to the worst of passions; and, thus nursed, educated, and daily exercised in tyranny, cannot but be stamped by it with odious peculiarities. The man must be a prodigy who can restrain his manners and morals undepraved by such circumstances. ... With the morals of the people, their industry also is destroyed; for, in a warm climate, no man will labor for himself who can make another labor for him." See (Jefferson 1785)

323 See (Gordon-Reed 2008)

324 "Comparing them by their faculties of memory, reason, and imagination, it appears to me that in memory they are equal to the whites; in reason much inferior, as I think one could scarcely be found capable of tracing and comprehending the investigations of Euclid; and that in imagination they are dull, tasteless, and anomalous." See (Jefferson 1785)

325 For Jefferson preventing freedmen from entering or living in Virginia, see (Ferling 2002)

326 For "Laws, to be just, must give a reciprocation of right", see (Jefferson 1785)

327 An Act to prevent the farther importation of Slaves (Virginia General Assembly, 5 Oct 1778)

328 The freed population of Virginia rose from 1 percent in 1782 to more than 7 percent in 1810. See (Kolchin 2003)

329 For Jefferson on colonisation, see (Jefferson 1785)

330 "We must await, with patience, the workings of an overruling Providence, and hope that that is preparing the deliverance of those our suffering brethren." Letter from Jefferson to Jean Nicolas de Meusnier, 26 June 1786

331 Writing to Robert Morris in 1786, George Washington said: "I hope it will not be conceived ... that it is my wish to hold the unhappy people who are the subject of this letter in slavery. I can only say, that there is not a man living who wishes more sincerely than I do, to see a plan adopted for the abolition of it."

332 For Northern emancipation, see (Berlin 2003), Chapter 9, pp228-55

333 For the impact on manumission of slaves, of wheat replacing tobacco, see (Berlin 2003)

334 For the number of freed slaves in Delaware and Maryland, see the US Census Bureau data for 1860

335 Quakers refused to report deaths to Anglican authorities during the Great Plague which preceded the Great Fire of London. This was cited by Samuel Pepys as a reason the authorities were unsure about the true mortality rates: "But it is feared that the true number of the dead this week is near 10,000 – partly from the poor that cannot be taken notice of through the greatness of the number, and partly from the Quakers and others that will not have any bell ring for them." See Pepys' *Diary*, 31 August 1665

336 Initially, naval forces were unable to seize ships with no slave-cargo, giving slavers an incentive to throw slaves overboard if they were at risk of being captured. It took years before the navies assigned to police the Middle Passage had enough fast ships to overtake the Baltimore clippers used by slavers.

337 Despite the heavy death-toll from tropical disease, more than one sixth of British naval resources would eventually be dedicated to ending the slave trade, with support from the us Navy from the 1820s onwards. They freed 150,000 people in transit on the Middle Passage between 1808 and 1860, and seized 1,600 ships which could not be readily replaced. For statistics relating to the Royal Navy in West Africa, see Jo Loosemore, *Sailing Against Slavery* (BBC programme, 24 Sept 2014)

338 For Franklin's estimate of slave mortality, see (Berlin 2003), p186

339 Franklin pointed to the impact of free-soil policies on neighbouring states in 1796: "The present prices of lands in Pennsylvania are higher than they are in Maryland and Virginia, although they are not of superior quality; (among other reasons) because there are laws here for the gradual

abolition of slavery, which neither of the two States above mentioned have at present, but which nothing is more certain than they must have, and at a period not remote." Letter from Washington to Sir John Sinclair, 11 December 1796

340   The United States had 1.2 million slaves in 1810, rising to 4 million by 1860. See census data and (Kolchin 2003)

341   For banning black members from slave congregations, see (Berlin 2003), p361

342   An Act to amend the several laws concerning slaves (Virginia General Assembly, 25 Jan 1806)

343   A key architect of the treaties which led to the Trail of Tears was a Scots-Irish Presbyterian from South Carolina, whose antagonism to the Anglican gentry of Charleston shaped his ideas on tyranny. John Caldwell Calhoun would serve as a Congressman, Senator, Secretary of State, Secretary of War, and Vice President under two us Presidents.

344   "Slavery a positive good": John C. Calhoun Senate speech, 5 February 1837

345   "I may say with truth, that in few countries so much is left to the share of the laborer, and so little exacted from him, or where there is more kind attention paid to him in sickness or infirmities of age. Compare his condition with the tenants of the poor houses in the more civilised portions of Europe – look at the sick, and the old and infirm slave, on one hand, in the midst of his family and friends, under the kind superintending care of his master and mistress, and compare it with the forlorn and wretched condition of the pauper in the poor house."

346   For more on the break-up of slave families, see (Morgan 2002)

347   Jefferson on slave-women bringing capital, in a comment made to one of his overseers

348   Calhoun believed that the rise in the population of the North, allied to the rise in power of the federal government, would turn anti-slavery sentiment into a moral imperative: "A large portion of the Northern States believe slavery to be a sin, and would consider it as an obligation of conscience to abolish it if they should feel themselves in any degree responsible for its continuance. . . . Already it has taken possession of the pulpit, of the schools, and, to a considerable extent, of the press; those great instruments by which the mind of the rising generation will be formed. However sound the great body of the non-slaveholding States are at present, in the course of a few years they will be succeeded by those who will have been taught to hate the people and institutions of nearly one-half of this Union. . . . Be assured that emancipation itself would not satisfy these fanatics – that gained, the next step would be to raise the negroes to a social and political equality with the whites; and that being effected, we would soon find the present condition of the two races reversed. They and their northern allies would be the masters, and we the slaves. . . . It is easy to see the end. By the necessary course of events, if left to themselves we must become, finally, two people."

349   Whigs and Democrats had controlled federal government between them for decades, and the political vacuum which followed the demise of the Whig Party led to the temporary collapse of two party politics. Popular frustration with the obsessive focus on slavery mounted, as hundreds of thousands of Irish and German Catholic immigrants poured into the North.

350   For the scandal among the Massachusetts Know Nothing party in relation to sexual impropriety in convents, see (Anbinder 1992)

351   Moral abhorrence of slavery was highest where the threat to prosperity posed by Emancipation was lowest. In Ireland, the African-American activist Charles Lenox Remond got sixty thousand people to sign a petition calling for the abolition of slavery. In America, the Democratic Party parlayed fears about competition for jobs into hostility towards abolitionism. Irish stevedores refused to work with African-Americans in New York. In the Draft Riots of 1863, Irish immigrants burnt down the Colored Orphan Asylum, as well as churches where African-Americans worshipped.

352   Lincoln launched his campaign using biblical rhetoric to brilliant effect: "A house divided against itself cannot stand. . . . Either the opponents of slavery will arrest the further spread of it, and place it where the public mind shall rest, in the belief that it is in the course of ultimate extinction; or its advocates will push it forward, till it shall become lawful in all the States, old as well as new – North as well as South." Lincoln's "House Divided" speech, Springfield, Illinois, 16 June 1858

353   Douglas was the architect of the Kansas-Nebraska Act, which allowed slavery north of the Missouri Compromise line. He believed that slavery should be allowed where the local white electorate approved it – a doctrine known as Popular Sovereignty. Douglas principle of self-government, Ottawa, Illinois, 21 August 1858

354   Douglas accused Lincoln of being an Abolitionist. It was one thing to argue that slavery should not be allowed in new territories, but insisting on abolition in existing states was an extreme position. "Government on the white basis", Chicago, 9 July 1858

355   Lincoln: "a universal feeling, whether well or ill-founded, cannot be safely disregarded". Ottawa,

Illinois, 21 August 1858

356   "Base alloy of hypocrisy": Letter from Abraham Lincoln to Joshua Speed, 24 August 1855

357   Frederick Douglass "freedom from prejudice", in (Douglass 1909). Douglass said that Lincoln "was the first great man that I talked with in the United States freely, who in no single instance reminded me of the difference between himself and myself, of the difference of color", putting Lincoln on a higher plane than principled abolitionists such as Salmon Chase.

358   Lincoln attempted to square the circle on inequality by considering proposals to re-settle freed slaves in Africa. Physical difference social and political equality, Ottawa, Illinois, 21 August 1858

359   "Right to eat the bread", speech made at Ottawa, Illinois, 21 August 1858

360   "I hate it because of the monstrous injustice of slavery itself. I hate it because it . . . enables the enemies of free institutions, with plausibility, to taunt us as hypocrites – causes the real friends of freedom to doubt our sincerity, and especially because it forces so many really good men amongst ourselves into an open war with the very fundamental principles of civil liberty—criticizing the *Declaration of Independence, and insisting that there is no right principle of action but self-interest.*" Opposition to slavery was a matter of right and wrong: "They are the two principles that have stood face to face from the beginning of time; and will ever continue to struggle." Lincoln, Alton, Illinois, 15 October 1858

361   "Freeport Doctrine and Popular Sovereignty", speech made at Freeport, Illinois, 27 August 1858

362   "Public sentiment is everything", speech made at Ottawa, Illinois, 21 August 1858

363   Presidents spent the first weeks of their term hearing requests from potential office-holders and appointing thousands of judges, military commanders, district attorneys, civil servants and postmasters across the United States.

364   For the replacement of federal officials by Lincoln, see (Sandburg 1939), Vol. IV, p105, and the "Presidential Patronage" section on *mrlincolnandfriends.org*

365   Four states outlined their reasons for secession in detailed Declarations of Causes. Georgia referred to Northern attempts to contain "and finally abolish slavery in the States where it exists". South Carolina said: "These [Northern] States have assumed the right of deciding upon the propriety of our domestic institutions; and have denied the rights of property established in fifteen of the States and recognised by the Constitution; they have denounced as sinful the institution of slavery, [permitting societies] whose avowed object is to disturb the peace and eloign the property of the citizens of other States." The refusal of Northern states to enforce the Fugitive Slave Act amounted to a breach of the compact under which the Constitution had been ratified by all the states, freeing the Lower South from their obligations under the Constitution. With the election of Abraham Lincoln, "On the 4th day of March next, this party will take possession of the Government. It has announced that the South shall be excluded from the common territory, that the judicial tribunals shall be made sectional, and that a war must be waged against slavery until it shall cease throughout the United States."

366   For the "Better Angels of our nature" speech, see Lincoln's First Inaugural Address, 4 March 1861

367   "Secession nothing but revolution", see Robert E. Lee's letter to his son, 23 January 1861

368   Using a figure of 761,000 war deaths (350,000 Confederate, 411,000 Union) from J. David Hacker (Hacker, A Census-Based Count of the Civil War Dead Dec 2011) and an estimate of 2.8 million individuals serving in the armies (750,000 Confederate, 2,078,000 Union) from (Long 1971). For the implications on Civil War historiography, see (Hacker, Recounting the Dead 2011)

369   Death-toll higher than other wars combined. See (McPherson, Battle Cry of Freedom 1988)

370   For "Emancipation as an indispensable necessity", see Lincoln's letter to Albert G. Hodges, 4 April 1864

371   In Louisiana, 99.5 percent of black voters were disenfranchised by 1910. See (Pildes 2000)

372   Plessy v. Ferguson, Supreme Court 163us537 (1896)

373   Loving v. Virginia 388us1 (1967)

374   "With some the word liberty may mean for each man to do as he pleases with himself, and the product of his labor; while with others the same word may mean for some men to do as they please with other men, and the product of other men›s labor. . . . The shepherd drives the wolf from the sheep's throat, for which the sheep thanks the shepherd as a liberator, while the wolf denounces him for the same act as the destroyer of liberty, especially as the sheep was a black one . . . the wolf's dictionary, has been repudiated." "Wolf's dictionary has been repudiated", Lincoln Address at a sanitary fair, Baltimore, Maryland, 18 April [1864]

375   For uv deficiency as an explanation for depigmentation, see https://www.sciencemag.org/news/2015/04/how-europeans-evolved-white-skin

376 Opponents of Brexit, nicknamed "Remoaners" in the British tabloid press, have been accused of crying wolf over the potential risks posed by leaving the European Union, three decades after the break-up of the Soviet Union, and two decades after a peace agreement ended violence in Northern Ireland.

377 Belief without evidence was the definition of faith proffered by Richard Dawkins (Dawkins 2008). Apart from failing the George Michael test, the definition begs the question of what constitutes evidence: astronomers lack the ability to run full-scale experiments, but their idea of the likely impact of Shoemaker-Levy 9 prior to its collision with Jupiter would hardly be described as faith. On the other hand, a Christian citing the biblical view that God is Love (1 John 4) could argue that there was ample evidence for its existence.

378 "Belief without good reason" also fails the George Michael test for popular definitions of faith, although cynics might support its matrimonial relevance. Just saying. See (Pinker 2018), p30

379 In April 1962, John F. Kennedy hosted a dinner for Nobel Prize winners of the Western Hemisphere. Welcoming the dignitaries, jfk quipped: "I think this is the most extraordinary collection of talent, of human knowledge, that has ever been gathered together at the White House, with the possible exception of when Thomas Jefferson dined alone." Jefferson was the drafter of the Declaration of Independence, polymath, diplomat, statesman, visionary supporter of the Louisiana Purchase, poster-child for the Enlightenment and third President of the United States. A man who wrote that all men are created equal, and, as we have seen, exploited his slaves both sexually and financially.

380 For intellectually lightweight *philosophes*, see (Pinker, The Better Angels of our Nature 2011), p184

381 For "No Hitler, no Holocaust", see (Pinker, The Better Angels of our Nature 2011) p 343

382 For Voltaire's anti-Semitism, see (Voltaire 1771), quoted by (Hertzberg 1968)

383 For moral retardation, see (Pinker, The Better Angels of our Nature 2011), p658

384 For teleological historicism, see (Popper 2011)

385 For Engel's "false consciousness" quote, see his letter to Franz Mehring, 14 July [1893]

386 For more on the parlous state of French finances in 1789, see (Sargent and Velde 1995)

387 The Declaration of the Rights of Man and of the Citizen, issued by the French National Constituent Assembly, 27 August [1789]

388 The national Festival of Reason was celebrated on 10 November [1793]

389 For more on the death-toll in the Vendée uprising, see the *Dictionnaire de la Contre-Révolution (2011)*

390 Festival of the Supreme Being, celebrated on 8 June [1794]

391 For "Slowness of judgement equal to impunity", see Robespierre *Report on the Principles of Political Morality, 5 February 1794*

392 For the death-toll in the Napoleonic Wars, see (Gates 2003)

393 Personifying the general will dampened dissonance. Unlike Christians sanctifying Holy War, or Enlightenment slavers who believed that all men are created equal, there were no contradictions to trouble moral zeal. The "general will" was whatever the Dear Leader said it was. For criticism of the general will, see (Berlin and Hardy 2002)

394 For "Was ever such a prize won with so little innocent blood?" see letter from Jefferson to William Shore, 3 January 1793

395 The 1848 revolutions were preceded by economic and agricultural crises in much of Europe. For data on poor potato yields in Europe in the 1840s, see (Grada 2006)

396 For Marx's history of class struggles, see (Marx, The Communist Manifesto 1848)

397 For shortening agonies through revolutionary terror, see (Marx, Victory of the Counter-Revolution in Vienna 1848)

398 For more on the Commune, see (Horne 2007)

399 Corruption was limited by capping pay, as well as ensuring that the Commune was "formed of the municipal councillors, chosen by universal suffrage in the various wards of the town, responsible, and revocable at short terms". Public awareness of communism soared throughout Europe after 1870. The leaders of the German Workers Party were tried for treason the following year. After the prosecution read *The Communist Manifesto into the record, Marx and Engels were able to print a German edition without legal repercussions*; this was followed by hundreds of editions, in more than thirty languages, over the next forty years. For Marx and Engels' praise of the Commune, see (Marx, The Civil War in France 1871)

400 For Lenin, the execution of his elder brother, Sasha, for conspiring to kill Tsar Alexander III, had blurred the line between revolutionary socialism and personal vendetta. Political crises had roiled

the Russian Empire since the assassination of Tsar Alexander II in 1881, by the group Narodnaya Volya, or "People's Will". The People's Will were predominantly lapsed Orthodox atheists, but state and media figures scapegoated the Jewish minority for Alexander's assassination.

Most Jews lived in the Pale of Settlement, a region annexed by Russia after the destruction of the Polish state in 1795. The May Laws of 1882 imposed quotas on Jewish students, doctors and lawyers, and prevented observant Jews from farming, buying land or living outside designated towns in the Pale of Settlement. The anti-Semitic backlash, including pogroms in multiple locations in 1881 and the deportation of twenty thousand Jews from Moscow a decade later, was supported by the Okhrana, the Tsarist secret police. More than two thousand Jews died in pogroms in 1903 and 1905, following the defeat of Russia in the Russo-Japanese War. In the thirty-odd years between the assassination of Tsar Alexander II in Saint Petersburg and the assassination of Franz Ferdinand in Sarajevo, more than 2 million Jews left the Russian Empire, often for the United States. Radicalised urban Jews who remained often joined revolutionary organisations.

For "excessive magnanimity on the part of the revolutionary Communards", see (Lenin 1908)

401   For more on the Constituent Assembly, see (Fitzpatrick 2008)
402   For more on the Treaty of Brest-Litovsk, see (Fitzpatrick 2008)
403   For more on the death-toll in the Russian Civil War, see (Fitzpatrick 2008)
404   For rephrase ?the deportation and murder/killing of Cossacks, see (Gellately 2007)
405   When Nikita Khrushchev denounced Stalin at the 20th Congress of the Soviet Union in 1956, he entitled his speech: "The Personality Cult and Its Consequences". After Stalin assumed power, his rivals were airbrushed from popular accounts. He described himself as modest, but he accumulated grandiloquent titles like "Brilliant Genius of Humanity", "Great Architect of Communism" and "Gardener of Human Happiness". Poems, songs, anthems, prizes, streets, villages, towns and cities were named for him, and Soviet art, statuary, textbooks, newspapers, newsreels, radio and rallies honoured his achievements. Stalin mocked his cult at a New Year's Eve Party in 1935, according to Arvo Tuominen. See "The Cult of Personality and Its Consequences", 20th Party Congress, 25 February 1956
406   Stalin was denounced by ?Nikita Khruschev at a closed session of the 20th Congress of the Communist Party of the Soviet Union, 25 February 1956
407   For Stalin's quote on "enemies of the people", see (Volkogonov 1991)
408   For the death-toll in the Gulag, see (Snyder, Bloodlands 2010), pp27-8
409   For the Polish Military Organisation (a group financed by the Polish government to foment unrest in the Soviet Union), see (Snyder, Bloodlands 2010), pp89-94, 98-100, 135
410   For Soviet intelligence belief in a secret Polish-Japanese pact, see (Snyder, Bloodlands 2010), pp37-8
411   For Stalin's "liquidation" of Kulaks "as a class", see (Snyder, Bloodlands 2010), p25
412   For acts of Ukrainian resistance, see (Snyder, Bloodlands 2010), p 84
413   "Dizzy With Success", (Stalin 1931)
414   For the famine in Kazakhstan being the fault of a local party boss, see (Snyder, Bloodlands 2010), p35
415   For Vsevelod Balytski, the head of security in Ukraine, see (Snyder, Bloodlands 2010), pp43-5
416   For Stalin's policy of sealing the border with Ukraine, see (Snyder, Bloodlands 2010) p 45
417   For the death-toll in the Ukraine famine, see (Snyder, Bloodlands 2010), pp21-58, especially p53
418   For Koestler's "enemies of the people" quote, see (Snyder, Bloodlands 2010), p54
419   For Walter Duranty's views on mortality from malnutrition, see the New York Times, 31 March 1933, p13. Duranty suggested in the same article that you cannot make an omelette without breaking eggs.
420   In a New Yorker review of Daniel Kalder's The Infernal Library: On Dictators, the Books They Wrote, and Other Catastrophes of Literacy (Henry Holt 2019), Adam Gopnik highlights the fact that Stalin was a clear thinker and a good writer, who gave literary advice and notes to playwrights such as Alexander Afinogenov. See (Gopnik 2019)
421   For the suppression of votes at the 17th Party Congress, see (Fitzpatrick 2008)
422   For Central Committee deaths in the Great Terror, see (Snyder, Bloodlands 2010), p75, and pp65, 72-3 and 81
423   For the source of Nikolai Yeshov's claim that subversives were castrating prize sheep, see (Snyder, Bloodlands 2010), p75
424   For the death-toll in the Great Terror of Soviet Poles compared with other Soviets, see (Snyder, Bloodlands 2010), p104
425   For the Butovo death-toll, see (Snyder, Bloodlands 2010), p83

426   For the sentence for owning rosary beads in the Gulag, see (Snyder, Bloodlands 2010), p96

427   Some of the most prominent members of the Soviet Communist Party, including Trotsky, Kamenev, Litvinov and Zinoviev, were of Jewish origin; prior to the Great Terror, more than half of the General Officers in the Soviet nkvd, the successor to the Cheka, were Jewish. For the execution of Nikolai Yeshov, see (Snyder, Bloodlands 2010), p108

428   Stalin called for "the liquidation of the reactionary clergy in our country".

429   For the results of the Census of 1937, see (Snyder, Bloodlands 2010), p79

430   For the Nazi Party's vote-share in 1928, see (Geary 1988)

431   For more on hyperinflation in Weimar Germany, see (Taylor 2013)

432   Traditional historiography connects the spread of anti-Semitic conspiracy theories in the West to the translation of *The Protocols of the Elders of Zion into German and English* from 1919 onwards, but such ideas were in circulation long before the October Revolution.

In the trenches of 1915, many British troops were gripped by a new thriller written by John Buchan. The opening pages of *The 39 Steps*, whch is set just before the outbreak of the First World War, feature an American agent, named Scudder, who talks of a conspiracy "to get Russia and Germany at loggerheads . . . the anarchist lot thought it would give them their chance . . . to see a new world emerge. . . . The capitalists would rake in the shekels, and make fortunes by buying up wreckage. Capital . . . had no conscience and no fatherland. . . . Besides, the Jew was behind it, and the Jew hated Russia worse than hell. . . . Do you wonder? For three hundred years they have been persecuted, and this is the return match for the pogroms. The Jew is everywhere, but you have to go far down the backstairs to find him. . . . If you're on the biggest kind of job, and are bound to get to the real boss, ten to one you are brought up against a little white-faced Jew in a bath chair with an eye like a rattle-snake. Yes, sir, he is the man who is ruling the world just now, and he has his knife in the Empire of the Tsar, because his aunt was outraged and his father flogged in some one-horse location on the Volga."

Those who read on to read Chapter Four would discover this Jewish plot was "eye-wash", a canard to throw the real enemy, a German secret society called "the Black Stone", off the scent. By the end of the Great War, however, for many anti-Semites, hare-brained Jewish conspiracy theories seemed eerily prophetic.

The Anglo-Irish journalist Phillip Graves definitively exposed *The Protocols of the Elders of Zion as a forgery in 1921, but it had a* "truthiness" to it that many anti-Semites found irresistible. It wrapped the creation of the Soviet Union, and the incomprehensible slaughter of the First World War, into a neat package which displaced responsibility for the bombs, shells, tanks, torpedoes, mines, machine-guns and chemical weapons away from civilised, enlightened society.

Henry Ford wrote: "The only statement I care to make about *The Protocols is that they fit in with what is going on. They are* sixteen years old, and they have fitted the world situation up to this time." By the mid-1920s, Ford had paid for and organised the distribution of half a million copies of *The Protocols in the United States.*

Hitler alluded to suggestions that *The Protocols were a forgery in Mein Kampf:* "the important thing is that with positively terrifying certainty they reveal the nature and activity of the Jewish people and expose their inner contexts as well as their ultimate final aims".

The threat of "Judeo-Bolshevism" became a core tenet of the German *Einsatzgruppen, as they pre-emptively massacred the Jewish population of Soviet Eastern Europe during the Second World War.*

433   For the Nazi Party's vote-tally in 1928 and 1932, see (Geary 1998). Thirty-seven percent of the vote amounted to 13.7 million voters.

434   For the demographics of Nazi voters, see (Geary 1998)

435   For *Kulturkampf Catholic* Church closures, see (Steinhoff 2006)

436   Judeo-Bolshevist conspiracy theory has been attributed to Alfred Rosenberg as well as *The Protocols of the Elders of Zion.*

437   Martin Heidegger became Rector of the University of Freiburg in April 1933, became a member of the Nazi Party in May 1933, and wrote speeches to students in praise of Adolf Hitler.

438   "Aryan physics" fizzled out after Heisenberg's mother called Himmler's mother to ask if the attacks could stop. Heisenberg was allowed to use the ideas of Bohr and Einstein, but he was not allowed to mention their names.

439   Number of Einsatzgruppen leaders with PhDs (Snyder, Bloodlands 2010) p 126

440   For the number of Jews recorded in the 16 June 1933 census, including Saar, see the United States Holocaust Memorial Museum

441   Five of the 117 founders of the Fasci Italiani di Combattimento were Jewish. According to the Bu-

reau of Jewish Social Research, Italian Jews accounted for 0.12 percent of the population in 1919 (43.000 out of 36.55 million). See also (Brustein 2003)

442   Two hundred and thirty of the marchers were Jewish. See (Brustein 2003)

443   Margheritta Sarfatti wrote *Dux, the biography of Mussolini, in 1926. One of the great what-ifs of history is whether active deterrence of a resurgent Germany might have delayed or prevented the carnage* which was to follow. All the major powers saw the need for rearmament after 1932, with British military plans no longer assuming that a major conflict was at least a decade away. The French had been trying to divide Germany since the fragmentation of the Habsburg Holy Roman Empire in the religious wars of the sixteenth century. They were beaten out of sight in the Franco-Prussian War of 1870, and lost nearly 2 million young lives in the defence of France in the Great War. Even before the Anschluss with Austria and the seizure of the Sudetenland, the German population was more than 60 percent (or 25 million people) larger than that of France in 1932.

In the six years before the start of the Second World War, Hitler rebuilt the German army, reoccupied the Rhineland, provided aid to Franco in the Spanish Civil War, annexed the military resources of the Sudetenland, unified Germany and Austria, and seized the remaining portion of the Czech Republic, as well as creating a client-state in Slovakia. The only world-leader who resisted him was Mussolini, who mobilised the Italian army in an old-school show of force at the Brenner Pass, after Nazis attempted a coup in Austria in 1934. Having approved the assassination of the Austrian Chancellor, Engelbert Dollfuss, by the local ss, Hitler was forced into a humiliating climbdown.

Diplomacy in the 1930s still relied on the concept of a stable equilibrium between major powers, recognising a right to control weaker nations within their sphere of influence, without interference from rivals. In 1934, Austria was within the Italian sphere of influence; this was why Mussolini felt entitled to threaten war against Germany if Hitler did not back down. President James Monroe had placed Latin America within the us "sphere of influence" in 1823, when he said that any intervention by a foreign country would be "the manifestation of an unfriendly disposition towards the United States". The role of statecraft was to offset weight and counterweight, so that a balance of power was maintained. This delicate clockwork was credited with preventing all-out war in western Europe for a century after Napoleon.

Woodrow Wilson suggested an alternative strategic doctrine after the debacle of the Great War. The Austro-Hungarian, Ottoman and Russian Empires had been dismembered, and the political map of Europe had to be redrawn. Wilson argued that the sovereignty of all nations, great and small, should be guaranteed by the international community acting in concert. This became known as "collective security". Frontiers should be based on the democratically expressed wishes of the local population – a principle known as self-determination. A League of Nations should be created to police disputes.

The idea was popular among the general public, but failed to gain traction among statesmen, all of whom sought exceptions which favoured their own national interests. The subsequent carve-up, under the Treaty of Versailles, left large ethnic minorities on the wrong side of borders, especially in Czechoslovakia and Poland. Congress was loathe to see the United States embroiled in foreign wars under a League of Nations mandate, or to replace the Monroe Doctrine with collective security, and refused to ratify the Treaty of Versailles. Absent the United States, the League of Nations became a paper tiger.

With no prospect of a cohesive supra-national deterrent, Mussolini forged an Anglo-French alliance to contain German pretensions in Austria, and to ensure that Italy had a free hand in Abyssinia. The Stresa Front, an alliance between Italy, France and the United Kingdom, split apart in months, as Britain unilaterally signed a Naval Pact with Germany, France agreed a Mutual Assistance Pact with the Soviet Union, and public outrage over the invasion of Abyssinia trumped private assurances of indifference over Italian adventures in the Horn of Africa. Roughly 7 percent of the population of Ethiopia would die in the subsequent Italian occupation.

With the public clamouring for oil sanctions which would cripple Italy, French and British statesmen told "good strong lies" over plans to accommodate Italian colonial ambitions. For Mussolini, it was reminiscent of the humiliating Vittoria Mutilata in the Great War, when the victorious allies had refused to honour secret territorial claims which had been promised to Italy in 1915. Having cast around for partners to encircle Germany, Mussolini concluded that he would have to make peace with Hitler instead, and shifted gear accordingly. The Italian Axis with Germany was announced in October 1936, paving the way for the German Anschluss with Austria less than two years later.

444   For supporters of eugenics, see (Brignell 2010)
445   For sterilising the "feeble-minded" in Britain, see (Brignell 2010)
446   Quoted in the Holocaust Exhibition, Imperial War Museum, London
447   *ibid.*
448   The Aktion T4 Program formally ended in August 1941, but the killings of disabled adults and children continued until the end of the war. See (Lifton 1986)
449   For acolytes, the rationalist, pseudo-scientific morality in *Mein Kampf superseded flawed religious scriptures, giving an alternative narrative of human evolution. Alfred Rosenberg proposed the creation of a Reich Church, with a copy of Mein Kampf and a sword placed on the altar. Himmler sought the revival of German pagan deities. Following the arrest of members of the Confessing Church, the Minister for Church Affairs, Hans Kerrl, said in 1937:* "Positive Christianity is National Socialism. . . . National Socialism is the doing of God's will. . . .God's will reveals itself in German blood. . . . Dr Zoellner and Count Galen have tried to make clear to me that Christianity consists in faith in Christ as the son of God. That makes me laugh. . . . No, Christianity is not dependent upon the Apostle's Creed. . . . True Christianity is represented by the party, and the German people are now called by the party and especially the Fuehrer to a real Christianity. . . . The Fuehrer is the herald of a new revelation."
    The German state had attempted to silence religious criticism since the height of the *Kulturkampf, when the 1871 Pulpit Law forbade political sermons, ostensibly to separate* Church from State. Hitler endorsed the proposal for a unified church which repudiated the Hebrew Bible, or Old Testament, and re-cast Jesus as an Aryan freedom-fighter against the Jews. Some offshoots of the German Evangelical Church did reject the Old Testament. Other Christians mounted a pusillanimous defense of the Hebrew Bible, pointing to the frequency with which God punished the Israelites for their sinful ways as an argument for its retention. For the most part, however, the mainstream churches refused to compromise the integrity of the canonical Christian Bible by abandoning its roots in Judaism.
    Like Hitler, key Nazi figures such as Reinhard Heydrich, the architect of the Final Solution, and the Minister of Propaganda, Joseph Goebbels, were raised in the Catholic faith, but came to see it as incompatible with National Socialism (as was Goebbels' five-year liaison with Else Janke, who was half-Jewish). Goebbels confided in his diary that Hitler would not allow him to publicly disown his Catholic heritage "for tactical reasons". In private, Hitler did not share Hans Kerrl's optimism that Christianity could be Nazified. He described it as "the noblest of intentions, but I don't believe the thing's possible, and I see the obstacle in Christianity itself. As for the men close to me, who, like me, have escaped from the clutches of dogma, I've no reason to fear that the church will get its hands on them. We'll see to it that the church cannot spread abroad teachings that conflict with the interests of the State. We shall continue to preach the doctrine of National Socialism, and the young will no longer be taught anything but the truth. In the long run, National Socialism and religion will no longer be able to exist together."
450   For the claim that Gospel teachings were fabricated by Saint Paul, see (Snyder, Black Earth: The Holocaust as History and Warning 2015), p6
451   For "preserving the species, see (Snyder, Black Earth: The Holocaust as History and Warning 2015), p3
452   For Judeo-Christian teachings as a denial of natural order, see (Snyder, Black Earth: The Holocaust as History and Warning 2015), p6
453   In *Table Talk, Boorman quotes Hitler: "the teachings of Christianity are a rebellion against the natural law of selection by struggle and survival of the fittest".* For Hitler's quote on Jewish "pestilence", see (Snyder, Black Earth: The Holocaust as History and Warning 2015), p8
454   The public opposition of religious groups, including the Jehovah's Witnesses and the Protestant Confessing Church, was problematic for the Nazi regime. It was one thing to refuse consent for the removal of the Hebrew Bible from the Christian canon, but active dissent threatened the authority of the Nazi Party. To make matters worse, one of the leading Lutheran pastors in the Confessing Church, Martin Niemoller, was a decorated U-Boat officer, who had won the Iron Cross in the Great War. When, in 1936, Niemoller denounced the anti-Semitic and anti-Christian interference of the Nazi Party in religious affairs, seven. hundred pastors were arrested, and Niemoller and other Confessing Church leaders were sent to concentration camps. Not all survived. In later life, survivors regretted that they had focused purely on ecclesiastical independence, rather than issuing a polemic against the persecution of all groups. As Niemoller wrote: "First they came for the Socialists, and I did not speak out, because I was not a Socialist. Then they came for the Trade Unionists, and I did not speak out, because I was not a Trade Unionist. Then they came for the Jews, and I did not

speak out, because I was not a Jew. Then they came for me, and there was no one left to speak for me."

The Confessing Church could be suppressed because it did not speak for most German Protestants, who were reluctant to see the church interfere in political affairs. Only one Christian denomination had the moral authority to speak for nearly 40 percent of Germans, and a history of political organisation against an overweening state. The Roman Catholic Church signed a Concordat with the Reich in 1933, but by 1937 Pope Pius XI felt compelled to speak out against Nazi breaches of the accord, especially their control of education, as well as condemning racism ("Whoever exalts race . . . is far from the true faith in God"), defending the Hebrew Bible ("Whoever wishes to see banished from church and school the Biblical history and the wise doctrines of the Old Testament, blasphemes the name of God"), supporting freedom of worship ("Laws which impede this profession and practice of Faith are against natural law") and condemning the utilitarian Nazi value system ("what is morally indefensible, can never contribute to the good of the people"). The "enemy of Holy Scripture . . . oversowed the cockle of distrust, unrest, hatred [and] defamation . . . against Christ and His Church".

The Papal Encyclical *Mit brennender Sorge* ("With Burning Concern"), written in German rather than Latin, was prepared in secrecy and smuggled into Germany, where 300,000 copies were printed and read out on one of the busiest days in the church calendar, Palm Sunday. Despite reports that Hitler was furious, critics argue that the encyclical was too oblique. The condemnation of Reich government behaviour can only refer to the Nazis, but neither the party nor National Socialism are explicitly named, nor is Hitler name-checked as the "mad prophet" sowing "pantheistic confusion", "neopaganism", the idolisation of the state or "the so-called myth of race and blood". The document defends freedom of worship, but no mention is made of the persecution of practising Jews, still less the attacks on Communists, who were the subject of *Divini Redemptoris, a scathing Papal Encyclical put out two days before Mit brennender Sorge was read from the pulpit. The day after the* encyclical was promulgated, the Gestapo shut down twelve printing presses which had facilitated its publication. The anticipated crackdown against senior Roman Catholic clergy did not materialise, but hundreds of lay-people were arrested. *Mit brennender Sorge could have been blunter and more comprehensive in its critique,* but that would, at best, have redounded to the reputation of Pope Pius XI. The bigger problem was that the condemnation of Nazi practices could not be parlayed into effective, sustained political opposition within a totalitarian state.

455 For American Plantation as a template for *Lebensraum,* see (Snyder, Black Earth: The Holocaust as History and Warning 2015), pp12-14, 21

456 The Hunger Plan was prepared by Herbert Backe, a failed PhD student in agriculture who was dismissive of the scientific potential to raise food-yields from German territory.

457 For the terms of the Hunger Plan, see (Confino 2014), p163

458 For the target death-toll from the Hunger Plan, see (Confino 2014), p163

459 For Heydrich and Operation Tannenburg, see (Snyder, Black Earth: The Holocaust as History and Warning 2015), pp106-7

460 For the Polish projected death-toll under the Hunger Plan, see (Confino 2014), p163

461 For teaching Polish children pidgin German, see (Snyder, A New Approach to the Holocaust 2011)

462 For the quote from *Volkischer Beobachter,* see (Confino 2014), p219

463 For house of cards, see (Snyder, Black Earth: The Holocaust as History and Warning 2015), pp19-20

464 For the Erich Koch quote, see (Snyder, Black Earth: The Holocaust as History and Warning 2015), p18

465 For the Wehrmacht death-toll on the Eastern Front, see (Confino 2014), p193

466 For the wearing of the Star of David in Germany in September 1941, see (Snyder, Black Earth: The Holocaust as History and Warning 2015), p166

467 For the prospect of Jews killing all "Aryan" Germans, see (Snyder, Black Earth: The Holocaust as History and Warning 2015), p166

468 Churchill's "crime without a name" radio broadcast, 24 August [1941]

469 For the Jewish death-toll in Latvia, Lithuania, Ukraine and Belarus by December 1941, see (Snyder, Black Earth: The Holocaust as History and Warning 2015), p192

470 For more on the participation by lawyers in the Holocaust, see (Snyder, Black Earth: The Holocaust as History and Warning 2015), pp40, 43, 144-5

471 For Victors Bernhard Arajs, see (Snyder, Black Earth: The Holocaust as History and Warning 2015), pp169-72, 176

472 For the death-toll in Lithuanian pogroms, se (Snyder, Black Earth: The Holocaust as History and Warning 2015), p149

473 The persecution of the Jewish minority in Lithuania had begun with the Soviet invasion of the Baltic following the Molotov-Ribbentrop Pact. For the Soviet Union, the establishment of a socialist republic required the destruction of the capitalist state which preceded it. In Poland, this meant the execution by the nkvd of 21,892 captured prisoners of war (21,891 males and one female), who represented the leadership cadre of Polish society, including nearly half the Officer Corps of the Polish army. In the Baltic, it meant establishing a system of collaboration and denunciation of "class enemies" by the local population, leading to their execution or deportation. With their heavy presence in commercial life, Jewish businessmen were front and centre. Before the Soviet invasion, Karlis Ulmanis, the American-educated Latvian leader, had afforded Jewish citizens the full protection of the state. Antanas Smetona, the Lithuanian autocrat, had made public his hostility to "zoological nationalism and racism". Both Latvia and Lithuania accepted Jewish refugees, and far-right anti-Semitic groups were suppressed and proscribed. With the arrival of the Soviets, 83 percent of the businesses targeted by the nkvd were owned by Lithuanian Jewish citizens, who accounted for less than 8 percent of the population. Those deported to the Siberian Gulags would be spared the annihilation of the Holocaust, but the targeting of minority firms reinforced the vulnerability to scapegoating of those who were left behind. Despite this, "spontaneous" pogroms were a failure in the Holocaust.

474 Georg Duckwitz was designated "Righteous Among The Nations" by Yad Vashem

475 For the Zofia Kossak story, see (Bazalgette 2017), pp14-15

476 For Mother hitching pants, see (Snyder, Black Earth: The Holocaust as History and Warning 2015), p188

477 For the rescue of Sara Sonja Griffin, see (Bazalgette 2017), pp 15-16

478 For Kurt Trimborn's aid to Eleazar Bernstein and his shooting of Jews, see (Snyder, Black Earth: The Holocaust as History and Warning 2015), p251

479 Back home, people endorsed traditional anti-Semitism, but not depictions of Jews as hordes of rats to be exterminated. By 1942, 20 million Germans had seen the wildly popular costume drama *Jew Suss, where the villain was banished at the end; but audiences were repelled by the documentary The Wandering Jew, which closed in* thirty-five out of thirty-six Berlin cinemas within a few weeks of opening. For the relative popularity of *Jew Suss versus The Wandering Jew*, see (Confino 2014), pp 171-3

480 For Franz Stahlecker on emotional strain, see (Snyder, Black Earth: The Holocaust as History and Warning 2015), p166

481 For Friedrich Jeckeln and the "sardine method", see (Snyder, Black Earth: The Holocaust as History and Warning 2015), p176

482 Walter Rauss, quoted in Holocaust Exhibition, Imperial War Museum, London

483 Wannsee Conference, 20 January [1942]

484 For the death-toll from starvation of Soviet pows, see (Snyder, Black Earth: The Holocaust as History and Warning 2015), p194

485 Hitler's "prophecy" that Jewish people would be eradicated was made in the Berliner Sportpalast arena, 30 January [1942]

486 For "more humane to kill than to starve", see (Snyder, Black Earth: The Holocaust as History and Warning 2015), p203

487 For the exterminations at Treblinka, Belzec and Sobibor extermination, see (Snyder, Black Earth: The Holocaust as History and Warning 2015), p202

488 For the detah-toll at Auschwitz, see (Snyder, Black Earth: The Holocaust as History and Warning 2015), p210

489 For the Jewish death-toll in France and the Netherlands, see (Snyder, Black Earth: The Holocaust as History and Warning 2015), p242

490 For the Jewish death-toll by end of the Second World War II, as well as of Roma, gay and disabled people, see (Snyder, Bloodlands 2010), pp379-80

491 For the number of Polish Jewish survivors in Gulags, see (Snyder, Black Earth: The Holocaust as History and Warning 2015), p 219. For a Jewish account of life in a concentration camp, see (Levi 2004)

492 In his documentary *The Fallen of World War II* (2015), Neil Halloran estimates that there were 70 million fatalities.

493 For the homicide rate in the west versus the east, see (Pinker, The Better Angels of our Nature 2011), p103

494 For homicide rates in Canada and the United States, see (Pinker, The Better Angels of our Nature 2011), p116

495   For the ten-fold drop in violence in California between 1840 and 1910, see (Pinker, The Better Angels of our Nature 2011), pp102-6

496   Inspired by the ideas of the Enlightenment and the French Revolution, the feminist Mary Wollstonecraft wrote *A Vindication of the Rights of Woman: With Strictures on Political and Moral Subjects in 1792. Rejecting the idea that middle-class women were assets to be traded in marriage, she argued that they should have a liberal education* in order to become true "companions" to their husbands, to educate their children, to act as role-models to servants, and to avoid the objectification and vanity she associated with aristocrats: "taught from their infancy that beauty is woman's sceptre, the mind shapes itself to the body, and, roaming round its gilt cage, only seeks to adorn its prison".

The change in attitudes can be seen two decades later in the work of Jane Austen. She revolutionised English literature through her development of the novel, providing a realistic portrait of domestic life for the rural middle class. Pressure is often put on her heroines to consider an "advantageous" match, but they are not compelled to go ahead with such a match; they are responsible for choosing who to marry.

Austen's role-models are self-made couples who work as partners, such as Admiral and Mrs Croft, who sailed around the world together. When Mrs Croft seizes the reins in order to prevent their carriage from hitting a post, Austen says it is "no bad representation of the general guidance of their affairs".

497   After the Fugitive Slave Act of 1850 forced Northern states to return runaway slaves, Harriet Beecher Stowe wrote *Uncle Tom's Cabin, which reinforced racial stereotypes but delivered a damning verdict on the cruelties of human bondage. Uncle Tom's Cabin* had a profound influence on Northern attitudes towards the institution of slavery before the Civil War, becoming the best-selling book of the nineteenth century after the Bible, and moving public opinion from regret or indifference to active political opposition.

Free African-Americans were already eloquent advocates for change, with the testimony of former slaves such as Frederick Douglass having a profound effect on the Abolitionist movement. In the 1840s, the Baptist, Presbyterian and Methodist churches all split into Northern and Southern sections over the question of whether slavery was a moral evil – for which perpetrators were accountable before God.

Harriet Beecher Stowe exposed the cognitive dissonance of the churches in a key to *Uncle Tom's Cabin:* "The Methodist Church is . . . peculiarly situated upon this subject, because its constitution and book of discipline contain the most vehement denunciations against slavery of which language is capable."

Some of the most powerful advocates for emancipation were also champions of equal rights for women. Sojourner Truth was an emancipated slave from New York who became the first woman to successfully sue a white man to return her son, who had been illegally sold down to Alabama. In 1851, Sojourner Truth spoke on equal rights in Akron, Ohio, at the Women's Convention:

> I want to say a few words about this matter . . . I have plowed and reaped and husked and chopped and mowed, and can any man do more than that? I have heard much about the sexes being equal. I can carry as much as any man, and can eat as much too, if I can get it. I am as strong as any man that is now. As for intellect, all I can say is, if a woman have a pint, and a man a quart – why can't she have her little pint full? You need not be afraid to give us our rights for fear we will take too much, for we can't take more than our pint'll hold.

> The poor men seems to be all in confusion, and don't know what to do. Why children, if you have woman's rights, give it to her and you will feel better. You will have your own rights, and they won't be so much trouble. I can't read, but I can hear. I have heard the Bible and have learned that Eve caused man to sin. Well, if woman upset the world, do give her a chance to set it right side up again.

> The lady has spoken about Jesus, how he never spurned woman from him, and she was right. When Lazarus died, Mary and Martha came to him with faith and love and besought him to raise their brother. And Jesus wept and Lazarus came forth. And how came Jesus into the world? Through God who created him and the woman who bore him. Man, where was your part? But the women are coming up blessed be God and a few of the men are coming up with them.

> But man is in a tight place, the poor slave is on him, woman is coming on him, he is surely between a hawk and a buzzard.

498   The history of the twentieth century would have been very different if Lenin, Stalin or Mao had listened to German socialist Rosa Luxemburg. Less than three weeks after co-founding the Ger-

man Communist Party, she was beaten, shot and thrown into the Landwehr Canal by right-wing Freikorps paramilitaries. Her body was not found until six months later, at the beginning of July 1919. She continues to be remembered for her passionate advocacy of plural social democracy. Rosa wrote that "Freedom only for the members of the government, only for the members of the Party . . . is no freedom at all. Freedom is always the freedom of dissenters. . . . Without general elections, without freedom of the press, freedom of speech, freedom of assembly, without the free battle of opinions, life in every public institution withers away, becomes a caricature of itself, and bureaucracy rises as the only deciding factor. . . . There is no democracy without socialism, and no socialism without democracy." (Luxemburg 1920)

499   The Nineteenth Amendment to the Constitution reads: "The right of citizens of the United States to vote shall not be denied or abridged by the United States or by any State on account of sex."

500   In December 1955, Rosa Parks refused to go to the back of the bus. She was sitting in the "colored" zone in Montgomery, Alabama, but when the white area filled, the driver slid the "colored section" sign further down, and told four black passengers that they had to move.

Mrs Parks remembered the driver, James Blake. Twelve years earlier, he had insisted that she buy her ticket at the front of the bus, before disembarking and re-entering the colored section at the rear. When she argued with him, he had left her in the rain.

There had been too many indignities. Too many lynch-mobs. Too many acquittals. She was "tired of giving in". She refused to move, and she was arrested. Five days later, the Montgomery Improvement Association was created to lead a boycott of city buses. It lasted for 381 days under the leadership of its president, a young minister by the name of Martin Luther King, until the Supreme Court ruled that segregation of the Alabama bus system was unconstitutional in Browder v. Gayle.

Talking to NPR nearly forty years later, Rosa Parks said: "I did not want to be mistreated, I did not want to be deprived of a seat that I had paid for. It was just time . . . there was an opportunity for me to take a stand to express the way I felt about being treated in that manner. I had not planned to get arrested. I had plenty to do without having to end up in jail. But when I had to face that decision, I didn't hesitate to do so because I felt that we had endured that too long. The more we gave in, the more we complied with that kind of treatment, the more oppressive it became."

Rosa Parks was part of a dignified and peaceful civil rights campaign which brought the dissonance of racism home to American society as a whole. Mamie Clark was an African-American psychologist who showed how damaging segregation was to the mental health of young children. Her Masters thesis was entitled "The Development of Consciousness of Self in Negro Pre-School Children." She found that both black and white children preferred white dolls over black dolls, and children who correctly drew themselves as black or brown would draw others who were non-white in a lighter shade than their actual skin-colour when asked what colour they should be.

Mamie's research was put to good use in a lawsuit against the city of Topeka, Kansas. In order to attend third grade, a little girl called Linda Brown had to walk six blocks to catch a bus to Monroe Elementary School, which was a mile away. Sumner Elementary School was only seven blocks from her home, but it was for whites only. Her father and twelve other parents filed a class action against the Board of Education.

With her husband Kenneth Clark, the first African-American president of the American Psychological Association, Mamie provided expert testimony to the Supreme Court before they made a unanimous ruling in Brown v. Board of Education in 1954 that even if schools were of a similar standard, segregation was "inherently unequal". The ruling stated that "The effect is greater when it has the sanction of the law, for the policy of separating the races is usually interpreted as denoting the inferiority of the negro group. A sense of inferiority affects the motivation of a child to learn."

501   Spending on education rose seven-fold in real terms between 1955 and 2015 in the uk alone. See https://www.ifs.org.uk/tools_and_resources/fiscal_facts/public_spending_survey/education

502   For the impact of paternity leave on (Bregman 2017), pp 143-4

503   See (Research n.d.)

504   See research by Borrell Associates. Online advertising in 2016 had increased 900 percent compared with the 2012 election.

505   Theresa Hong, the Digital Content Director for the Trump campaign, later said: "Without Facebook, we wouldn't have won." See (Osnos, Ghost in the Machine: Can Mark Zuckerberg fix Facebook before it breaks democracy? 2018)

506   Among the advertisements listed in the indictment are the following:

6 April 2016: "You know, a great number of black people support us saying that #HillaryClintonIsNotMyPresident"

7 April 2016: "I say no to Hillary Clinton / I say no to manipulation"

19 April 2016: "JOIN our #HillaryClintonForPrison2016"

10 May 2016: "Donald wants to defeat terrorism . . . Hillary wants to sponsor it"

19 May 2016: "Vote Republican, vote Trump, and support the Second Amendment!"

24 May 2016: "Hillary Clinton Doesn't Deserve the Black Vote"

7 June 2016: "Trump is our only hope for a better future!"

30 June 2016: "#NeverHillary #HillaryForPrison #Hillary4Prison #HillaryForPrison2016
#Trump2016 #Trump #Trump4President"

20 July 2016: "Ohio Wants Hillary 4 Prison"

4 August 2016: "Hillary Clinton has already committed voter fraud during the Democrat Iowa
Caucus."

10 August 2016: "We cannot trust Hillary to take care of our veterans!"

14 October 2016: "Among all the candidates Donald Trump is the one and only who can defend
the police from terrorists."

19 October 2016: "Hillary is a Satan, and her crimes and lies had proved just how evil she is"

507   The indictment indicates that the hackers created false us personas, operating social media pages and groups designed to attract us audiences. These groups and pages, which addressed divisive us political and social issues, falsely claimed to be controlled by us activists. They also used the stolen identities of real us persons to post on social media accounts they controlled. These accounts reached significant numbers of Americans for the purposes of interfering with the us political system, including the presidential election of 2016.

508   The indictment claims that the Internet Research Agency started to make claims of voter fraud by the Democratic Party through their us personas and groups on social media, buying advertisements on Facebook. In August 2016, they began buying ads promoting a post on their Facebook account "Stop A.I." The post said that "Hillary Clinton has already committed voter fraud during the Democrat Iowa Caucus". They also tweeted that allegations of voter fraud were being investigated in North Carolina on their Twitter account @TEN_GOP. In November, they tweeted on @TEN_GOP: "#VoterFraud by counting tens of thousands of ineligible mail-in Hillary votes being reported in Broward County, Florida."

509   The indictment claims that the Internet Research Agency created thematic group pages on social-media sites, particularly Facebook and Instagram, which addressed a range of issues, including immigration (using names including "Secured Borders"), Black Lives Matter (with names including "Blacktivist") and religion (including "United Muslims of America" and "Army of Jesus"). They also created regional groups within the United States with names including "South United" and "Heart of Texas". Around 2015, they began to buy advertisements on social-media sites to promote their social-media groups.

510   The indictment states that in the latter half of 2016, they began to encourage us minority groups not to vote in the presidential election, or to vote for a third-party candidate. In October, they used their Instagram account "Woke Blacks" to post the following: "[A] particular hype and hatred for Trump is misleading the people and forcing Blacks to vote Killary. We cannot resort to the lesser of two devils. Then we'd surely be better off without voting AT ALL." They bought an advertisement in November to promote a post on their Instagram account "Blacktivist" which read, in part: "Choose peace and vote for Jill Stein. Trust me, it's not a wasted vote." In early November, they used their "United Muslims of America" social-media accounts to post anti-vote messages such as: "American Muslims [are] boycotting elections today, most of the American Muslim voters refuse to vote for Hillary Clinton because she wants to continue the war on Muslims in the middle east and voted yes for invading Iraq."

511   The indictments states that they bought political advertisements on social media in the names of us persons and entities. They staged political rallies inside the United States. Without revealing their Russian identities and affiliation, they posed as us grass-roots entities and citizens, and solicited and paid real us citizens to promote or disparage candidates. Posing as us persons, some of the defendants communicated with unwitting individuals associated with the Trump campaign and with other political activists to coordinate political activities.

512   The indictment claims that the defendants illegally used the social-security numbers and dates of birth of real us citizens without those persons' knowledge or consent. Using these means of identification, they opened accounts at PayPal, created fake drivers' licences and posted on social media using the identities of these us victims. They also obtained false identification documents to use as proof of identity in maintaining accounts and buying advertisements on social-media sites.

513   See (Marantz 2020)

514   After the Cold War, people were reluctant to shed American blood on foreign soil. A disastrous intervention against warlords in Somalia fatally stayed the hand of President Clinton in Rwanda. For a detailed assessment of the Bosnian genocide by the un Commander on the ground, see (Dallaire 2004). Clinton responded in Bosnia with an air campaign which helped prevent the recurrence of massacres like Srebrenica, where eight thousand Muslim men and boys were murdered by their Bosnian Serb neighbours. See (Power 2007), pp401-41. Jihadis were radicalised in the Middle East as populations soared and their prospects dwindled. More than half the population of mena (the Middle East and North Africa) is under twenty-five, and mena has the highest regional youth-unemployment rate in the world (Middle East, 27.2 percent; North Africa, 29 percent), according to the World Economic Forum (Eide and Rösler 2014). Tensions in authoritarian regimes would lead to the attacks on the World Trade Center in 1993 and 2001, as well as the nascent protests of the Arab Spring. The presence of us troops in Saudi Arabia was cited as a reason for the 9/11 attacks. Polling in the Middle East by Gallup in May 2008 confirmed the hostile perception of the us bases in Saudi Arabia and Egypt among the local population (Ray 2009). Libyan intervention toppled the regime of Muammar Ghadaffi, without replacing it with a stable, pluralist democracy. Transparency International ranked Libya among the ten most corrupt states in the world in 2016. See https://www.transparency.org/country/LBY. Red lines were crossed in Syria on the use of chemical weapons without consequence. See (Kessler 2013). The soaring yes-we-can rhetoric of President Obama was distilled into a pithy aphorism on foreign affairs: "Don't do stupid shit." The President who tried to minimise American entanglement in unwinnable wars, prevent a Great Depression, and pioneer a new federal health care program after decades of legislative stalemate, spoke at a Commencement Ceremony at the United States Military Academy in West Point on 28 May 2014 about reining in "America's willingness to rush into military adventures". A war-weary nation sought to disengage from Iraq and Afghanistan in ways which were consistent with honour and security. For the growth of Islamic State, see (Nagus 2006)

515   The Migrant Offshore Aid Station (moas) charity had a fifteen-fold increase in donations within twenty-four hours of the pictures being published. See (Henley 2015)

516   The National Police Chiefs Council found that hate crimes remained 14 percent higher months after Brexit. See (Mortimer 2016)

517   uk intelligence officials estimated in May 2017 that three thousand British Muslims had "active Jihadist leanings", with a further twenty thousand posing a "residual risk". See (O'Neill, et al. 2017)

518   When Twitter increased the tweet limit to 280 characters, Trump was quoted as saying: "It's a good thing, but it's a bit of a shame because I was the Ernest Hemingway of 140 characters." See (Woodward 2018), p207

519   Stephen Colbert definition of "truthiness", aired on *The Colbert Report*, 17 October [2005]

520   Liberal commentators have been hyperbolic in criticising President Trump for everything from his effusive praise of Kim Jong-un to his tenuous grasp of hurricane trajectories and his eagerness to broker a peace-deal with the Taliban, at the risk of losing perspective. See https://www.washingtonpost.com/opinions/2019/09/10/with-taliban-invite-camp-david-trump-continues-his-desecration-norms/

521   Trump's enthusiastic endorsement of the new Crown Prince cooled somewhat following the murder of the Saudi Arabian journalist Jamal Khashoggi at the Saudi Consulate in Turkey.

522   See https://thehill.com/homenews/sunday-talk-shows/429322-saudi-foreign-minister-blames-khashoggi-killing-on-officials

523   See *Foreign Policy* magazine: https://foreignpolicy.com/2019/02/12/jared-kushner-and-the-art-of-humiliation/

524   For talking to enlisted soldiers, see (Woodward 2018), pp 124-5

525   For the disastrous war in Afghanistan, see (Woodward 2018) p 315

526   Trump to Secretary of State Tillerson: "But how many more deaths? How many more lost limbs? How much longer are we going to be there?" See (Woodward 2018), p125

527   Bob Woodward recounts that officials had to rein in President Trump's desire to re-negotiate free-trade deals with South Korea, where Special Access Programs allowed the us to detect a North Korean icbm launch within 7 seconds, versus 15 minutes from Alaska. See (Woodward 2018), prologue

528   No one seemed to see the implications of meeting with representatives of a foreign power in order to get dirt on a domestic opponent. According to Steve Bannon, they were so guileless that they met in plain sight in Trump Tower without bringing their own lawyers into the room. Bannon said that removing Comey would turn a third-tier story into the biggest in the world. Trump's attorney, John

Dowd, described the original *New York Times story as "horseshit" since opposition research to get dirt was commonplace. See* (Woodward 2018), p197. On 8 June 2018, James Comey testified that the *Times* story on Trump aides' contacts with senior Russian intelligence officials "in the main was not true". See (Woodward 2018), p85

529   For Rex Tillerson calling Trump a "fucking moron", see (Woodward 2018), p225

530   For a tweet on bleeding from a facelift, see (Woodward 2018), p205

531   For the resignation of cnn journalists, see (Grynbaum 2017)

532   According to Thomas Wolff, the Trumps sleep in separate bedrooms – the first time this has happened since the Kennedy administration. If he isn't busy in the evenings, Donald Trump will eat a cheeseburger in bed while watching TV and calling business friends and associate he admires.

533   See Suzanne Lynch in https://www.irishtimes.com/news/world/us/americans-go-to-polls-in-most-consequential-election-in-us-history-1.4398700

534   Loving v. Virginia 388us1 (1967)

535   The death-toll in the Belgian Congo was 8 million. See (Hochschild 1999). The French government suppressed a similar report on abuses in the French Congo in 1905. German records of the 1904 rebellion of the Herero and Nama in south-west Africa were destroyed in 1926. Tens of thousands of civilians were killed through starvation, dehydration, disease and exhaustion. Some were used in medical experiments. The Supreme Commander of German forces, Lieutenant-General Lothar von Trotha, saw the uprising as the "beginning of a racial struggle". He believed "that the nation as such should be annihilated", and drove women and children into the desert to die of thirst, where his troops could not be "infected by their diseases". The official journal of the German General Staff, *Der Kampf* ("The Struggle"), praised von Trotha's use of the desert in "the extermination of the Herero nation".

536   Overrun by Scots (Bardon 2012), p304

537   For James I being refused the title "King of Great Britain", see (Bardon 2012), p111

538   For the proportion of immigrants to the United States between 1970 and 2015, see the cdc report on us Healthcare, 2016

539   See the McKinsey Global Institute report on the impact of immigration written by (Woetzel, et al. 2016). Also, on the impact of emigration on the Developing World, see (Bregman 2017)

540   For the reversal of homicide rates (and others) in the 1990s and 2000s, see (Pinker, The Better Angels of our Nature 2011), pp378-481

541   For the reduction in inter-state warfare, see (Pinker, The Better Angels of our Nature 2011), p302

542   Virginia Page Fortna report, quoted in (Pinker, The Better Angels of our Nature 2011), pp314-5

543   Trade as a propotion of GDP has risen from 24.14 percent of gdp in 1965 to 58.04 percent in 2015. https://data.worldbank.org/indicator/NE.TRD.GNFS.ZS

544   See the graph of democracies around the world in (Pinker, The Better Angels of our Nature 2011), p279

545   Also known as the Massacre of 1391

546   For the defenestration of Prague, see (Wilson 2011)

547   The investigations of blood-libel and poisoning a well are cited in (Confino 2014), pp103-4. The Gestapo apparently apologised to a man named Blumenthal in the blood-libel case in Manau, but when three peasants in a bar complained about the mistreatment of suspects in an alleged poisoning of a well in Frankenwinheim, Stormtroopers forced them to shout that they were servants of the Jews.

548   For the 1851 mortality rate in Liverpool and Okehampton, see (Daunton 2004). For uk life expectancy for the poorest decile in 2013, see uk Census data for males and females.

549   "As the heavenly bodies, once thrown into a certain definite motion, always repeat this, so is it with social production as . . . effects, in their turn, become causes, (Marx, Das Kapital 1867 - 1883). As a proponent of "scientific socialism", to use Engel's phrase, the value of Marxist thinking lies in its predictive power. The extent to which Marx changed his mind in the light of new evidence is a bone of contention among keepers of the flame. There are few scientific disciplines where revisionism is bandied around as a pejorative.

550   For more on income inequality and stagnation, see (Piketty 2013)

551   For the 2017 survey by the Public Religion Research Institue, see https://www.prri.org/

552   Daniel Kahneman received a Nobel Prize in Economics for work on the behavioural implications of loss-aversion.

553   Trump's negative advertising was far more likely to have a policy basis than Hillary Clinton's. See

https://www.vox.com/policy-and-politics/2017/3/8/14848636/hillary-clinton-tv-ads

554 Or at least more excuses. In *The Righteous Mind*, Jonathan Haidt quotes the experiments of David Perkins, who found that people with higher iqs were able to provide more arguments in favor of their "gut" opinions on social issues, but did not come up with more arguments against. See (Haidt 2012), pp 94-5

555 Khalid Shaikh Mohammed was held in Guantánamo for helping to plot the 9/11 attacks. See (Blake 2017)

556 Coulibaly's rationalisation was recorded by rtl Radio, which had called the market: http://edition.cnn.com/2015/01/10/world/france-market-shooting-scene/index.html

557 For partisan bias, see (Bloom 2016)

558 But conforming to tribal norms does not mean that we believe in them. Robb Willer of Stanford University ran an experiment asking subjects to taste what they were told were two different wines; the samples were both from the same bottle. More than half the subjects agreed that one was far superior to the other, after being told that all bar one of their fellow reviewers thought this way. Then they found out that the last reviewer thought they tasted the same. If the subjects were asked to rank their peers in wine-tasting publicly, they gave the dissenter a low score, but if asked to rank them privately, the dissenting reviewer got a higher score.

559 In President Trump's statement on withdrawing from the Paris Climate Accord, he said: "I cannot in good conscience support a deal that punishes the United States – which is what it does – the world's leader in environmental protection, while imposing no meaningful obligations on the world's leading polluters. I was elected to represent the citizens of Pittsburgh, not Paris." See (Woodward 2018), p194

560 See "Key takeaways on Americans' views of guns and gun ownership" by Ruth Igielnik and Anna Brown https://www.pewresearch.org/fact-tank/2017/06/22/key-takeaways-on-americans-views-of-guns-and-gun-ownership, based on the Pew data; the *Washington Post* article "Everyone knows Americans own more guns than residents of any other country. But why?" by Amanda Erickson, 4 October 2017; the bbc's "America's gun culture in 10 charts", 21 March 2018; and the *Guardian* article "The gun numbers: just 3 percent of American adults own a collective 133 million firearms. Facts show owning more than 40 guns is actually fairly common in the United States, and violence falls most heavily on the country's poorest neighborhoods", Lois Beckett in New York, @loisbeckett, 15 Nov 2017

561 A significant proportion of those who voted for President Trump abhorred his behaviour but were willing to hold their noses because he could secure a pro-life majority on the Supreme Court. Jurists on both sides of the debate believe that the legal rationale behind Roe v. Wade was flawed and needs to be overhauled, but that does not mean the Court will determine when a foetus acquires the rights of a person. Apart from the metaphysical connotations of the word, personhood is a key concept in law, defining who or what has standing to enforce their rights before the courts. The Supreme Court in Citizens United decided that Limited Liability Corporations are persons in a legal sense, with the capability not only to make and enforce contracts, but to form Super-PACs which can influence presidential elections under First Amendment rights to free speech. Citizens United v. Federal Elections Commission 558us310 (2010). The Supreme Court also ruled that slaves were property, rather than persons, in the Dred Scott case which presaged the American Civil War. Dred Scott v Sandford, 6 March [1857, 60us393].

562 Roughly half a billion legal terminations have occurred around the world since the Supreme Court ruling in Roe v. Wade. 336 million terminations had occurred under the One Child policy in China by 2013, according to the Chinese Health Ministry (Moore 2013). According to the Guttmacher Institute, approximately 60 million terminations have taken place in the United States alone. Other data-sets suggest that more than 45 million terminations have occurred, but have not provided a complete estimate across the United States. Termination statistics are difficult to compile because individual states do not have to report data. Balancing the conundrum of reproductive rights and foetal rights led President Clinton to state that "no one knows when biology turns into humanity". See "No one knows when biology turns into humanity" (Clinton 2004), p229. For a detailed discussion of hard-wired traits, see (Pinker, The Blank Slate 2002), and for evidence of a hard-wired moral sense, see (Bloom, Just Babies: The Origins of Good and Evil 2013)

563 The anterior cingulate does not develop until week 26 (Templeton, et al. 2010)

564 Some states seeking to dissuade women from choosing terminations have sought mandatory sonograms prior to any other procedure being carried out. Sonograms can be highly invasive in the early stages of gestation. Speech by Kellyanne Conway to the March for Life in Washington DC, 27 January [2017]

565 Defence of abortion first published in (Thomson 1971)

566   Because she had a rare blood type, no one else could be hooked up to provide life support. The violinist will die without her sustenance for the next nine months. Thomson argues that it is morally praiseworthy to keep the violinist alive, but not morally obligatory. The public agrees. Critics argue that the thought-experiment is flawed in a number of ways. To replicate the kinship of mother to child, the violinist should be a close genetic relative. More importantly, the scenario denies the woman agency in the decision to provide life-support. For the percentage of public agreeing with moral obligations under kidnap and consensual scenarios, see (Hauser 2006), pp249-50

567   Planned Parenthood v. Casey ruling on viability. Arguably, advances in stem-cell research could see the point at which unique human life begins moved outward, if procedures in utero alter our RNA.

568   It is estimated that 91.9 percent of abortions in the United States occur by the end of week 13. See (Pazol, et al. 2010)

569   For US opinion on abortion, see http://news.gallup.com/poll/1576/abortion.aspx

570   For opinion polls on termination on economic grounds or after the first trimester, see http://news.gallup.com/poll/1576/abortion.aspx

571   Approximately 40 percent of children living with single mothers in the United States are below the poverty line, compared to 11 percent of children living with both parents. See the US Census Bureau, 2016, Table C8:
Poverty Status, Food Stamp Receipt, and Public Assistance for Children Under 18 Years by Selected Characteristics

572   When James Comey was Deputy Attorney General in the Bush administration after 9/11, he was met with hostility when he said that enhanced interrogation techniques were illegal. He had to rush to the hospital bed of the ailing Attorney General, John Ashcroft, to prevent White House staff from doing "an end run" around him, and asked the then Director of the FBI, Robert Mueller, to order his agents to prevent his forcible removal by the Secret Service. Comey put the inability of White House staff to see the legal realities of interrogation down to confirmation bias, concluding that "doubt is not weakness, it is wisdom".

573   In *The Righteous Mind,* Jonathan Haidt highlights the research of Antonio Damasio on subjects whose ventromedial prefrontal cortex, which is involved in emotional and moral judgements, had been damaged. Relying on their dorsolateral prefrontal cortex to make decisions led to a continuous loop of evaluating pros and cons. Their ability to make any decision which did not rely on simple maths was compromised. They felt nothing when looking at images of delight or horror, and relationships with their loved ones broke down. See (Haidt 2012), pp39-41

574   Their charter states that "MSF provides assistance to populations in distress, to victims of natural or man-made disasters, and to victims of armed conflict. They do so irrespective of race, religion, creed, or political convictions. . . . MSF observes neutrality and impartiality in the name of universal medical ethics and the right to humanitarian assistance and claims full and unhindered freedom in the exercise of its functions. . . . Members undertake to respect their professional code of ethics and maintain complete independence from all political, economic, or religious powers."

575   Orbinski went on: "No doctor can stop a genocide. No humanitarian can stop ethnic cleansing, just as no humanitarian can make war. And no humanitarian can make peace. These are political responsibilities, not humanitarian imperatives. . . . Let me say this very clearly: the humanitarian act is the most apolitical of all acts, but if its actions and its morality are taken seriously, it has the most profound of political implications. And the fight against impunity is one of these implications."

576   #BlackLivesMatter includes gay and transgender members, illegal immigrants, the disabled and those with criminal records.

577   The movement has not been without its critics. Deroy Murdock challenged the notion that innocent black people are simply gunned down by police as "one of today's biggest and deadliest lies". *Washington Post* data on fatal police shootings suggest that white people are killed nearly twice as often, and that the proportion of black fatalities was relatively lower than the rate of violent crime perpetrated by African-Americans. Homicide spikes in some cities prompted fears that police were not as active in enforcing the law as they should be following #BlackLivesMatter protests in Ferguson, but no evidence could be found for this at a national level.

578   Malala featured in a *New York Times* documentary and in TV programs in Urdu, Pashtun and English.

579   The attack was criticised by the President of Pakistan, the Secretary-General of the United Nations, and President Barack Obama.

580   MeToo had earlier antecedents. When, a decade earlier, in 2006, a community organiser called Tarana Burke was confronted with a thirteen-year-old girl who told her she had been sexually assaulted, she didn't know what to say. Later, she wished she had just replied: "Me too."

581   In his recent book, *War On Peace,* Ronan Farrow has shown that the hollowing out of the State Department since the end of the Cold War has left America bereft of experienced diplomats at a time when complex regional, ethnic, tribal and sectarian conflicts risk dragging American troops into "military adventures". If the War on Terror topples one enemy only to strengthen another, then American ingenues need to think more strategically about foreign interventions.

582   In *Defense of American Liberties: A History of the* ACLU by Samuel Walker, Second Edition, Southern Illinois University Press, 1999

583   Not everyone will agree that mandatory violence-prevention programmes impair freedom of conscience by insisting that chauvinist or aggressive language is problematic. Nor would everyone defend a Christian a cappella group which dismisses a gay member.

584   Similar bias-reporting policies are in place at 153 out of 467 campuses across the United States, according to thefire.org.

585   See (Haidt 2012)

586   Recent studies at Princeton have shown that people support morally optimistic judgements which support friends and loved ones, even when they are not supported by evidence. See (Cusimano and Lombrozo 2020)

587   Amos Tversky addressed the University of New York at Buffalo on the topic of "Historical Interpretation: Judgement Under Uncertainty", focusing on the cognitive biases under which all historians labour. Lecture quoted by (Lewis 2017). Tversky once questioned why history wasn't more interesting, since most of it was made up.

588   As quoted by Kyle Reese

589   Jewish thinkers had a profound influence on the Enlightenment, and in the battle for civil rights the Jewish community contributed heavily to the NAACP.

      The Society of Friends, better known as the Quakers, took a leading role in the abolition of slavery, the War of Independence and engagement with Native Americans.

      The American Friends Service Committee works today to combat Islamophobia, end mass incarceration and discrimination, build peace, and defend immigrant rights and economic justice.

590   For the idea that war is obsolete, see (Hariri, Homo Deus 2015)

591   For the suggestion that our forebears were "morally retarded", see (Pinker, The Better Angels of our Nature 2011)

592   As Peter Ward and Donald Brownlee say in *Rare Earth,* we have no idea whether complex life can even evolve in the absence of a neighbouring gas giant to take out asteroids, plate-tectonics to regulate the biosphere, a strong magnetic core to reflect cosmic radiation, a disproportionately large moon to stabilise the planetary axis of rotation, oxygen (from the right type of bacteria), water (from the right sort of meteorites), and an orbit in the "goldilocks" region of a star with just enough mass to generate a consistent level of energy over billions of years. For the fragility of intelligent life, see (Peter D. Ward 2004)

593   For Russian manipulation of news-feeds, see (Clarke and Volz 2017)

594   Vasily Grossman on kindness, quoted in (Snyder, Black Earth: The Holocaust as History and Warning 2015), p319

595   For Hariri's "biological" reinterpretation of the Declaration of Independence, see (Hariri, Sapiens 2014), p123

Bibliography

Anbinder, Tyler G. 1992. *Nativism and Slavery*. Oxford: Oxford University Press.

Arendt, Hannah. 2009. *The Origins of Totalitarianism*. London: Benediction Classics.

Armitage, Simon J., Sabah A. Jasim, Anthony E. Marks, Adrian G. Parker, Vitaly I. Usik, and Hans-Peter Uerpmann. 2011. "The southern route 'out of Africa': evidence for an early expansion of modern humans into Arabia." *Science*, January: 453-56.

Arnett, Peter. 1968. "Major Describes Moves." *New York Times*, 8 February.

Asbridge, Thomas. 2005. *The First Crusade*. London: The Free Press.

Aslan, Reza. 2013. *Zealot*. New York: Random House.

Babcock, Linda, and George Loewenstein. 1997. "Explaining bargaining impasse: the role of self-serving biases." *Journal of Economic Perspectives:* 109-26.

Bain, Henry. 2012. "Errors in the Constitution - Typographical and Congressional." *Prologue Magazine*, Vol 44 Fall: No 2.

Bainton, Roland H. 1978. *Here I Stand: A Life of Martin Luther*. Nashville: Pierce & Smith.

Balaresque, Patricia, Georgina R. Bowden, Susan M. Adams, Ho-Yee Leung, Turi E. King, Zoe H. Rosser, Jane Goodwin, and Jean-Paul Moisan. 2010. "A Predominantly Neolithic Origin for European Paternal Lineages." *PLOS Biology*, 19 January.

Balter, Michael. 2011. " 'Was North Africa the launch pad for modern human migrations?'." *Science*, January: 20-23.

Barbero, Alessandro. 2004. *Charlemagne: Father of a Continent*. Oakland: University of California.

Bardon, Jonathan. 2012. *The Plantation of Ulster*. Dublin: Gill and Macmillan.

Bass, Gary J. 2013. *The Blood Telegram*. New York: Alfred A. Knopf.

Bazalgette, Peter. 2017. *The Empathy Instinct*. London: John Murray.

Behrendt, Stephen D. 2005. "Transatlantic Slave Trade." In *Africana: The Encyclopedia of the African and African-American Experience*, by Henry Louis Gates and Kwame Anthony Appiah. Oxford: Oxford University Press.

Behringer, Wolfgang. 2004. *Witches and Witch-Hunts: A Global History*. Oxford: Wiley-Blackwell.

Berlin, Ira. 2003. *Many Thousands Gone*. Cambridge, Massachusetts: Harvard University Press.

Berlin, Isaiah, and Henry Hardy. 2002. *Freedom and Its Betrayal: Six Enemies of Human Liberty*. Princeton: Princeton University Press.

Bibliowicz, Abel Mordechai. 2013. *Jews and Gentiles in the Early Jesus Movement: An Unintended Journey*. Palgrave MacMillan.

Blake, Andrew. 2017. "Khalid Sheikh Mohammed, 9/11 Mastermind, blasts Obama in newly released letter from Gitmo." *Washington Times*, 10 February.

Blickle, Peter. 1981. *The Revolution of 1525: The German Peasants War from a New Perspective*. Baltimore: Johns Hopkins University Press.

Bloom, Paul. 2016. *Against Empathy*. London: The Bodley Head.

——. 2013. *Just Babies: The Origins of Good and Evil*. New York: Broadway Books.

Boehm, Christopher. 2012. *Moral Origins*. New York: Basic Books.

Bokenkotter, Thomas. 1979. *A Concise History of the Catholic Church*. New York: Image Books.

Bonatto, Sandro L., and Francisco M. Salzano. 1997. "A single and early migration for the peopling of greater America supported by mitochondrial DNA sequence data." *Proceedings of the National Academy of Sciences of the United States of America*, 4 March: 1866-1871.

Borst, Arno. 1974. *Les Cathares*. Paris: Payot.

Boswell, James. 1791. *The Life of Samuel Johnson LLD*. London.

Brands, H. W. 2012. *Ulysses Grant in War and Peace*. New York: Anchor.

Brecht, Martin. 1999. *Martin Luther: The Preservation of the Church Volume 3, 1532-1546.* Minneapolis: Fortress Press.

Bregman, Rutger. 2020. *Humankind: A Hopeful History.* New York: Little, Brown and Company.

——. 2017. *Utopia for Realists.* London: Bloomsbury.

Briggs, Robin. 1996. *Witches and Neighbors: The Social And Cultural Context of European Witchcraft.* New York: Viking.

Brignell, Victoria. 2010. "The eugenics movement Britain wants to forget." *New Statesman,* 9 December: Politics Section online.

Brustein, William L. 2003. *Roots of Hate: Anti-Semitism in Europe Before the Holocaust.* Cambridge: Cambridge University Press.

Bryner, Jeanna. 2008. "Graffiti triggers crime, littering, study shows." *NBC News,* 20 November.

Buchan, John. 1915. *The Thirty-nine Steps.* London.

Buntgen, Ulf, Willy Tegel, Kurt Nicolussi, Michael McCormick, David Frank, Valerie Trouet, Jed. O. Kaplan, Franz Herzig, and Karl-Uwe Huessner. 4 Feb 2011. "2500 Years of European Climate Variability and Human Susceptibility." *Science:* 578-82.

Butterfield, Fox. 1979. "Hanoi Regime Reported Resolved To Oust Nearly All Ethnic Chinese." *New York Times,* 12 July.

Buultjens, Ralph. 1983. "What Marx Hid." *New York Times,* 14 March.

Cahill, Thomas. 1995. *How the Irish Saved Civilisation.* London: Hodder and Stoughton.

Campbell, Gwyn. 2003. *The Structure of Slavery in Indian Africa and Asia.* London: Routledge.

Carneiro, Robert L. 1970. "A Theory of the Origin of the State." *Science,* Vol. 169, 21 August: 733-8.

Cawthorne, Nigel. 1996. *Sex Lives of the Popes.* London: Prion.

Christakis, Nicholas A. 2019. *Blueprint: The Evolutionary Origins of Good Society.* New York: Little, Brown Spark.

Chrysostom, John. 387. *Adversos Judaeos.* Antioch: John Chrysostom.

Churchill, Winston S. 1948. *The Gathering Storm.* New York: Houghton Mifflin.

Clark, Christopher. 2006. *Iron Kingdom: The Rise and Downfall of Prussia, 1600-1947.* Cambridge, Massachusetts: Belknap Press.

Clarke, Toni, and Dustin Volz. 2017. "Trump acknowledges Russia role in U.S. election hacking: aide." *Reuters,* 8 January.

Clarkson, Chris, Zenobia Jacobs, Ben Marwick, Richard Fullagar, Lynley Wallis, Mike Smith, Richard G. Roberts, et al. 2017. "Human occupation of Northern Australia by 65,000 years ago." *Nature,* 20 July: 306-10.

Clement. 80-98. *Letter to the Corinthians.* Rome: Clement.

Clinton, William Jefferson. 2004. *My Life.* London: Hutchinson.

Collins, Francis S. 2007. *The Language of God.* New York: Free Press.

Confino, Alon. 2014. *A World Without Jews.* New Haven: Yale University Press.

Constantine, and Licinius. 313. *Edict of Milan.* Milan: Roman Empire.

Corish, Patrick J. 1967. "The Origins of Catholic Nationalism." In *A History of Irish Catholicism,* by Patrick J. Corish, 15-18. Dublin: Gill and Macmillan.

Cowen, Richard. 2011. *Exploiting the Earth.* Baltimore: John Hopkins University Press.

Cross, F. L., and E. A. Livingstone. 2005. "Apostolic Succession." In *The Oxford Dictionary of the Christian Church.* Oxford: Oxford Univerity Press.

Crow, David, and Robin Harding. 2014. "US governors order Ebola quarantine." *Financial Times,* 25 October.

Cusimano, Corey, and Tania Lombrozo. 2020. *Morality justifies motivated reasoning.* Princeton: Princeton University Department of Psychology.

Dallaire, Romeo. 2004. *Shake Hands with the Devil.* London: Arrow Books.

Daunton, Mark. 2004. "London's 'Great Stink' and Victorian Urban Planning." *BBC History,* 4 November.

Dawkins, Richard. 2008. *The God Delusion.* New York: Houghton Mifflin.

——. 1989. *The Selfish Gene.* New York: Oxford University Press.

Diamond, Jared. 1999. *Guns, Germs, and Steel.* New York: W. W. Norton & Company Inc.

Dikötter, Frank. 2010. *Mao's Great Famine: The History of China's Most Devastating Catastrophe, 1958-62.* New York: Walker and Company.

Dith Pran, Sidney Schandler. n.d. *The Killing Fields.*

Dorney, John. 2012. "War and Famine in Ireland, 1580-1700." *theirishstory.com,* 3 January.

Douglass, Frederick. 1909. "Lincoln and the Colored Troops." In *Reminiscences of Abraham Lincoln*, by Allen Thorndike Rice. New York.

Dumas, Samuel. 1923. *Losses of Life caused by War*. Oxford.

Durand, John D. 1974. *Historical Estimates of World Population: An Evaluation*. Population Center Analytical and Technical Reports, Pennsylvania: University of Pennsylvania.

Easting, Robert. 1997. *Visions of the Other World in Middle English*. Martlesham: Boydell and Brewer.

Ebrey, Patricia Buckley. 2005. *China: A Cultural, Social and Political History*. Belmont: Wadsworth Publishing.

Editorial. 1862. "Excitement in Brooklyn." *New York Times*, 5 August.

Edmond Awad, Sohan Dsouza, Azim Shariff, Iyad Rahwan, Jean-Francois Bonnefon. 2020. "Universals and Variations in Moral Decisions Made in 42 Countries with 72,000 Participants." *PNAS: Proceedings of the National Academy of Sciences of the United States of America*, 4 February: 2332-7.

Edwards, Mark. 2004. *Printing, Propaganda and Martin Luther*. Minneapolis: Augsburg Fortress Publishers.

Ehrman, Bart D. 2012. *Did Jesus Exist?* New York: HarperOne.

Eide, Espen Barth, and Philipp Rösler. 2014. *Rethinking Arab Employment*. Geneva: World Economic Forum.

Emerson, Newton. 2004. *The Portadown News*. Dublin: Gill & Macmillan.

Engen, Robert. Autumn, 2011. "S. L. A. Marshall and the Ratio of Fire." *Canadian Military History*: 39-48.

Eusebius. 339. *Vita Constantini*. Caesarea: Eusebius Pamphili.

Eusebius, and G. A. Williamson. 1965. *The History of the Church from Christ to Constantine*. Baltimore: Penguin.

Evans, Richard J. 2004. *The Coming of the Third Reich*. London: Penguin.

Ferling, John. 2002. *Setting the World Ablaze: Washington, Adams, Jefferson and the American Revolution*. Oxford: Oxford University Press.

Festinger, L. 1962. "Cognitive Dissonance." *Scientific American*: 93-107.

Fischer, Ruth. 1948 and 2013. *Stalin and German Communism*. Cambridge, Massachusetts: Harvard University Press.

Fitzpatrick, Sheila. 2008. *The Russian Revolution*. Oxford: Oxford University Press.

Foner, Eric. 2010. *The Fiery Trial*. New York: W. W. Norton & Co.

Fossier, Robert. 1986. *The Cambridge Illustrated History of the Middle Ages, 950-1250*. Cambridge: Cambridge University Press.

Freeman, Charles. 2002. *The Closing of the Western Mind*. New York: Vintage Books.

Friedman, Alan. 1993. *Spider's Web: The Secret History of How the White House Illegally Armed Iraq*. New York City: Bantam Books.

Fry, Douglas P. 2013. *War, Peace and Human Nature: The Convergence of Evolutionary and Cultural Views*. Oxford: Oxford University Press.

Furedi, Ann. 2016. *The Moral Case for Abortion*. London: Palgrave Macmillan.

Gandhi, M. K. 2009. *What Jesus Means to Me*. Ahmedabad: Navajivan Trust.

Gates, David. 2003. *The Napoleonic Wars, 1803-1815*. London: Pimlico.

Geary, Dick. 1998. "Who Voted for the Nazis?" *History Today*, Volume 48, Issue 10, October: Third Reich.

Gellately, Robert. 2007. *Lenin, Stalin and Hitler: The Age of Social Catastrophe*. New York: Knopf.

George, Andrew R. 2003. *Epic of Gilgamesh*. Oxford: Oxford University Press.

Gibbon, Edward. 1776-1789. *Decline and Fall of the Roman Empire*. London: Strahan and Cadell.

Gibbons, Ann. 2014. "Three-part ancestry for Europeans." *Science*, 5 September: 1106-7.

Gilbert, J. T. 1861. *A History of the City of Dublin*. Dublin: James Duffy.

Goldewijk, Kees Klein, A. H. W. Beusen, and Peter Janssen. June 2010. "Long term dynamic modelling of global population and built-up area in a spatially explicit way: HYDE 3.1." *The Holocene*: 1-9.

Goodwin, Doris Kearns. 2005. *Team of Rivals*. London: Penguin.

Gopnik, Adam. 2019. "Tyrant Chic: Analyzing the Modern Dictator." *New Yorker*, 23 December: 84-9.

Gordon-Reed, Annette. 2008. *The Hemingses of Monticello*. New York: W. W. Norton & Co.

Grabbe, Lester L. 2014. "Jesus Who Is Called the Christ: References to Jesus Outside Christian Sources." In *"Is This Not The Carpenter?" The Question of the Historicity of Jesus*, by Thomas S. Verenna and Thomas L. Thompson, 61-7. London: Routledge.

Grada, Cormac O. 2006. *Ireland's Great Famine*. Dublin: University College Dublin Press.

Graney, Christopher M., and Dennis Danielson. Jan 2014. "The Case Against Copernicus." *Scientific American*: 72-7.

Grebler, Leo. 1940. *The Cost of the World War to Germany and Austria-Hungary*. New Haven, Connecticut: Yale University Press.

Green, David B. 2014. "1298: In Germany, the Start of a Wave of Massacres." *Haaretz*, 20 April: This Day in Jewish History.

Greene, Joshua. 2013. *Moral Tribes*. New York: The Penguin Press.

Grossman, David. 1996. *On Killing: The Psychological Cost of Learning to Kill in War and Society*. New York: Back Ray Books.

Grynbaum, Michael M. 2017. "3 CNN Journalists Resign after Retracted Story on Trump Ally." *New York Times*, 26 June.

Hacker, J. David. Dec 2011. "A Census-Based Count of the Civil War Dead." *Civil War History:* 307-48.

——. 2011. "Recounting the Dead." *New York Times*, 20 September.

Haidt, Jonathan. 2012. *The Righteous Mind*. New York: Vintage Books.

Halberstam, David. 1992. *The Best and the Brightest*. New York: Ballantine.

Hamilton, Marcus J., Bruce T. Milne, and Robert S. Waler: James H. Brown. 2007. "Nonlinear scaling of space use in human hunter-gatherers." *Proceedings of the National Academy of Sciences* 4765-9.

Hannum, Hurst. 1989. "International Law and Cambodian Genocide: The Sounds of Silence." *Human Rights Quarterly:* 82-138.

Hare, Brian, and Vanessa Woods. 2020. *Survival of the Friendliest: Understanding Our Origins and Rediscovering Our Common Humanity*. New York: Random House.

Hariri, Yuval Noah. 2015. *Homo Deus*. London: Vintage.

——. 2014. *Sapiens*. London: Vintage Books.

Hauenstein Center, The. 2012. "How many of our Presidents owned slaves?" *Slaveholding Presidents*, 29 May.

Hauser, Mark D. 2006. *Moral Minds*. New York: Ecco.

Henley, Jon. 2015. "Britons rally to help people fleeing war and terror in Middle East." *The Guardian*, 3 September.

Hertzberg, Arthur. 1968. *The French Enlightenment and the Jews: The Origins of Modern Anti-Semitism*. New York: Columbia University Press.

Hitchens, Christopher. 2009. *God Is Not Great*. New York: Twelve, Hachette Book Group.

Hitler, Adolf. 1925. *Mein Kampf*. Munich: Eher Verlag.

Hochschild, Adam. 1999. *King Leopold's Ghost: A Story of Greed, Terror and Heroism in Colonial Africa*. Boston: Houghton Mifflin.

Hoffrogge, Ralf. 2015. "Working-Class Politics in the German Revolution: Richard Müller, the Revolutionary Shop Stewards and the Origins of the Council Movement." *Historical Materialism*

Holt, Mack P. 2005. *The French Wars of Religion*. Cambridge: Cambridge University Press.

Horne, Alistair. 2007. *The Fall of Paris: The Siege and the Commune 1870-71*. London: Penguin.

Hubble, Edwin. 1924. "Andromeda Galaxy (island universe) discovered." *New York Times*, 23 November.

Huber, Michel. 1931. *La Population de la France pendant la Guerre*. Paris.

Hughes, Philip. 1947. *History of the Church: Volumes 1 and 2*. London: A. & C. Black.

Hurd, Douglas. 2007. *Robert Peel*. London: Phoenix.

Hutcheson, Francis. 1725. *Inquiry concerning Moral Good and Evil*. Dublin.

Hutton, Ronald. 1993. *The Pagan Religions of the Ancient British Isles: Their Nature and Legacy*. Oxford: Wiley-Blackwell.

Jefferson, Thomas. 1785. *Notes on the State of Virginia*. Paris.

Jerryson, Michael K. 2007. *Mongolian Buddhism: The Rise and Fall of the Sangha*. Chiang Mai: Silkworm Books.

Johnpoll, Bernard K. 1995. "Why They Left: Russian-Jewish Mass Migration and Repressive Laws, 1881-1917." *American Jewish Archives:* 17-54.

Johnson, Boris. 2014. *The Churchill Factor*. London: Hodder & Stoughton.

Johnson, Samuel. 1775. *Taxation No Tyranny*. London.

Josephus, Flavius. 100? *Against Apion*. Rome: Flavius Josephus.

——. 93. *Antiquities of the Jews*. Rome: Vespasian.

Joyce, Rosemary A., Richard Edging, Karl Lorenz, and Susan D. Gillespie. 1986. *Olmec Bloodletting: An Iconographic Study*. Oklahoma: Oklahoma University Press.

Kahneman, Daniel. 2011. *Thinking, Fast and Slow.* New York: Farrar, Straus and Giroux.

Kamen, Henry. 2014. *The Spanish Inquisition: Fourth Edition.* New Haven: Yale University Press.

Keeley, Lawrence H. 1996. *War Before Civilization: The Myth of the Peaceful Savage.* New York: Oxford University Press.

Keizer, Kees, Siegwart Lindenberg, and Linda Steg. 2008. "The Spreading of Disorder." *Science:* 1681-85.

Kelly, Raymond C. 2003. *Warless Societies and the Origin of War.* Ann Arbor: The University of Michigan Press.

Kessler, Glenn. 2013. "President Obama and the 'red line' on Syria's chemical weapons." *Washington Post,* 6 September.

Khruschev, Nikita. 1956. *The Personality Cult and Its Consequences.* Moscow.

Kirianov, Iiuri Iloich. 2005. *Socio-political protest of Russian workers in the years of the First World War. July 1914-February 1917.* Moscow: Institut rossiiskoi istorii RAN.

Kissinger, Henry. 1994. *Diplomacy.* New York: Simon and Schuster.

Kolchin, Peter. 2003. *American Slavery, 1619-1877.* New York: Hill & Wang.

Lactantius, Lucius Caecelius Firminianus. 315. *De Mortibus Persecutorum.* Rome: Constantine.

Lambert, Malcolm D. 1998. *The Cathars.* Oxford: Wiley, Blackwell.

Landa, Diego de, and William Gates. 2012. *Yucatan Before and After the Conquest: An English Translation.* New York: Dover Publications.

Lenin, V. I. 1908. "Lessons of the Commune." *Zagranichnaya Gazeta, No. 2,* 23 March.

Levi, Primo. 2004. *If This Is a Man & The Truce.* London: Abacus.

Levitt, Steven D., and Steven J. Dubner. 2005. *Freakonomics: A Rogue Economist Explores the Hidden Side of Everything.* New York: William Morrow.

Lewis, Michael. 2017. *The Undoing Project.* London: Allen Lane.

Lewy, Guenter. 1978. *America in Vietnam.* New York: Oxford University Press.

Lifton, R. J. 1986. *The Nazi Doctors: Medical Killing and the Psychology of Genocide.* New York: Basic Books.

Lindberg, Carter. 2009. *A Brief History of Christianity.* Hoboken, New Jersey: John Wiley & Sons.

Long, E. B. 1971. *The Civil War Day By Day: An Almanac 1861-1865.* New York: Doubleday.

Longerich, Peter. 2015. *Goebbels: A Biography.* New York: Random House.

Loughran, Trish. 2007. *The Republic in Print: Print Culture in the Age of U.S. Nation Building, 1770-1870.* New York: Colombia University Press.

Luther, Martin. 1520. *On the Babylonian Captivity of the Church.*

Luxemburg, Rosa. 1920. *The Russian Revolution.* Berlin.

Madden, Thomas F. 2004. "The Real Inquisition." *National Review,* 18 June: The Corner.

Madison, James. 1787. *Vices of the Political System of the United States.* Philadelphia.

Mandela, Nelson. 1994. *The Long Walk to Freedom.* Philadelphia: Little, Brown & Co.

Manning, Patrick. 1992. "The Slave Trade: The Formal Demographics of a Global System." In *The Atlantic Slave Trade: Effects on Economies, Societies and Peoples in Africa, the Americas, and Europe,* by Joseph E. Inikori and Stanley L. Engerman, 117-44. Durham, North Carolina: Duke University Press.

Marantz, Andrew. 2020. "#Winning." *New Yorker,* 9 March: 44-55.

Marshall, S. L. A. 1947. *Men Under Fire.* Oklahoma: University of Oklahoma Press.

Martin, Andy. 2013. "The Persistence of the 'Lolita Syndrome'." *New York Times,* 19 May.

Martin, F. X. 2008. "Overlord Becomes Feudal Lord." In *A New History of Ireland, Volume II,* by Art Cosgrove, Chapters 2, 3 and 4. Oxford: Oxford University Press.

Marx, Karl. 1891. "Critique of the Gotha Program." *Die Neue Zeit.*

——. 1867-1883. *Das Kapital.* Hamburg: Verlag von Otto Meisner.

——. 1848. "Victory of the Counter-Revolution in Vienna." *Neue Rheinische Zeitung,* 27 October.

——. 1871. *The Civil War in France.* London: International.

——. 1848. *The Communist Manifesto.* London.

McCullough, Michael E. 2020. *The Kindness of Strangers: How a Selfish Ape Invented a New Moral Code.* New York: Basic Books (Hachette).

McEvedy, Colin, and Richard M. Jones. 1978. *Atlas of World Population History.* London: Penguin.

McPherson, James M. 1988. *Battle Cry of Freedom.* New York: Oxford University Press.

——. 2008. *Tried By War.* London: Penguin.

Meredith, Fionola. 2016. "The end of a life in the womb doesn't compare with the taking of any other life." *Irish Times,* 26 October.

Michael, Robert. 2008. *A History of Catholic Anti-Semitism: The Dark Side of the Church*. New York: Palgrave Macmillan.

Milgram, Stanley. 1974. *Obedience to Authority: An Experimental View*. New York: Harper Collins.

Mill, John Stuart. 1859. *On Liberty*. London: John W. Parker & Son.

Milne, H. J. M., and T. C. Skeat. 1981. "Scribes and Correctors of the Codex Sinaiticus." In *Manuscripts of the Greek Bible: An Introduction to Palaeography*, by Bruce M. Metzger. Oxford: Oxford University Press.

Mizugaki, Wataru. 1987. "Origen and Josephus." In *Josephus, Judaism and Christianity*, by Louis Harry Feldman and Gohei Hata. Boston: Brill.

Mooallem, John. 2017. "Neanderthals Were People Too." *New York Times*, 11 January: Magazine section.

Moore, Malcolm. 2013. "336 million abortions under China's one-child policy." *Telegraph*, 15 March.

Morgan, Marcyliena H. 2002. *Language, Discourse and Power in African-American Culture*. Cambridge: Cambridge University Press.

Morris, Edmund. 2001. *Theodore Rex*. New York: Random House.

Mortimer, Caroline J. 2016. "Brexit caused lasting rise in hate crime, new figures show." *Independent*, 8 September.

Nagus, Stephen. 2006. "Call for Sunni State in Iraq." *Financial Times*, 15 October.

Nelles, Paul. 2007. *The Uses of Orthodoxy and Jacobean Erudition: Thomas James and the Bodleian Library*. Oxford: Oxford University Press.

O'Neill, Sean, Fiona Hamilton, Fariha Karim, and Gabriella Swerling. 2017. "Huge scale of terror threat revealed: UK home to 23,000 jihadists." *Times*, 27 May.

O'Halloran, Marie. 2013. "Irish bog bodies 'may have been victims of climate change'." *Irish Times*, 28 November.

O'Neill, Domhnall, and Edmund Curtis (trans). 1317. *Remonstrance of the Irish Chiefs to Pope John XXII*. Cork: University College Cork.

Osnos, Evan. 2018. "Ghost in the Machine: Can Mark Zuckerberg fix Facebook before it breaks democracy?" *New Yorker*, 17 September: 32-47.

——. 2018. "Ghost in the Machine: Can Mark Zuckerberg fix Facebook before it breaks democracy?" *New Yorker* Magazine, 17 September: 32-47.

Paine, Thomas. 1987. *The Thomas Paine Reader*. London: Penguin Classics.

Pakenham, Thomas. 1992. *The Scramble for Africa: White Man's Conquest of the Dark Continent from 1876 to 1912*. New York: Avon Books.

Pazol, Karen, Andreea A. Creanga, Kim D. Burley, Brenda Hayes, and Denise J. Jamieson. 2010. *Abortion Surveillance – United States, 2010*. Atlanta: Centers for Disease Control and Prevention.

Pegg, Mark Gregory. 2001. *The Corruption of Angels: The Great Inquisition of 1245-1246*. Princeton: Princeton University Press.

Peter D. Ward, Donald Brownlee. 2004. *Rare Earth*. New York: Copernicus Books.

Phillips, Charles, and Alan Axelrod. 2004. *Encyclopedia of Wars*. New York.

Phillips, Melanie. 2015. "Bush was wrong on Iraq, says Rumsfeld." *Times*, 6 June.

Piketty, Thomas. 2013. *Capital in the Twenty-first Century*. Cambridge, Massachusetts: Belknap Press.

Pildes, Richard H. 2000. "Democracy, Anti-Democracy and the Canon." *Constitutional Commentary, Volume 17*: 295-319.

Pinker, Steven. 2018. *Enlightenment Now*. New York: Penguin Random House.

——. 2011. *The Better Angels of our Nature*. New York: Viking.

——. 2002. *The Blank Slate*. London: Allen Lane.

Pitulko, V. V., P. A. Nikolsky, E. Yu. Girya, A. E. Basilyan, V. E. Tumskoy, S. A. Koulakov, S. N. Astakhov, E. Yu. Pavlova, and M. A. Anisimov. 2004. "The Yana RHS Site: Humans in the Arctic Before the Last Glacial Maximum." *Science*, 2 January: 52-6.

Popper, Karl. 2011. *The Open Society and Its Enemies*. Abingdon: Routledge Classics.

Power, Samantha. 2007. *A Problem from Hell*. London: Harper Perennial.

Pryor, Francis. 2004. *Britain* BC. London: Harper Perennial.

Radzinsky, Edvard. 1993. *The Last Tsar: The Life and Death of Nicholas II*. New York: Anchor.

Ragsdale, Lynn. 1998. "Vital Statistics on the Presidency." *Congressional Quarterly Press* 132-8.

Raphael, Ray. 2013. "Thomas Paine's Inflated Numbers." *Journal of the American Revolution,* 20 March.

Ray, Julie. 2009. "Opinion Briefing: U.S. Image in Middle East/North Africa." *Gallup.com,* 27 January.

Research, National Bureau of Economic. n.d. *Working Paper.* 2020.

Rosa Parks, Gregory J. Reed. 1996. *Dear Mrs Parks: A Dialogue with Today's Youth.* New York: Lee & Low Books.

Rosen, William. 2008. *Justinian's Flea: The First Great Plague and the End of the Roman Empire.* London: Penguin.

Russell, Bertrand. 1945. *A History of Western Philosophy.* New York: Simon & Schuster.

Russell, Jeffrey Burton. 1984. *Witchcraft in the Middle Ages.* Ithaca: Cornell University Press.

Salisbury, Harrison E. 1992. *The New Emperors.* New York: Avon.

Sally, David, and Elisabeth Hill. 2006. "The development of interpersonal strategy: Autism, theory-of-mind, cooperation and fairness." *Journal of Economic Psychology:* 73-97.

Sandburg, Carl. 1939. *Abraham Lincoln: The War Years.* New York: Harcourt.

Sargent, Thomas J., and Francois R. Velde. 1995. "Macroeconomic Features of the French Revolution." *Journal of Political Economy:* 474-518.

Scarre, Jeffrey, and John Callow. 2001. *Witchcraft and Magic in Sixteenth- and Seventeenth-Century Europe.* Basingstoke: Palgrave.

Scholasticus, Socrates. 439. *Historia Ecclesiastica.* Constantinople: Socrates Scholasticus.

Schulze, Hagen. 2000. *Weimar. Deutschland 1917-1933.* Munich: btb.

Sedekides, Constantine, Rosie Meek, and Mark D. Alicke. 2013. "Behind Bars but Above the Bar: Prisoners Consider Themselves More Pro-social than Non-Prisoners." *British Journal of Social Psychology,* December.

Sheehan, Neil. 1988. *A Bright Shining Lie.* London: Pimlico.

Shirer, William L. 1960. *The Rise and Fall of the Third Reich.* London: Secker & Warburg.

Smith, David A. 2015. *The Price of Valor: The Life of Audie Murphy, America's Most Decorated Hero of World War II.* Washington DC: Regnery History.

Snyder, Timothy. 2015. *Black Earth: The Holocaust as History and Warning.* New York: Tim Duggan Books.

——. 2010. *Bloodlands.* New York: Basic Books.

——. 2011. "A New Approach to the Holocaust." *The New York Review of Books,* 23 June.

Sobel, Dava. 2000. *Galileo's Daughter.* London: Fourth Estate.

Spenser, Edmund. 1596. *A View of the Present State of Ireland.* Cork: celt.ucc.ie.

Stalin, Joseph. 1931. *Dizzy With Success.*

Steinhoff, Anthony J. 2006. "Christianity and the Creation of Germany." In *Cambridge History of Christianity, Volume 8,* by Sheridan Gilley and Brian Stanley, 282-300. Cambridge: Cambridge University Press.

Stowe, Harriet Beecher. 2008. *Uncle Tom's Cabin.* New York: Signet.

Sullivan, Karen. 2011. *The Inner Lives of Medieval Inquisitors.* Chicago: University of Chicago Press.

Sumption, Jonathan. 2000. *The Albigensian Crusade.* London: Faber and Faber.

Sykes, Bryan. 2006. *Blood of the Isles.* London: Corgi Books.

Tachios, Anthony Emil N. 2001. *Cyril and Methodius of Thessalonica: The Acculturation of the Slavs.* New York: St Vladimir's Seminary Press.

Taleb, Nassim Nicholas. 2007. *The Black Swan.* London: Penguin.

Taylor, Frederick. 2013. *The Downfall of Money: Germany's Hyperinflation and the Destruction of the Middle Class.* London: Bloomsbury Press.

Templeton, Allan, Richard Anderson, Toni Belfield, Stuart Derbyshire, Kay Ellis, Jane Fisher, Maria Fitzgerald, et al. 2010. *Fetal Awareness: Review of Research and Recommendations for Practice.* London: Royal College of Obstetricians and Gynecologists.

Tertullian. 197. *Apolegeticum.* Carthage: Tertullian.

——. 208 or earlier. *On the Prescription of Heretics.* Carthage: Tertullian.

1985. *The New Jerusalem Bible.* London: Darton, Longman and Todd.

Thomlinson, Ralph. 1975. *Demographic Problems: Controversy over Population Control.* Ecino, California: Dickenson Publishing.

Thomson, Judith Jarvis. 1971. "A Defense of Abortion." *Philosophy & Public Affairs:* fall.

Trevor-Roper, Hugh Redwald. 1953. *Adolf Hitler: Secret Conversations.*

Trivers, Robert L. March, 1971. "The Evolution of Reciprocal Altruism." *Quarterly Review of Biology:* 35-57.

Trueman, C. N. 2015. *Population and the Thirty Years War.* London: historylearningsite.co.uk.

Turchin, Peter. 2015. *Ultrasociety: how 10,000 years of war made humans the greatest cooperators on earth.* Storrs, Connecticut: Beresta Books.

Turner, Robert F. 1975. *Vietnamese Communism: Its Origins and Development.* Stanford: Hoover Institution Publications.

Unknown. 1903. *The Protocols of the Elders of Zion.* Moscow, Detroit: Henry Ford.

Volkogonov, Dmitri. 1991. *Stalin: Triumph and Tragedy.* New York: Prima Publishing.

Voltaire. 1771. *Letter of Memmius to Cicero.* Paris: Voltaire.

Waal, Frans de. 2006. *Primates and Philosophers.* Princeton: Princeton University Press.

Walker, Samuel. 1999. *In Defense of American Liberties: A History of the ACLU.* Carbondale: Southern Illinois University Press.

Wallace, Max. 2003. *The American Axis: Henry Ford, Charles Lindbergh and the Rise of the Third Reich.* New York: St. Martin's Press.

Weinryb, Bernard Dov. 1973. *The Jews of Poland: A Social and Economic History of the Jewish Community in Poland from 1100 to 1800.* Philadelphia: Jewish Publication Society.

Wendorf, Fred. 1968. "Site 117: A Nubian Final Paleolithic Graveyard near Jebel Sahaba, Sudan." *Prehistory of Nubia* 954-5.

White, Lynn Townsend. 1966. *Medieval Technology and Social Change.* Oxford: Oxford University Press.

Wikstrom, Per-Olof. 2012. *Peterborough Adolescent and Young Adult Development Study.* ESRC research project, Cambridge: University of Cambridge Institute of Criminology.

Wilson, Peter H. 2011. *The Thirty Years War: Europe's Tragedy.* Cambridge, Massachusetts: Belknap Press.

Woetzel, Jonathan, Anu Madgavkar, Khaled Rifai, Frank Mattern, Jacques Bughin, James Manyika, Tarek Elmasry, Amadeo Di Lodovico, and Ashwin Hasyagar. 2016. *People on the Move: Global Migration's Impact And Opportunity.* San Francisco: McKinsey Global Institute.

Wolgemuth, Kathleen L. 1959. "Woodrow Wilson and Federal Segregation." *Journal of Negro History,* 158-73.

Woodward, Bob. 2018. *Fear: Trump in the White House.* New York: Simon & Schuster.

Wright, Robert. 2000. *Non Zero.* New York: Vintage Books.

——. 1995. *The Moral Animal.* New York: Vintage Books.

Xing, Song, Maria Martinon-Torres, Jose Maria Bermudez de Castro, Xiujie Wu, and Wu Liu. 2015. "Hominin teeth from the early Late Pleistocene site of Xujiayao, Northern China." *American Journal of Physical Anthropology,* February: 224-40.

Zhivotovsky, Lev A., Noah A. Rosenberg, and Marcus W. Feldman. May 2003. "Features of Evolution and Expansion in Modern Humans, Inferred from Genome-wide Micro-satellite Markers." *American Journal of Human Genetics:* 1171-1186.

Index